Existence and Actuality

A. W. G.
1984

Existence and Actuality

Conversations with Charles Hartshorne

Edited by John B. Cobb, Jr., and Franklin I. Gamwell

The University of Chicago Press • Chicago and London

JOHN B. COBB, JR., is Ingraham Professor of Theology, School of Theology at Claremont, and Avery Professor of Religion, Claremont Graduate School. FRANKLIN I. GAMWELL is dean and associate professor of ethics and society at the Divinity School of the University of Chicago.

The University of Chicago Press, Chicago 60637
The University of Chicago Press, Ltd., London
© 1984 by The University of Chicago
All rights reserved. Published 1984
Printed in the United States of America

93 92 91 90 89 88 87 86 85 84   5 4 3 2 1

Library of Congress Cataloging in Publication Data
Main entry under title:

Existence and actuality.

A selection of papers presented at a conference held at the Divinity School, University of Chicago, in the fall of 1981.
Includes index.
1. Hartshorne, Charles, 1897–   —Congresses.
I. Hartshorne, Charles, 1897–   . II. Cobb, John B.
III. Gamwell, Franklin I.   IV. University of Chicago.
Divinity School.
B945.H354E95   1984   230'.092'4   84-2476
ISBN 0-226-11122-9
ISBN 0-226-11123-7 (pbk.)

Contents

Preface

After joining the faculty in philosophy at Harvard University in 1925, where he began editing the collected papers of C. S. Peirce, Charles Hartshorne also served as an assistant to Alfred North Whitehead. "I am becoming a Whiteheadian without ceasing to be a Peircean," he once said to Whitehead. Subsequently, Hartshorne became the most forceful and convincing interpreter of Whitehead, and to him belongs principal credit for shaping the influence of process philosophy upon contemporary philosophical theology. But Hartshorne pursued this course because he found in Whitehead's thought the most systematic formulation of convictions at which he had previously arrived, in some cases with the help of Peirce. Accordingly, his intellectual adventure has been, above all, one of philosophical construction, appropriating Whitehead and Peirce especially for his own metaphysical statement. In the Preface to an early volume, Hartshorne wrote: "To the mountainous—I had almost said monstrous—mass of writing devoted to 'philosophical theology,' what can there be to add? I answer simply, if without apparent modesty, there is exactitude, logical rigor." More than anyone else in this century, Charles Hartshorne has fulfilled this commission and, in doing so, has presented a comprehensive proposal which merits an assessment equally thorough and rigorous.

This volume is designed to honor Hartshorne's achievement by contributing to that assessment. Most of the essays included were originally presented at a conference on his thought held at the Divinity School of the University of Chicago in 1981. In 1928, Charles Hartshorne left Harvard to join the faculty of the Department of Philosophy at the University of Chicago; in 1943, he was jointly appointed to the faculty of the Divinity School and thereby to the Federated Theological Faculty, which also served Chicago Theological Seminary, Disciples Divinity House, and Meadville Theological

Seminary, and he held this joint appointment until leaving Chicago in 1955. Thus, the Department of Philosophy, the Divinity School, and these other theological institutions collaborated with the Center for Process Studies, Claremont, California, in sponsoring the 1981 conference. At an opening banquet, Hartshorne himself was the featured speaker, and his autobiographical remarks on that occasion, "How I Got That Way," are included as the initial presentation in this volume.

The ordering of the essays that follow is not important to a reading of them. On the one hand, each is written as a more or less independent discussion with Hartshorne. On the other hand, precisely because coherence is, for Hartshorne, a criterion of adequate metaphysical formulation, a discussion of any one aspect of his thought implies comments upon his philosophy as a whole. For both reasons, then, one may without loss read in the volume as one prefers. Nonetheless, a broad pattern informs the organization. An opening essay on Hartshorne's methodology is followed by eight others: the initial four focus in one fashion or another on Hartshorne's discussion of theism and the latter four attend to other aspects and implications of his thought. In this way, the volume is designed to affirm Hartshorne's contributions to the wider metaphysical enterprise even while it recognizes his chief interest, philosophical theology.

At the conference in his honor, Hartshorne responded to each paper. These replies, together with similar replies to those papers not read at the conference itself, are also included herein, the reply to each essay directly following it. As a consequence, these pages display Hartshorne reflecting at considerable length upon his own proposal in light of interpretations and criticisms offered. It is for this reason that the volume is subtitled "Conversations with Charles Hartshorne." The volume's title was suggested by a comment included in Hartshorne's response to the essay by R. M. Martin. Perhaps no other single claim better summarizes the constructive metaphysics which Hartshorne has advanced than his distinction between existence and actuality, upon which rests, among other things, his formulation and defense of neoclassical theism. "I rather hope," Hartshorne comments, "to be remembered for this distinction." The future of philosophy will be its own judge of Hartshorne's most original contributions. But his colleagues and students who have written here are persuaded that he belongs to that small class of philosophers who merit enduring attention and appreciation within the philosophic adventure. It is, therefore, our privilege to recommend him to his successors. In doing so, we also intend to express our profound gratitude and respect to Charles Hartshorne.

We also gratefully remember two of the participants in these conversations, Eugene H. Peters and George Wolf, who died in 1983.

John B. Cobb, Jr.
Franklin I. Gamwell

Charles Hartshorne

How I Got That Way

What causes an individual's choice of a philosophy? If to cause means to strictly determine, my philosophy holds that nothing causes such a choice. There are no literally sufficient conditions in the past for our present ways of thinking, or even for the precise happenings in inanimate nature. However, there are necessary conditions without which the thinkings or the happenings would have been impossible. There are also probabilities, weighted possibilities, or what Popper calls propensities. How a philosopher thinks is partly explained by biological inheritance and environmental influence from conception on.

What then made it possible, perhaps probable, that the oldest of five sons of Francis Cope Hartshorne (called Frank by his wife) would develop something like my kind of metaphysics? At least three features of that metaphysics, which I call neoclassical, need explaining. It is, in an obvious sense, religious; it at least tries to be clear and rational; it is both respectful of tradition and yet iconoclastic. My first suggestion is that these three traits were also in my parents. Frank Hartshorne was a sincerely pious Episcopal minister, son of an Episcopal mother and a Quaker father. My father did not merely proclaim his piety, he lived by it. Moreover, it was an attractive form of piety. He saw Christianity as a religion of love and took seriously the two sayings that God is love and that love for God and fellow creatures sums up Christian (and Judaic) ethics. He was essentially affectionate, gentle, and fair in his treatment of others. He had compassion for poor and underprivileged persons. Himself the son of a rich man, he disagreed strongly with the richest man in his church, who expected employees in his iron mill to work a twelve-hour day.

My mother, Marguerite Haughton Hartshorne, was the daughter of a pious and scholarly Episcopal minister whom I recall as a gentle and sweet grandfather. One of Mother's brothers was also an earnest clergyman of the same religion. There was a touch of saintliness in Mother. If she ever acted notably selfishly toward anyone, it escaped my notice. Her piety, even more than Father's, was attractive. If she hated or envied anyone, that too escaped my notice. The biblical phrase, "in whom was no guile," applied to her well. Once, mostly by the fault of another, she got on a train without her ticket or money. No great deal! Anyone could see that Mother was honest, as well as a lady in the complete, old-fashioned sense, who had a secure place in the world. Mother did not do the cooking for the family, but she kept busy doing useful things. So did Father. I was once told by someone in a position to know, "You haven't a lazy bone in your body." This was true of my parents.

How philosophers think about religion may well depend largely on how they have encountered it in childhood and youth. A genuine religion of love has its appeal. This is especially true if the love includes an aspect of what Spinoza called intellectual love and the poet Shelley called love for intellectual beauty. Frank Hartshorne had a very vigorous mind; he had earned two higher degrees, one in divinity and one in civil law, and was given an honorary degree in canon law. He published or spoke in public, respectably I believe, on all three subjects. He had studied natural science and accepted the evolutionary view in biology. He was far from being a biblical literalist. In intellectual development his wife was not his equal, and this was something of a trouble to both of them, though they made the best of it and had a fairly good life together. Mother had deep insights into people. Both my parents were habitually cheerful and, especially Mother, had vivid appreciation for the humorous side of things. She loved the songs of Gilbert and Sullivan. Father loved classical music and poetry, especially Tennyson and Matthew Arnold.

You are not to think that these were inhumanly perfect individuals. In the phrase of Wordsworth for his wife, they were "not too good/for human nature's daily food." In my youth I saw faults enough in both parents, and the full measure of their stature has become clear to me only with my own maturing.

In the broad sense of rationality, Mother was perhaps slightly superior to Father. Her view of things could be counted on for sanity, especially her view of personal relations. Three examples. Once, when I was fussing about a girl whom I knew I did not love and did not want to marry, but who had charm and who had somehow offended my pride, Mother heard my story and simply said, "Charles, life is big." No more needed to be said. I had been making a mountain out of a molehill. Once when a parishioner undertook to explain to Mother that she should refer to her black laundress not as Mrs. Smith but simply as Lizzy, Mother said, "I am accustomed to calling her Mrs. Smith. I think I will continue to call her Mrs. Smith." Subject closed. Third example. My youngest brother, Alfred, brought home for us all to look over the first girl who had interested him. We all thought she was hopeless. She seemed extremely frail, for one thing, as though starved from infancy, and not especially well educated. Mother did not argue with Alfred. As she told me later, she simply said, "Alfred, marriage is a very serious matter. It is not enough to love a girl, you must know that you can continue to love her for years after you are married to her. It is not fair to the girl otherwise." No one in the family was unkind to the girl, certainly not Mother. Brother Henry did say to me, "If you're going to marry into the proletariat, at least you ought to get health." Henry was the one of us with a slight touch of cynicism, and the only one who did not survive his twenties.

Father's sermons were not especially eloquent. They were reasoned affairs, rather like an honest lawyer's brief. He definitely intended to be rational. He also had the combination you may have noticed in me of respect for tradition but also willingness to smash idols. Biblical literalism, the Bible as the absolute word of God, he thought rather ridiculous. Father also believed, though I was not aware of this when I was thinking out the question myself, that medieval theology, as set forth in scholasticism, was the deduction of absurd consequences from alleged axioms. Father held that the absurdity of the conclusions should have been taken as reason for giving up one or more of the axioms. I have a letter from him about this, written after he had read my book *Man's Vision of God*. The letter showed that my rejection of classical theism was something like an elaborated repetition of what Father went through fifty or sixty years earlier.

In thinking about my parents I am struck by the fact that they did not talk in clichés. Mother's "Life is big" is not a hackneyed use of the word "big." Indeed I have never otherwise encountered it. Mother liked to say of someone she had known for a long time, "So and so has *developed*." This was high praise. In her diary she wrote, "Charles is a merry child." "Henry is such a comical baby." There was an aunt who, alone among the many relatives, had a reputation for selfishness, and who had kept a grown-up son as handy-man around the house but was finally persuaded by another aunt to let the son go to Labrador to take part in a philanthropic project there. Then she had sent a telegram to the persuading aunt, "James has gone to Labrador as you wished. Hell here." "And of course," said my mother, "She was the hell." Father's speech was similarly unhackneyed. Once when the family was packing up to go home from summer vacation Father found me reading a book with my unpacked things all around. "You're a model of inefficiency" was his summary of the situation. What neater way could there have been to make instantly clear to me that my role must be to turn myself right away into a model of efficiency? It comes to this: I and my five siblings had parents who used language creatively, as well as grammatically. When to his observation that, though he liked the main thrust of my *Man's Vision of God* he failed to find in it any discussion of sin, I replied "I have a paragraph on sin," his comment was a simple, "A paragraph!"

My parents talked and wrote (Mother in letters and a diary) well and to the point. They also told us no lies. Not much about sex, but no wrong things.

In our family of eight, plus a cook and a so-called (and well-called) mother's helper, quarrels were almost unknown and, as brother Richard recently put it, none lasted overnight. I have sometimes been said to like everyone. This would be even more true of my mother. And Father was not a man to quarrel much, though with one relative who irritated him he did have something of a quarrel. Although I argued with both parents, Mother complaining of this, I do not recall accusing them of unkindness in their treatment of me. Once when, as an adult, I defended myself mildly in answer to Father's letter objecting to my behavior in delaying repayment of a loan from him, no date of repayment having been specified, he replied, referring to his letter, "It was a fault of long-standing: that of overarguing a good case. And I did not do you justice." When I wrote that I had decided to become a philosopher, he wrote a letter giving his opinion of philosophy, stressing the fact that in that subject there is "not one certainty." I defended my choice of subject; his next letter began, "An excellent *apologia* for philosophy." When brother Richard announced his choice of mathematics for a subject, this was accepted; when with some apprehension he wrote a year later that he had changed his aim and would be a geographer, Father wrote saying that he liked that subject better than mathematics. All the time the family had hoped that one of the five sons would volunteer to become a clergyman; when none did, no fuss was made. We were all given financial assistance to do whatever we felt we could do best. True, the money came largely from Father's father, who left a fifth of a million-dollar estate to each of his five children.

That I was not aware, while working out my philosophy of religion, how much I was repeating some aspects of the paternal train of thought was partly a consequence of the facts that, from the age of fourteen on, I was much away from home at boarding school or college, in the army, studying in Europe, as instructor or research Fellow at Harvard, or otherwise occupied, all of which meant that I was seldom exposed to Father's sermons. Nor did we ever do much discussing of metaphysical issues, apart from the long letter mentioned, which came after my beliefs were largely formed. Yet it can hardly have been without considerable paternal influence that I became the kind of philosophical theist that I am.

The boarding school was small, Episcopalian, and for financial reasons went out of existence long ago. Its headmaster and founder, Dr. Gardner, was a clergyman somewhat like Father, trained in science which he taught in such a way as to make one appreciate its intellectual beauty. From him, as from Father, I heard nothing, so far as I recall, about a conflict between biblical creation and Darwinian evolution. I cannot remember having ever had to fight my way out of the trap some now quaintly call creation biology. That is what neo-Darwinian biology is for some of us. Later at Haverford, by wonderful luck, I had a course on evolution by a young man whose name I forget who skillfully taught the theory as then understood (1916). It was a fine course in theorizing. I have never consciously not been an evolutionist.

In the boarding-school years several events were perhaps more important than anything the school officially did for me through its teachers. During a vacation visit at home I happened to pick up my Father's copy of *Emerson's Essays,* which I read entire. This changed my life substantially. I also, during a Christmas vacation in 1912, saw and bought a copy of the first convenient, and even by today's standards excellent, bird guide, by Chester A. Reed. Returning to school, which was admirable for birding, being small and in the country, with nothing but fields, woods, and streams for miles around, I began to learn the small land birds of eastern Pennsylvania and in a few years knew them fairly completely without any assistance from others except the Reed's guide. The ultimate result of this new interest was that I came later to philosophize to some extent as a biologist and also to write seriously in a small branch of biology, the study of singing birds as such. My book, called *Born to Sing,* published fifty-eight years after I left boarding-school, is unique. Not since Aristotle, probably, had anyone in his work dealt so seriously with philosophy *and* ornithology.

Another change in those years was that, after an unduly delayed, major operation for appendicitis, I began to write poetry, writing the first poem in the hospital itself. For years I continued in this activity, and developed the ambition to be a poet, of course a great poet! During my college career this changed into the aim of being a writer indeed, but in prose. Some of the poems were about birds, and were so reminiscent of Wordsworth that a sophisticated friend who read one of them said to me, "You little Wordsworth!"

Another decisive event, near the end of the boarding-school experience, was that I read Matthew Arnold's criticism of Christianity called *Literature and Dogma.* This was my first encounter with a clear-cut attack on conventional Christianity. Emerson's essays were veiled attacks that somehow did not register as such. Arnold's book was almost like an explosion in my mind. My parents learned about this and were more or less upset but said little. I recall my father's remark, "I have not tried to mold you." This was true, though Mother had seen to it that we heard a fair number of Father's sermons and went to Sunday school. Eventually Father gave me his reason for being a Christian. Like Dr. Johnson, he thought the coming to be of the church could only be explained by the miraculous resurrection of Jesus as recounted in the Gospels. A fine Orientalist, Jeremy Ingalls, has written a book taking this position. It is a historical argument; she says that, while she does not attempt to refute metaphysical arguments, she does not trust herself to judge them. My response to her is that, while I do not trust myself to refute historical arguments, I have some trust in my ability to judge metaphysical ones.

After Arnold, my only options were to drop all theological beliefs—except perhaps Arnold's desiccated formula: "The enduring power not ourselves that makes for Righteousness"—or else to become a philosopher. It took four years, two of them in the army medical corps, to make this clear to me.

At Haverford College was Rufus Jones, a scholar in mysticism, reputedly a mystic himself, and probably the most philosophical theologian in the history of the American Society of Friends. A disciple of Josiah Royce, also of the Cornell school of idealism which sought to combine relativity and absoluteness, infinity and finitude in the idea of the supreme reality, he was reasonably open-minded and tolerant. He once said, "Every philosophical system has an impasse in it somewhere." I took his course on the history of Christian doctrine, and heard him give many talks in Quaker meetings and other gatherings involving the entire college.

Jones had us read Royce's *Problem of Christianity,* a very singular book, even for Royce. The chapter on community was another writing that changed my life. Never, after reading that, would self-interest theories of motivation have much appeal for me. Royce shows that, apart from participation in the lives of others, there is no self to be concerned about. Later on, Whitehead and Peirce, and eventually Buddhism, made the point even clearer. Sympathy, participation, is more fundamental than any concern for the ego, the mere personal career. David Hume brought the West close to the Buddhist "no-soul, no-substance" doctrine. Curiously, Hume did not use this aspect of his ontology in writing his ethics, with its contention that sympathy is not derivative from self-interest. All of these motifs are united in Whitehead, and all but the clear rejection of substance as relevant to ethics and as implying the primacy of unit-events rather than unit-things or persons, were in Peirce. An additional point, stressed by Buddhism and Whitehead, is that since we all die, the self is a wasting asset, unless there is something immortal to which our lives are contributions. It was no huge step to seeing all this from the way I was thinking soon after entering the army from my sophomore spring at Haverford.

At Haverford I did some reading on my own of works relevant to philosophizing, which after Arnold was a continuing activity. I read Coleridge's *Aids to Reflection,* the poet-philosopher's rehash of German idealism, of which I had then read nothing. I do not recall being excited by this book, but it must have done something to me. What did excite me was H. G. Wells's novel, *Mr. Britling Sees It Through.* In this wartime writing, Wells set forth, with wonderful eloquence, a kind of theism derivative from William James's notion of a finite God. Wells later rejected this view and reverted to his previous agnosticism. But I still think that a paragraph or two in this novel gives matchless expression to some aspects of the case for theism, provided the dismal idea of theological determinism is clearly ruled out. Wells wrote another religious novel, *The Bishop,* in which he got rather lost in theological speculations. Considering the limitations of James's idea of a finite deity, I can easily understand that Wells's satisfaction with this doctrine was not lasting. But he did strongly reinforce my own tendency toward a theism of some form, and his book led me to read, while in the army, James's *Varieties of Religious Experience,* a thrilling adventure. This work, Royce's book on Christianity, and Augustine's *Confessions* were the three writings by great philosophers, commonly so regarded, that I had read when I reached Harvard after the war was over.

While at Harvard I kept in touch with Rufus Jones. He led me to read the essays by J. E. Creighton, the Cornell idealist. Eventually I read nearly all the idealists, American, British, some of the French, and quite a good deal of Hegel, Fichte, and Schelling. This is one difference between me and many of my still living and younger contemporaries, that they have tended to avoid idealists in general. Charles Morris, not long before he died, told me that he regarded me as "the greatest *living* idealistic philosopher." This was measured praise since, as Morris knew, most of the great idealists were dead, including Peirce and Whitehead.

In childhood the people we encounter are the great influences. In my youth and early manhood, however, I think that it was books and essays which counted most. What made me once and for all an indeterminist, for example, was James's essay, "The Dilemma of Determinism." Later the chief reinforcement and generalization of the same position was Peirce's "Doctrine of Necessity Examined." None of my teachers had much to do with this decision. Lewis and Perry were then determinists. (Lewis later changed his mind but did not, so far as I know, publicly announce this change.) My joint rejection of dualism and materialism, that is, my idealism or psychicalism, came initially from no teacher but from my own experience, interpreted, as I later found Croce interpreting experience—in his aesthetics, which he regarded as prior to ontology for reasons that I also had in mind. Whitehead once told me that it was his reason for rejecting the concept of mere, dead matter.

At Harvard there were the idealist Hocking, whose poetic intuitions seemed to me profound, but whose arguments seemed mostly loose and unsatisfying (nevertheless it was he who convinced me that God was not immutable); Ralph Barton Perry, whose criticism of idealism and monism were challenging and impressive in their apparent rigor; and two brilliant logicians, Sheffer and Lewis. With these last two I had the most courses. Thus my intention to think rationally, which I had somehow had ever since reading Emerson (not that there was much logic in his writing) was reinforced and clarified. I think it was in my father's spirit.

My doctoral dissertation, "The Unity of Being," was a fantastically bold and comprehensive project. I stated my position on many of the philosophical problems to which my teachers had introduced me, for instance the question of internal and external relations; and I gave arguments for the positions. None of this work has been published, though many of the ideas expressed in later writings are more or less clearly anticipated in it. As I recall, Peirce and Whitehead are not mentioned. I then had read nothing of Peirce and had never seen Whitehead or read any of his metaphysical works.

Two years of postdoctoral study in Europe followed, mostly in Germany. These, and the two years in the army, are about the only years since the age of sixteen when I did not write for publication in some form, even if only a poem. In Europe I listened to Husserl and Heidegger; the idealists Kroner, Natorp, and Rickert; the Platonist Jonas Cohn, the Kantian Ebbinghaus; also Nicolai Hartmann; and Max Scheler.

After these influences I was simultaneously exposed, during my second and last stay in an official capacity at Harvard, from 1925 to 1928, to the writings of Peirce and the writings and presence of Whitehead. I already knew the general kind of metaphysics that could be convincing to me. But my experience was deficient on the side of exact science. That was the side Peirce and Whitehead were uniquely equipped to illuminate.

One of my teachers as a graduate student at Harvard had been the brilliant psychologist Troland, who happened to be a psychicalist, influenced by a founder of his science, Fechner. So the three scientists who influenced me most were, on this point, on my side. Later the great geneticist at the University of Chicago, Sewall Wright, became a fourth man of genius I could look to for support on this issue. Peirce and Whitehead were theists; Wright and possibly Troland were not.

An important difference in philosophers is the extent to which they have had to break away from manifestly vulnerable religious ideas. The most common form of this phenomenon is the reaction to the problem of evil in its classical formulation. The concept of omnipotence which generates this problem was never, so far as I know, the belief of any of my teachers, and definitely not of my father. He repudiated the idea that what happens to us is determined by divine fiat. He accepted the libertarian view of human freedom, and there was nothing like predestination in his theology. I am convinced that he did not accept the dogma of divine immutability. For him, classical theism, as found in the scholastics and in modern philosophy down to Kant, was neither biblical nor intelligently modern. Thus my, for some, too scornful attitude toward the scholastic theology was something I came to naturally enough. It was also reinforced by reading Nicolas Berdyaev.

To some extent then my thinking can be causally explained. Arnold's mode of rejection of any supernatural role for Jesus still influences me, and Whitehead's objective immortality in God is all that I make of ''Heaven.'' As for Hell I recall not a word about it from my early life. But I do believe that love, sympathy, participation, apply to reality on all levels from atoms to deity. And these ideas are also found in Peirce and Whitehead. But my basic convictions about them were derived not from these philosophers but partly from my being surrounded from birth with the reality in question; partly from Emerson's essays and the works of James and Royce; partly from the poems of Shelley and Wordsworth (which similarly influenced Whitehead); and most of all from my own experience, reflected upon especially during my two years in the army medical corps, when I had considerable leisure to think about life and death and other fundamental questions. What I owe to Peirce and Whitehead concerns technical matters of method, definition, rational reasons for and against, relations between metaphysics and science, relations to intellectual history.

This then is something like an answer to the question, "What caused my philosophical development?"

However, I have overlooked the most important single influence of all on my writing. If I were to describe, so far as this is possible, the company I have enjoyed with my most intimate companion of fifty-five years, whose name when I met her was Dorothy Eleanore Cooper, the reader in response could not do better than to quote one of Jane Austen's characters: "That is not good company, that is the best company." It was also the most helpful for one concerned with nature, science, philosophy, liberal religion, and good writing—all of which my wife had learned to appreciate before I met her. Without her I might have had opinions not widely different from those I have had; but I view the chances as slight that I would have been able to formulate them nearly so well and adequately as I have done. My wife has had her ambitions and many talents and skills, and I have tried to further those, for one thing by not expecting her to be a routine dishwasher and housecleaner, so far as I could prevent it. But any efforts I have made to this end are but little compared to the unfailing persistence and skill with which, in a remarkable variety of ways, she has furthered my aims, and enabled me to be actually what my first thirty years made possible.

Eugene H. Peters

1

Methodology in the Metaphysics of Charles Hartshorne

For Charles Hartshorne, a metaphysical statement is a unique form of statement. It is to be distinguished from empirical (that is, factual) assertions, which if true at all are true contingently. Metaphysical statements, if true, are true not contingently but necessarily. The point is that a metaphysical truth does not itself stand for a fact but for a principle, one which obtains for all facts, actual or possible. Such a principle is, to use Hartshorne's phrase, a universal correlate of fact.[1] A metaphysician, then, seeks to identify and formulate principles which, though inescapable, are nonetheless missed or denied through confusion, inconsistency, or lack of definite meaning.

Necessary truths may of course fail to qualify as metaphysical. Consider, for example, the mathematician's claim that 97 is a prime number. Though that claim could never be false, and is therefore true necessarily, it may be taken as a hypothetical truth. That is, if there were ninety-seven elements in a set, they could not be arranged in the manner of a set of elements which were not prime. Yet there need be no set of ninety-seven elements. Hypothetical necessities are, for Hartshorne, relations which hold among possibilities. And since possibilities are not unreal, truths such as "97 is a prime number" do in a sense tell us about the world. Yet, for Hartshorne, a hypothetical necessity is essentially a denial, a denial that any state of affairs could ever furnish an exception to the relation found in the hypothetical necessity. Be what they may, facts will never present ninety-seven elements that are nonprime. But to state what can never obtain does not suffice to tell us what does obtain—except among certain (that is, not among all) possibilities.

The metaphysical necessity, being a feature common to all factual possibilities, is categorical or nonhypothetical. This means it is illustrated by any and every fact. For though facts may each have incompatible alternatives, and in this sense be restrictive (that is, selective) of possibilities, facts are in no way restrictive of the universal correlates of fact. Hence, no matter which facts they are, the facts will exhibit those correlates. It follows that metaphysical principles are essentially positive, that they identify features, meanings, or characters which, while present in every actuality, yet exclude no conceivable entity or state of affairs. Hartshorne states: "Metaphysical truths may be described as such that no experience can contradict them, but also such that any experience must illustrate them."[2]

The truths of metaphysics, being categorical, apply positively to (are exhibited in) any actuality. But, we may ask, what if there were no actualities? In order for these truths to be applicable, there have to be facts to which they apply, facts in which they are illustrated. One should, for clarity, distinguish facts from actualities, facts being, for Hartshorne, states of affairs or contingent truths. It may "in fact" be clear and warm today. On the other hand, that state of affairs—the state of being clear and warm—may not obtain. Yet, if not, it is a fact that it does not. So what is not actual, but only possible, is as much a matter of fact as what is actual. This is only a way of stating that truths of fact may be either positive or negative, and that a truth of fact is such no matter whether it is positive or negative. Of course we may express a positive fact in a negative way. For example, we may say, "It's not cloudy or cold," when we find it clear and warm. Likewise a negative fact may receive positive expression—for example, when, as indicated by the context, we assert that it is clear and warm as a way of denying (say) fog and cold.

Now, for Hartshorne, there is an intrinsic negativity in every state of affairs that is merely possible. For he holds that the actual is the definite, the possible the more or less indefinite.[3] And this means that the possibility of X is deficient by comparison with the actuality of X. There is in an actuality positive quality or character which is absent in its possibility. We might, then, be led to pronounce the possibility a negative fact—relative to its actualization. But Hartshorne uses the term "negative fact" in the sense explained above; he does not take it to refer to the character of possibilities as such. Indeed, he refers to "positive possibility," an expression which would be confusing were possibilities as such taken to be negative facts.

The negative fact is a fact which is *alternative* to one which obtains; it is a state of affairs which might have been realized, or may be. It is "the road not taken"—a possibility not brought to fruition. The negative fact is not that possibility which *was* in fact realized, but that (or those) excluded by the realization, that (or those) incompossible with the fact realized. But if every positive fact entails negative facts (as alternatives excluded), is it also true that every negative fact entails positive facts? If not, then there could be negative facts excluded from realization by nothing positive, or, in other words, negative facts not really excluded at all. But a negative fact which has no positive bearing, no relevance in or for actuality, and which makes no empirical difference, is a privation and only that. Hartshorne repudiates the view that excluded alternatives are merely negative, and instead contends that any possible fact is partly positive.[4] And, since positive facts always entail negative facts, any possible fact is also partly negative. In brief, then, Hartshorne holds that any fact is a complex having both positive and negative aspects. I gather that Hartshorne is proclaiming a kind of "ontological principle" that the possible can never be sheared from its connections with actual things, that actuality is the base with respect to which all other things are relegated to their respective places.

Now, if any fact whatever is partly positive, never merely negative, then it follows that the things which are actual, had they been excluded from actualization, and thus remained possibilities, would have been excluded by alternative actualities, whatever actualities they might have been. So each actualization is an achievement of definite, positive content, yet an achievement which comes at the price of other actualities which might have been— and may yet be.

The supposition that metaphysical principles refer to factors which, though they pervade possibilities as universal ingredients, yet might fail to characterize actualities, since there need be none, is a supposition countermanded by Hartshorne. For that supposition violates what he calls the principle of positivity, that is, the principle that there can be no sheer absence or nonentity. Thus, we return to Hartshorne's characterization of metaphysical truth as categorical, as applicable positively to any actuality. Such truth then is ever-present, ever-exemplified.

But how has Hartshorne established his principle of positivity, or has he established it at all? The question is of importance because he uses that principle—the ineradicableness of the positive, or the primacy of the positive—as a weapon not only against those who espouse purely negative facts but against those who propose metaphysical principles which involve exclusive negativity. There are, we noted, nonfactual truths which are hypothetical. At least some of these truths are essentially negative. Hartshorne's example is: "Two apples and two apples are four apples."[5] This statement, he would hold, is analytic or empty, since it merely elucidates the import of certain terms in our language. It is really a denial, a denial that there might ever be an exception wherein two pairs of apples failed to make up a set of four apples. "It tells us nothing positive,"[6] says Hartshorne.

So there may be purely (or essentially) negative necessary truths, namely, hypothetical necessities. The point is that entities may be contingent, yet by nature or by definition rigidly require certain consequences or entailments. Hypothetical necessities, then, implicitly deny hypothetical (that is, imagined) denials of their analytic connections—such hypothetical denials being meaningless. Thus the negativity of such truths is *not* that of negative facts. Hypothetical necessities neither affirm nor deny the actuality of those entities to which they attribute the analytic connections.

But with metaphysical necessities we are talking about another species of nonfactual truth: the species whose members are positive necessities, illustrated in every fact. Still, our formulation is not quite accurate. Metaphysical truth is purely positive, but it applies primarily to *concrete* entities. Indeed, though Hartshorne accepts the formula that metaphysics explores "being *qua* being,"[7] he holds that metaphysics is the theory of concreteness.[8] The theory of concreteness will include a theory of abstractness, thus maintaining the crucial distinction between concrete and abstract. True, any entity can be thought, experienced, and valued. And any entity is a potential for becoming.[9] Yet such metaphysical claims must make room for the diversity of concrete and abstract, applying in one way to the concrete and in another to the abstract. There is, then, no single, perfectly general characterization neutral or indifferent to all differences among entities. We would reach a similar conclusion were we to take account of the distinction between the entities which are particulars and those which are the aggregates of particulars. So metaphysical truth is positive in being exhibited in every actual fact, yet it is not in precisely the same sense exhibited in mere groups of actualities, and is exhibited in possibilities with even greater qualification. When Hartshorne speaks, then, of metaphysical factors common to all possibilities, we understand him to be referring chiefly to factors any conceivable actuality (more accurately, any concrete singular or particular) will exhibit, not to factors which characterize possibilities or abstractions as such. But since possibilities are not nonentities, and are indeed factual—as are groups of actualities—we may wonder whether it is entirely appropriate to describe metaphysical truth as purely positive. Moreover, would we not be justified in distinguishing ontology, that is, the theory of being as such, from the theory of concreteness, since the system of all the basic types of entity must exhibit some commonality among those types, however formal and empty it may be?

If the theory of concreteness applies to concrete singulars in a way it does not apply to groupings of such singulars, or to abstractions, then there is a restrictedness about the theory. For example, if concrete happenings possess internal relations while abstract entities do not, then the theory of concreteness will apply with restriction. I do not mean that the theory of concreteness cuts off or excludes what might otherwise obtain, but that it relates properly and unqualifiedly (one might say unequivocally) only to actualities, not to other classes of entity. The entities of those other classes are not negative facts excluded by the metaphysical truths of the theory of concreteness. Indeed, for Hartshorne, the concrete is the inclusive form of reality, that from which all else is derivative.[10] So the possible and the actual do not stand related as adjacent realms, but as aspect or constituent is related to including whole. Even so, it remains true that metaphysical principles of the concrete whole need not apply to the aspects or constituents of the whole, or need not apply in the same way.

The positivity of metaphysical truth, then, is its universality as correlate of all (unit) actualities, of those which are and have been, as well as of those which are only possible or conceivable. It is this, I believe, which Hartshorne intends when he speaks of metaphysical statements as existential. They state those variables of which any and every actuality is, was, or is destined to be a value. It becomes even more obvious at this point why the principle of positivity—every negative fact has its positive side—is of such importance for Hartshorne. A merely negative fact, a sheer de facto absence or privation, would be a peculiar state of affairs to which metaphysical principles perhaps do not extend, unless they *do* apply unqualifiedly to the abstract and indefinite as well as to the concrete. And, as we have seen, metaphysics is the theory of the concrete. To admit purely negative facts is in effect to give an independence to possibilities, to sever them from their residency in and relevance for actuality, and thus to deny (and even invert) Hartshorne's contention that actualities are the concrete from which all else is abstractable as aspects or constituents. Much more is at stake for Hartshorne than a mere rejection of Platonism (which he finds unacceptable even in the guise of Whitehead's doctrine of eternal objects). For a purely negative fact, having no bearings in actuality, would make no empirical difference whatever and therefore could not be detected, unless by superhuman faculties. Nor could such a fact be easily imagined or conceived—at least not by humans—if indeed it could be imagined or conceived at all. But, further, if we grant to possibilities a self-sufficiency or independence, or a primacy with respect to actualities, we face ultimately the notion that there might have been (or may yet be) *only* nonactualities. With this notion the purely negative is accorded the status of a principle which does not now reign, but could reign, and might once have done so.

It matters little whether the *nothing* is taken as sheer possibility, or as the absence even of that. *Nothing* would be known to no one. Nor could it be. According to Hartshorne, what is beyond any and all knowledge or experience is simply meaningless.[11] It has perhaps not been sufficiently noticed that he is an idealist in holding that knowledge defines reality. "With Peirce, and all the idealists, if not all the metaphysicians, I submit that we must start with experience or knowledge, and in terms of it define 'reality.' "[12] Of course, it will not suffice to tell the pure negativist (he who denies that "something exists" is a necessary truth) that to be is to be known. For he asserts that were there no world, there would be neither knower nor known. Hartshorne's position, however, is that our statements simply lack meaning whenever we allege the sheer impossibility of X's being known (even by God). So it is not just that to be is to be known, but also that to be significant (as an utterance) or possible (as the extralinguistic referent of an utterance) is to be so for some conceivable knower. From this perspective, the metaphysical is that which could be absent from no conceivable experience, and hence is in principle unfalsifiable, since no experience could contradict it. Necessary existential truth (metaphysical truth) means to be capable, in principle, of being apprehended by any knower.

It is all-important to recognize that Hartshorne transforms the metaphysical issue into a question of verifiability and nonfalsifiability. Denials of metaphysical truth stand for or denote the wholly negative and at the same time the meaningless. For the denial of factors which are accessible to any knower represents a sheer negation and thus amounts to a denial of knowability itself, as well as of meaning. So a metaphysical truth may be identified as a statement which can never be known to be false, but is verified by any and every experience. Incidentally, while it is clear how the wholly negative can be said to imply the strictly unknowable, it is not clear how the strictly unknowable can be said to imply the wholly negative.[13] Hartshorne, I believe, intends both implications.

In any event, Hartshorne's practice is to call attention to the negativity of certain metaphysical claims. As metaphysical negations, they are—like the purely negative principle "nothing exists"—incapable ever of verification, and falsifiable by any experience whatever. Materialism, determinism, and atheism are each essentially denials, materialism being a denial of experience, determinism of creativity, and atheism of the unsurpassable form of experience and creativity. These doctrines could never be known to be true, since they exhibit nothing positive—no datum—to know or experience. Being exclusively negative (that is, presenting no incompatible positive correlate) they cannot possibly be true; hence, their contradictories are true a priori.

Thus theism (the existence of God) is true necessarily, granting that the idea of God itself is not confused or self-contradictory. Hartshorne says: "If there is no property whose instantiation excludes divinity (and I know of none), then *either* purely negative facts are possible, *or* the non-existence of deity is impossible."[14] Determinism may seem positive because "indeterminism" is linguistically negative. But to suppose that temporal advance is wholly predictable is to deny that the future brings genuine increase of actuality. So conceived, time would afford nothing to know or experience, since nothing would constitute the differences distinguishing past, present, and future. Rejecting the pure negativity of determinism leaves us indeterminism—of some sort or degree, short of absoluteness—as the metaphysical truth. A similar argument supports psychicalism. For the pure absence of feeling involves the presence of some property incompatible with feeling (unless we allow purely negative facts). Hartshorne grants that extremes of disunity or of monotony do exclude feelings, as, for example, in the case of rocks or perhaps trees. "But there are no facts showing that either reason [disunity or monotony] applies to the minute constituents of these things, or to the universe as a whole."[15] Since only these two properties exclude feelings, concrete actualities will always be characterized by feeling, though aggregates of such actualities, or their arbitrarily distinguished parts, may not be.

The basic simplicity of Hartshorne's view of metaphysical principles is not often noticed. All experience (even God's) must have data—something there, positively given. And any datum of experience is really present, though perhaps not where or when it is thought to be. On the other hand, what neither is nor can be a datum of experience, even for God, is unreal. Metaphysical error, as Hartshorne says, is recognized by its lack of positive meaning, by its failure to afford a datum of any sort for experience. We cannot of course observe that certain characters are common to all conceivable states of reality—though we may observe that they are common to some. But we can discern that certain claims can never furnish anything experienceable. They are therefore bereft of meaning (as indicated by unclarity or inconsistency) and so necessarily false. The proper method then is to seek to detect and eliminate metaphysical error while checking to see that our metaphysical assertions are supported by experience.

It may be argued that inanimateness, for example, is directly experienced, and if so is really there. The rock appears inert and dead. What appears *in fact* is a persisting, hard, colored surface enclosing a volume. "Inert" and "dead" are inferences which we take the appearances to imply. We infer the lack of individuality, of sensitivity, and of activity. "But where we fail to perceive individuality of action this negative fact, this failure, must not be turned into a positive affirmation, a success, the insight that no such individuality is present in that part of nature."[16] The minute, imperceptible constituents of the rock may very well be animate individuals. Our errors in perception concern, in part, our willingness to draw conclusions as to what is *not* given in experience—which can of course never be a datum.

The claim sometimes heard that Hartshorne is a rationalist can be seen, in light of our discussion, to be misleading.[17] Nonfactual truths, if categorical, are not about language or logic; they refer to the common aspects of all possibilities. Moreover, possibilities are states of affairs which are knowable or experienceable. "Once the connection with conceivable experience is broken," Hartshorne asserts, "we lose control over the meaning of our words."[18] If a statement could, in principle, receive no verification, it would be without meaning. So, while he is not an empiricist, Hartshorne is no philosophical linguist or logician; he is an experientialist, interested in the principles of experience as such. If Hartshorne is a rationalist, it is because experience possesses universal and inescapable features.

But what is the basis for Hartshorne's contention that meaning and truth are inseparable from conceivable experience? Sometimes, by way of argument, he will ask what does or could make something true. For example, he asks: "What 'makes' statements true for all the future?"[19] or "What could make it true that a final event had happened?"[20] Hartshorne suggests, through such examples, that to be true is to be true for some knower, ultimately for the divine knower. But, once more, is there a cogent justification for this idealist view? I think we have here a fundamental starting point in Hartshorne's philosophy, a starting point which represents his intuition: thought (meaningful discourse) is concerned with awareness, actual or possible, creaturely or divine. One of the problems is that some philosophers have had a rather different intuition. Leibniz, Schopenhauer, James, and Heidegger have asked why there is something rather than nothing—assuming thereby the meaningfulness of what could not possibly be known, of a pure negativity. Again, Kant's thing-in-itself, though transcendent of experience, is taken by Kant as real, not as impossible (as Hartshorne takes it). It is hard to see how Hartshorne could support his principle of "the unreality of the unknowable" without assuming it, since all his arguments seem to rest finally on that principle. Yet Hartshorne is critical of philosophers who, without proof, assume the truth of a doctrine. And so we must ask what support (beyond intuition) he can muster for his idealist principle.

Moreover, are there not statements which, while verifiable and in principle unfalsifiable, are by no means metaphysical necessities? Hartshorne considers "I am living."[21] He remarks that if "I" here refers to a definite subject other than God, then another subject could know its nonexistence. Yes, if, for example, Lincoln once said, "I am living," we could now falsify the statement; that is, we could find evidence for denying that Lincoln is alive. But I do not think this disposes of the matter. Suppose what is meant is that "I am living" is exclusively verifiable when, and only when, the subject (the "I") states it. In that case, the statement means: "I am living now, as I speak these words." Recall that Descartes held "that this proposition: *I am, I exist,* is necessarily true every time that I pronounce it or conceive it in my mind."[22] To take another example, consider the statement, "I (now) feel cold." If I am reporting, not misrepresenting, my experience, the assertion seems unfalsifiable: it could never be known to be false.

Since purely negative facts are taken to be meaningless because they would represent something unknowable, even by God, the axiom of positivity, that every fact must have positive aspects,[23] is, clearly, dependent on Hartshorne's idealist or experientialist postulate. What is less obvious perhaps is that another of Hartshorne's principles, the ultimate coincidence of real and logical possibility, depends on that same postulate. Thought, he holds, is concerned with at least potential awareness. Everything thinkable (logically possible) must then constitute a realizable datum, that is, a datum realizable somewhere at some time. But what of a logically possible state of affairs which is simply never realized? Presumably some alternative state of affairs would be forever actual, despite its never *having been* actualized—unless of course an endless, unbroken series of alternative states were successively realized. But, on this general hypothesis, the logically possible state would never itself become an experienceable datum, being ever excluded from realization.

Hartshorne repudiates any such hypothesis and holds rather that any actuality was once future: it could not be eternal. Indeed, whatever is eternal is noncontingent, that is, not a possibility at all; in this, Hartshorne holds, he is in agreement with Aristotle. The distinction between the logically possible and the really possible is pragmatic, not ultimate. So remote in our past, or in our future, is the time when the logically possible was, or will be, realizable, it has no relevance for ordinary purposes. The laws of nature are the most general of contingencies now prevailing, and for ordinary purposes possibilities excluded by those laws are regarded as "only logically possible," while possibilities not excluded by them (or by historical circumstances) are regarded as "really possible." But Hartshorne argues: "It is only because of lack of clarity or definiteness that really impossible descriptions appear to us as logically possible."[24] That is, it is because of lack of clarity or definiteness that we regard a description as only logically possible. Descriptons which are logically possible (which "make sense" and involve no contradiction) are also *really* possible—somewhere in space-time. So if there are other logically possible laws of nature, those now obtaining are not eternal but contingent, and must have had a genesis.

In general, there can be no eternal contingencies—whether laws of nature or more specific states of affairs; all contingencies must once have been future. Otherwise, "many things logically possible must always have been and always be really impossible."[25] And, once more, these things would themselves never furnish data for awareness. A possibility which was eternally only a logical possibility, though it would not be a *purely* negative fact, would nonetheless be an *eternally* negative fact, a privation never to be redeemed through actualization. "Possible worlds" are neither nothing at all nor actualities. "Possible worlds are . . . real possibilities, not merely logical ones."[26] In turn, real possibilities are experienceable (by some subject or other) as real future states. I remark that Hartshorne, who never breaks the connection of thought with conceivable experience, might be called an empiricist who has reflected seriously on the meaning of futurity.[27]

If "logically possible" implies "really possible," does the contrapositive hold? Are we to suppose that what cannot really occur (that is, what causality forbids) is logically excluded as well? Yes, if an event is always so related to its antecedent causal conditions, including causal laws, that these operate as limitations on it, the events of the past molding and restricting their immediate successors—though not deterministically. For then the character of each event is set within a context, often a narrow one, provided by its predecessor events, a context of real possibility. It is really impossible for an event to be out of its context; to be so would be for the event to be what it is not, which is logically impossible, that is, contradictory.

According to Hartshorne, all thought—if free of absurdity or inconsistency—represents something necessary (and so never simply future) *or else* something contingent (and so now future, or once future).[28] In either case, the modal concept is related to the experienceable, furnishing a potential datum for knowledge or awareness. But how convincing is Hartshorne's theory of the coincidence of logical and real possibility? Why should the two species of possibility not represent a strict dualism? And why should there not be eternal, if inexplicable, contingencies, positive or negative? I can think of no more fundamental answer, from Hartshorne's point of view, than the following: "only logically possible" affords nothing to experience, at least, nothing to experience directly, whereas real possibility is in principle experienceable (as futurity). Even if this answer is essentially true—and Hartshorne does not give it in so many words—we can once more challenge the logical dependence of being upon being known. The philosophers who have espoused a dualism of real and logical possibilities seem not to have been troubled by the prospect of what would, ever and always, be unexperienceable. Moreover, can we not think of cases in which something logically possible fails to be really possible? Or are we to accept Hartshorne's contention that in such cases we are just ignorant of the manner in which causal conditions have rendered the thing in question logically impossible? How could such a contention be justified, since we can never be aware of the extent or particularity of our ignorance?

Even Hartshorne's earliest writings disclose his experientialist orientation. Recall that his first book was *The Philosophy and Psychology of Sensation*. He conceives reality as the object of experience, that which is known or valued. Thus Hartshorne belongs broadly within the idealist tradition.[29] At one of the recent meetings of the American Philosophical Association, a young man who stood up to speak identified himself as "the last idealist in captivity." One might, on impulse, think it is Hartshorne to whom the phrase should apply. However, there are and will continue to be any number of idealists; "the last idealist" has yet to be born. And Hartshorne is by no means "in captivity"—though the man and his system are indeed captivating. We are accustomed to refer to the influence of Peirce and Whitehead on Hartshorne, and of course their influence on him is unmistakable. But at the core of Hartshorne's philosophy is, less obviously but just as surely, the idealist influence of his teacher W. E. Hocking and of Josiah Royce, who was Hocking's teacher, and perhaps even of the Quaker mystic Rufus Jones, Hartshorne's teacher at Haverford.

Notes

1. See Charles Hartshorne, *The Logic of Perfection and Other Essays in Neoclassical Metaphysics* (LaSalle, Ill.: Open Court, 1962), p. 296.
2. Ibid., p. 285.
3. See, for example, Charles Hartshorne, *Reality as Social Process: Studies in Metaphysics and Religion* (Glencoe, Ill.: The Free Press, 1953), p. 88.
4. See Hartshorne, *The Logic of Perfection*, p. 283.
5. See ibid.
6. Ibid.
7. See Charles Hartshorne, *Creative Synthesis and Philosophic Method* (LaSalle, Ill.: Open Court, 1970), p. 162.
8. See ibid., pp. 24–26.
9. See ibid., p. 26.

10. See ibid., p. 27.

11. See Hartshorne, *The Logic of Perfection,* p. 283.

12. Hartshorne, *Creative Synthesis and Philosophical Method,* p. 170. See also ibid., pp. 25–26, and Hartshorne, *The Logic of Perfection,* p. 296.

13. I have previously argued that each actual happening has a subjective uniqueness which defies appropriation—even by God. See my *The Creative Advance* (St. Louis: Bethany Press, 1966), pp. 125–28, and Hartshorne's reply in his Comment in *The Creative Advance,* pp. 140–41.

14. Charles Hartshorne, "The Structure of Metaphysics: A Criticism of Lazerowitz's Theory," *Philosophy and Phenomenological Research* 19 (December 1958): 236.

15. Ibid., p. 237.

16. Hartshorne, *Creative Synthesis and Philosophic Method,* p. 51.

17. See ibid., p. 97.

18. Ibid., p. 58.

19. Hartshorne, "The Structure of Metaphysics," p. 233.

20. Charles Hartshorne, "Real Possibility," *The Journal of Philosophy* 60 (October 1963): 602.

21. Hartshorne, *Creative Synthesis and Philosophic Method,* p. 170.

22. René Descartes, *Meditations on First Philosophy,* trans. Laurence J. Lafleur (Indianapolis: Bobbs-Merrill, 1960), p. 24.

23. See Charles Hartshorne, "Negative Facts and the Analogical Inference to 'Other Mind,' " no. 21 in *Dr. S. Radhakrishnan Souvenir Volume,* ed. J. P. Atreya et al. (Moradabad, India: Darshana International, 1964), p. 151.

24. Hartshorne, "Real Possibility," p. 594.

25. Ibid., p. 595.

26. Ibid., p. 597.

27. I add, as "circumstantial evidence" of Hartshorne's empirical bent, his lifelong interest in and writings about birdsong (of which the most important is his recent book *Born to Sing*), and in addition his high regard for Karl Popper.

28. See Hartshorne, "Real Possibility," p. 598.

29. But, in an earlier review, Hartshorne points out that even phenomenologists have failed to be sufficiently concrete in interpreting experience, and have tended to employ traditional and abstract conceptions, to the neglect of such ideas as feeling, willing, valuing, loving, and hating. See Charles Hartshorne, review of *Jahrbuch für Philosophie und phänomenologische Forschung,* by Edmund Husserl, in *The Philosophical Review* 38 (May 1929): 285.

Response by Charles Hartshorne

My good friend Peters is right. I am an idealist. So was Peirce, who said so, and Whitehead, who did not say so but who did affirm what he called "reformed subjectivism." So were Emerson, my first philosophical hero, and Royce, my second philosophical hero. I could greatly prolong the list, but must mention Leibniz and Bishop Berkeley. My first and really great teacher in psychology, L. T. Troland, was an idealist, in the psychicalist form. Several other psychologists that I took seriously and learned from were also of this persuasion. But, curiously enough, when I came to my first clear conviction on the materialism-dualism-idealism issue it was not of any particular philosopher or writer that I was thinking but of life and nature as I then experienced them while serving in a humble role in an army hospital. It was experience, not books, that convinced me and still does. I had not then read Leibniz or Berkeley, and knew nothing of Peirce or Whitehead. And the books in which Royce expounded his idealism were the ones I had not read. Emerson's essay declaring his idealism I had, I think, read, but long before; and I could not have given any but the vaguest account of what was in the book of Emerson's *Essays* that I read and was inspired by four or five years earlier.

It is important to distinguish several meanings of "idealism." In some writers it means the theory of universally internal relationships (as in Royce, many Anglo-Hegelians, Blanshard) or the theory that reality is so unitary that relations and a plurality of related terms are appearances not the reality (Bradley). By these definitions I am not an idealist, nor were Peirce or Whitehead. My idealism is less monistic than that of Royce or Bradley. This is not because of the influence of Peirce or Whitehead, but because of that of my Harvard teachers (Hocking, Perry, and Lewis) and of the writings of William James. Also my modicum of common sense. I read Bradley and Bosanquet and judged them perverse or extreme on this point.

Another meaning of idealism, which I call epistemological or subjective idealism, is that when we experience something, have it as immediate intuitive datum, it is nothing but a quality of our own mental state (Berkeley's or Locke's idea or Hume's impression). I used to challenge my friends to refute this view when I was reading Berkeley for the first time, but I do not recall having really believed it. What is given to us does qualify our mental state, but it is never merely such a quality. It has first of all its own status, independently of us as at the given moment, and it then becomes a constituent of our mental state as aware of (prehending) it. An independent reality is what we intuit, and the intuiting makes us dependent on it, not vice versa. Being given to a particular experience or momentary subject is an external or nonconstitutive relation for the reality that is given. In this sense solipsism is a metaphysical, not merely a practical, absurdity. It is nonsense. In this sense realism is metaphysically obligatory. Any metaphysical idealism must also be epistemologically realistic to be valid.

Being given to a particular experience, say E', is not constituent of what is given; this is the valid sense of realism. It is quite another matter to affirm that a reality might not be given at all, to any experience or subject. The human species, to take an analogous case, will exist so long as there are some human beings. Each of us continues the existence of the species. But no one of us, and no particular set of us, was required for that continuance. If not I, someone else might have done, and the same for you and you and you, whoever you are.

Return now to the question of the givens in experience. Whitehead rightly holds that it is inherent in being an event to be destined to be superseded by further events, to acquire the status of being past. Pastness is not an intrinsic character of past events. Pastness is an external relation. It is in and for the new events that the old are past, not for themselves. For or in themselves they were only present. They are past presents, because of the fact of being given to new presents. This actual being given is nothing to them. In memory, past experiences are given as such to present experiences. They were not so given to themselves. The most they could know in this respect was only that they were bound to become data for *some* future subjects able to objectify them.

Epistemological realism is entirely compatible with metaphysical idealism. It is subjects that depend on objects, meaning by objects simply what are given to subjects. But we know from memory, interpreted in an intuitively natural way, that past experiences or subjects can be given to present experiences or subjects. This is at least one way in which pastness can be explained in purely psychical terms. A present instance of the psychical has a past instance as its datum. In perception we have the other main way in which experiences have data. We know from physics and physiology that the thunder and lightning precede our experience of them. I follow Whitehead in generalizing this to include even events in the body as experienced. The neural disturbance that we feel as pain has just happened when we first experience it. Pain is not naturally taken as simply nonpsychical. The intuitively right description, in my judgment, is that pain is our participation in a bodily suffering that is first cellular and becomes ours by our act of participating in, sympathizing with, this bodily distress. In some cases at least the given is psychical.

Epistemological realism not only does not contradict metaphysical idealism, it greatly strengthens the case for it. It removes a host of paradoxes that idealism would otherwise involve. Perry's "fallacy of argument from the egocentric predicament" becomes irrelevant. What I now experience does not in the least depend upon my now experiencing it; however, this is not because its reality need not be experienced at all, but rather because being experienced by *someone* does not in the least entail being experienced by me. "To be is to be (destined to be) perceived (or remembered, or both)"—this is a formula that an infinity of possible instances could actualize. Similarly, that every event is destined to be superseded by successors for which it will be past is a general formula from which no particular instance is deducible. This is just logic. It never was good reasoning to derive epistemological idealism from metaphysical idealism.

To repeat, we experience as givens some realities that are themselves experiences, or have psychical character. Do we experience anything that is unequivocally nonpsychical? I put this question to myself in 1918 and gave a negative answer. Before me Berkeley put the question, less sharply perhaps, and gave the negative answer. So did Croce. I was delighted when I learned about their anticipatory agreement with a position I had arrived at. Thunder is growl-like, groan-like, and the negative psychical meaning of growls and groans is not a mere association by contiguity. (See my book on sensation.) Pains and physical pleasures are merely the most obvious cases of the psychical nature of the given. Whitehead told me that this was the reason for his rejection of materialism.

To have something actual or concrete as given is to feel its feelings. No one put this so simply and clearly as Whitehead did in his formula "feeling of feeling." But Peirce had the idea, and a hospital orderly had it, knowing nothing of Peirce or Whitehead. What only Whitehead had was the utter clarity of expression and analysis of the temporal and logical structure of physical prehension or feeling of feeling. In this "of" relation is the sociality of existence, its universally sympathetic duality of structure. Whitehead's rejection of the nearly universal assumption of the continuity of experiencing, his notion of unitary or quantum instances of prehending, is an important part of his achievement, distinguishing it from the views of Peirce or Bergson.

Realism, as process rationalism interprets it, is the self-transcendence of subjects in arriving at, and adding to, an independent, preexistent world. As to the units composing that world, we either take them to be universally subjects of some sort, presumably of many sorts mostly widely different from human subjects, or we know not what most of them are. The alternative to idealism is not materialism or a definite dualism but agnosticism. Matter is whatever fits the equations of physics and biology, whose account of matter is extremely abstract. What fills in the outlines we either can never know or we conceive it in terms of an indefinitely or completely generalized comparative psychology. The transcendence of the subject to reach independent objects is either social, sympathetic, or it is a leap in the dark. This is my deepest conviction, the hunch on which I feel happy to gamble.

I apologize to Peters for not dealing in detail with his essay. It happens that this is a time when I appear obligated to do a number of things simultaneously. I was surprised by his apparent equating of "rationalist" and "linguistic analyst or logician." I am not a distinguished logician, familiar with the *present* state of the subject. But neither was Spinoza or Leibniz, who are the classical rationalists. Nor was Whitehead, who called himself a rationalist. But I appeal to elementary logical principles far more than Bergson or William James, for example, did. Or than Heidegger did. I think George Lucas's term "process rationalist" applies to me. True enough, I am an experientialist, yes indeed.

My argument for the principle of positivity is that by accepting it we avoid many absurdities and incur no comparable ones. The alleged idea of *purely* negative facts plays no constructive role in science (Sir Karl Popper recognizes this in his doctrine that the datum of scientific observation is always something positive). It leads to the dismal paradox (among others) that, although there might have been nothing there is something—not that anything brought this about or could explain or make it possible, but still, in sheer arbitrariness, with no reason, condition, or cause, there is something. Why waste time and energy on such needless and useless formulations? In this regard, the Wittgenstein phrase is irresistible, it seems to me: "Language is here idling." If no experience could tell you what you mean, why suppose that you mean anything?

Schubert M. Ogden

2

The Experience of God:
Critical Reflections on Hartshorne's
Theory of Analogy

Simply in itself, "the experience of God" is ambiguous in that it can be construed both as a subjective and as an objective genitive phrase. If it is construed as the first, it means God's own experience as an experiencing subject, whether the experience be of God's self alone or also of some object or objects other than God. If it is construed as the second, it means someone's experience of God as experienced object, whether the experience be solely God's own or also that of some other subject or subjects. My contention is that this phrase will prove to be an important term in any adequate Christian theology insofar as, on either construction, it expresses a concept indispensable to the foundational assertions of such a theology. And this is so, I contend, precisely when, on both constructions, it is taken in its fullest sense—as meaning that God is both the subject and the object of experience, not only reflexively in relation to self, but also nonreflexively in relation to others. The reasons for this contention can be explained in three steps.

First of all, by "Christian theology" is properly meant either the process or the product of critically reflecting on the Christian witness of faith so as to be able to evaluate any and all claims as to its meaning and truth. If the constitutive assertion of this witness, however expressed or implied, is specifically christological, in that it is the assertion, in some terms or other, of the decisive significance of Jesus for human existence, the metaphysical implications of this assertion are specifically theological in that they all either are or clearly imply assertions about the strictly ultimate reality that in theistic religious traditions is termed "God." In this sense, the foundational assertions of Christian witness and theology, as distinct from their constitutive assertion, are all assertions about God; and this means that, in the very same sense, the concept expressed by "God" must be as indispensable to Christian theology as to the witness of faith on which it is the reflection.

Second, a Christian theology can be adequate in a given situation only insofar as its assertions as formulated, whether expressed or implied, satisfy the specific requirements in the situation for being at once appropriate and credible: *appropriate,* in the sense that they are congruent in meaning with the assertions of the Christian witness as normatively represented in the witness of the apostles; and *credible,* in the sense that they are worthy of being believed by the same standards of critical judgment as properly apply to any other assertions of the same logical type or types. If this rule holds good of all the assertions of Christian theology, it obviously applies to theology's foundational assertions about God. The adequacy of any such assertion depends on satisfying all that is specifically required by appropriateness and credibility alike, given some historical situation with its limits and opportunities.

Third, in our situation today, the specific requirements of these two criteria are such that no theology can be adequate unless it makes the assertion of the experience of God, by which I mean that it must assert, in some formulation or other, that the strictly ultimate reality termed "God" is the object as well as the subject of experience, and this in relation to others as well as to self.

One part of this assertion is made necessary by what we now take to be specifically required by the criterion of credibility. If in earlier situations the standards of critical judgment that properly applied to foundational theological assertions allowed for appeals to authorities of various kinds to settle the issue of their credibility, for us today all such appeals can have at most a provisional validity. Sooner or later, appeal must be made beyond all mere authorities to the ultimate verdict of our common human experience, which alone can establish the credibility even of theological assertions. This means, then, that God must be asserted to be in some way the object of human experience, else the foundational theological assertions could never be established as worthy of being believed.

The other part of the assertion is made just as necessary by what we now see to be the specific requirements of the criterion of appropriateness. One of the most assured results of the application of historical-critical methods of study to the tradition of Christian witness is the soundness of Pascal's famous judgment that the God of the philosophers is not the God of Abraham, Isaac, and Jacob. Provided this judgment is taken as it should be, not as formulating a timeless principle, but as relative to the classical philosophy that Pascal clearly had in mind in making it, it can claim the full support of contemporary historical, including biblical, theology. So far from being the God of classical philosophy, who is in no way related to others and whose sole object of experience is self, the God of Christian scripture as well as of the Hebrew patriarchs is consistently represented as the supremely relative one, who is related to all others as well as to self by the unique experiences of creation and redemption. And if this is true of scripture, it is no less true of the normative witness of the apostles of which the Old and New Testaments are the primary source. This is to say, then, that God must be asserted to be in some sense the subject of the experience of others as well as of self, lest the foundational assertions of Christian theology fail to be congruent in meaning with the apostolic witness that is their norm.

And yet if assertion of the experience of God is thus seen to be necessary to any adequate contemporary theology, it is nevertheless a problematic assertion, and that in the one part as well as in the other. This becomes particularly clear when one takes account of certain basic presuppositions that are now widely shared by theologians as well as philosophers.

Partly as a result of the emergence of modern culture generally, especially science and technology, but also in part because of developments in philosophy associated, above all, with the work of Immanuel Kant, most of us have long since come to think of the several fields of human experience or reflection as much more clearly differentiated than earlier generations supposed them to be. Thus, if we now understand religion and morality, say, as forms of life and experience that are quite different from that of science, the same can also be said, mutatis mutandis, of our understanding of philosophy and metaphysics. We recognize that, whereas science can claim to be empirical in a straightforward sense of the word, the same is not true of any of these other forms of culture or modes of thought, whose empirical connections, if any, are either less direct or more difficult to specify. As a matter of fact, for many of us, neither religion as a form of life nor theology and metaphysics as modes of reflection are empirical at all in the strict sense in which science can be said to be so. On the contrary, they are as clearly differentiated from science as we take them to be, precisely because they spring from an interest or concern that is more than merely empirical and because the assertions they typically make or imply are not subject to any strictly empirical mode of verification. Consequently, whatever reservations we may have about Paul Tillich's dictum that "God is being-itself, not *a* being," we can only concur in its essential point about the uniqueness of God. We take for granted that, for religion as well as for philosophy, the question of God is extraordinary and cannot possibly be adequately answered on the same basis in experience or in the same terms and concepts as any ordinary question.

To the extent that presuppositions such as these are basic to our whole philosophical or theological approach, any talk about the experience of God, however construed, is bound to raise problems. If such talk is construed objectively, as asserting that God is in some way the object of human experience, the fact that "God" must be understood to express a nonempirical concept means that no empirical evidence can possibly be relevant to the question of whether the concept applies and that, therefore, God must be experienced directly rather than merely indirectly through first experiencing something else. Moreover, if "God" is correctly understood as in some sense referring to reality itself, its referent, if any, is evidently ubiquitous, and this implies that the experience of God is universal as well as direct—something unavoidably had not only by mystics or the religious but by every human being simply as such, indeed, by any experiencing being whatever, in each and every one of its experiences of anything at all. To become aware of such implications, however, is to realize at once why asserting the experience of God is, in this part of the assertion, indeed problematic. Even aside from the consideration that prevalent assumptions as to the limits of human experience scarcely allow for any such direct experience of God, the plain fact is that "God" does not appear to express a universally indispensable concept. On the contrary, the sheer existence of non- and even a-theistic religions and philosophies throughout culture and history is prima-facie evidence against the claim that the experience of God is a universal human experience.

The other part of the assertion, which construes "the experience of God" subjectively, as asserting God's own experience of others as well as of self, is hardly less problematic. To be sure, there is nothing new about the fact that the clear assertions or implications in scripture that God is really related to the world as Creator and Redeemer, and hence by experiences of love and care, judgment and forgiveness, create difficulties for theological reflection. It was precisely the attempt to cope with such difficulties that led the church fathers to appropriate Stoic and Hellenistic Jewish methods of allegorical interpretation and the medieval theologians to develop elaborate theories of analogy and nonliteral predication. But one may still question, I think, whether, prior to the emergence of the modern scientific world-picture and the sharp differentiation of the nonempirical claims of religion and metaphysics from the strictly empirical claims of science and ordinary language, these difficulties could be felt as acutely as most of us feel them today. At any rate, it was left to Christian theologians of the last two centuries to expressly try, in one way or another, to "overcome theism," and only in our own time have there been theologies of "radical demythologizing" and of "the death of God," as well as various attempts to salvage religious discourse by interpreting it exhaustively in noncognitive terms. This strongly suggests, I believe, that any assertion that God is the subject of the experience of others is certain to create a peculiar problem for theology today. However necessary such an assertion may be if justice is to be done to the normative Christian witness, it is bound to strike most of us as, on the face of it, a category mistake: the application of a merely empirical predicate to a subject that can be adequately conceived only as radically nonempirical.

But now the fact that the assertion of the experience of God is as problematic as I am arguing is directly connected with what I want to say about the work of Charles Hartshorne as a natural, or philosophical, theologian. One way, certainly, of making the claim for the extraordinary significance of Hartshorne's work for Christian theology is to say that he has done more than any other thinker on the scene to clarify, if not to solve, the problems raised by both parts of this assertion.

To be sure, his contribution toward solving the problems of asserting that God is directly experienced by every experiencing subject is less original and is matched or even excelled in important respects by the essentially similar solutions of other revisionary metaphysicians. Basically, his solution takes the form of distinguishing two different levels of human experience, or of more or less conscious thinking about experience, on only the deeper of which is there an experience of God that is both direct and universal. Since such unavoidable experience of God need not be consciously thought about at the higher level and, in fact, may even be absent or denied there, the assertion that God is directly experienced by every human being as such is in no way incompatible with the existence of non- or even a-theistic modes of thought. But, of course, this is very much the solution to the same set of problems that is offered by so-called transcendental Thomist thinkers, beginning with Joseph Maréchal and continuing down to Karl Rahner and Bernard Lonergan. In fact, if Hartshorne's solution can be said to surpass theirs in its explicitly psychicalist claim that God is somehow experienced not only by every human being but by every actual entity whatever, theirs can be said to go beyond his in its more fully elaborated metaphysics of knowledge or cognitional theory. Even so, Hartshorne clearly has his own contribution to make toward solving even this first set of problems; and if his own theory of human experience is hardly as fully developed as certain others, its basic axioms are arguably more adequate because better founded in experience itself.

But where his work clearly seems to me to be unsurpassed in every respect is in the contribution he has made toward clarifying the second set of problems raised by asserting the experience of God, which is to say, by the concept of God as also the subject of experience, of others as well as of self. By working out a neoclassical theory of nonliteral religious discourse consistent with his neoclassical theism generally, he has not only overcome the notorious contradictions involved in classical theism's use of analogy and other modes of nonliteral language, he has also given good reasons for thinking that our distinctively modern reflection about God results from two movements of thought, not simply from one. At the very same time that it has become clear that the theistic question cannot possibly be discussed as a merely empirical question, it has also become clear, on secular philosophical grounds as well as religious, that contingency and relativity can be as readily predicated of ultimate reality as necessity and absoluteness. To this extent, Hartshorne has spoken, as no one else has succeeded in doing, to the peculiar problem posed by the apparent category mistake of any talk about God as the subject of experience. In fact, his contribution in this respect has been so impressive that a number of us who work at the task of Christian theology have long proceeded as though he had, in effect, solved this second set of conceptual problems.

But as impressive as Hartshorne's achievement still seems to me to be in clarifying both sets of problems, I have become increasingly convinced that his attempted solutions to them also involve certain difficulties, some of which I take to be serious. As a matter of fact, unless I am mistaken, he can be said to succeed in solving one of these sets of problems only insofar as he must be said to fail in solving the other.

The source of these difficulties, I believe, is his theory of analogy, the attempt, in connection with his neoclassical theory of religious language, to establish a third stratum of meaning, or set of concepts and terms, distinct both from the set of plainly formal, strictly literal concepts and terms, on the one hand, and from the set of plainly material, merely symbolic or metaphorical concepts and terms, on the other. In attempting thus to establish analogy, of course, Hartshorne follows a precedent long since set by classical metaphysics and theology. Indeed, although he rarely makes use of the terms and distinctions of classical theories of analogy, the formal parallels between his own theory and that formulated by Thomas Aquinas are remarkably close. Still, as I already indicated, there are also important differences between Hartshorne's neoclassical theory of analogy and any classical theory such as Aquinas's.

For one thing, he is far more explicit in acknowledging that the whole superstructure of nonliteral predication, whether symbolic or analogical, rests on a base of strictly literal metaphysical claims. If Aquinas at least tacitly acknowledges this by making all analogical predications depend upon the clearly literal distinction between Creator and creature, he can also seem not to acknowledge it by flatly declaring that we cannot know of God *quid sit,* but only *an sit* or *quod sit.* In Hartshorne's case, however, the position is consistently taken that "whatever the qualifications, some abstract feature or *ratio* is implied, and this common feature must not be denied if anything is to be left of the analogy" (1945, 19). Another, even more important, difference between Hartshorne's and any classical theory is not formal, but material— namely, his demonstration that the strictly literal claims that must be made about God if there are to be any symbolic or analogical predications at all must be partly positive, not wholly negative, in meaning. It is just this demonstration, indeed, that enables him, as I said before, to overcome the contradictions between literal and nonliteral claims about God in the classical theistic tradition. By conceiving God as eminently relative, he is not only able to conceive God as also eminently nonrelative or absolute but is further able, without falling into contradiction, to make the symbolic or analogical assertions about God that are essential to theistic religious faith and worship.

There is no question, then, that Hartshorne's theory of analogy, however similar to classical theories, is free of some of their most obvious and intractable difficulties. But these are not the only, or even the most serious, such difficulties; and, as I now propose to show, it is rather less clear that he has succeeded in surmounting certain others as well. I shall begin by trying to clear up some more or less minor difficulties which appear to be more hermeneutical than substantive. Since some resolution of them is necessary to a coherent interpretation of Hartshorne's meaning, there is nothing to do but to work through them before discussing what I take to be the major difficulties of his theory.

In an essay entitled "The Idea of God—Literal or Analogical?" Hartshorne concludes an account of his panentheistic concept of God by asking explicitly, "What, in the foregoing account, is literal, and what is meta-phorical, or at least, analogical?" To this he replies: "The psychological conceptions, such as love, will, knowledge, are non-literal. For God's love or knowledge differ *in principle,* not merely in degree, from ours. The criterion of these non-literal concepts is precisely that they involve degrees, that they are affairs of more or less, of high and low. They are *qualitative.* Literal concepts are not matters of degree, but of all or none. They express the formal status of an entity. They classify propositions about it as of a certain logical type" (1956, 134). Hartshorne's main point here, presumably, is that non-literal concepts like "love" or "knowledge" differ from literal concepts in being matters of degree rather than of all or none. But he also appears to deny this when he says that God's love or knowledge differ from ours *"in princi-ple,* not merely in degree." What gives the appearance of contradiction, how-ever, is the assumption, which Hartshorne's essay says nothing to disabuse, that his one distinction between differing merely in degree and differing in principle corresponds exactly to his other distinction between being a matter of degree and being a matter of all or none. But my guess is that he is here implicitly depending on a distinction he explicitly introduces elsewhere that invalidates this assumption—namely, the threefold distinction between "in-finite," "finite," and "absolute" difference (see, e.g., 1957, 80f.). Assum-ing this distinction, which turns upon his more basic distinction between "all," "some," and "none," he can assert that God's love and knowledge differ in principle from ours without denying, as he appears to do, that the difference is still not absolute and hence expressible only in nonliteral con-cepts. In other words, what he means to say is that to differ in principle *is* to differ in degree, because it is not an absolute difference, but it is not to differ *"merely* in degree," because it is an infinite rather than a merely finite difference.

A second difficulty is connected with the statement, already quoted, that "Literal concepts are not matters of degree, but of all or none." What makes this and parallel statements in other writings problematic is that some of the very concepts that Hartshorne classifies as "literal" are elsewhere im-plied to be matters of degree rather than of all or none and are even said to be "analogical" when applied to God. Consider, for example, what he says about the polar concepts "absolute" and "relative."

In one place, where he expressly proposes a classification of theological terms, he speaks of "plainly literal terms like relative or absolute" (1970a, 155). Similarly, he tells us in another passage, whose larger context is closely parallel, that, although "God is symbolically ruler" and "analogically con-scious and loving," God is "literally both absolute (or necessary) in existence and relative (or contingent) in actuality" (1962, 140). Elsewhere, however, in a discussion of "analogical concepts and metaphysical uniqueness," he makes his usual point that the unique status of deity is "a double one" by arguing that "no other being, in *any* aspect, could be either wholly relative or wholly nonrelative. Thus, while all beings have some measure of 'absoluteness' or independence of relationships and some measure of 'relativity,' God, and only God, is in one aspect of his being strictly or maximally absolute, and in another aspect no less strictly or maximally relative. So both 'relative' and 'nonrelative' are analogical, not univocal, in application to deity'' (1948, 32). This argument is all the more striking because Hartshorne immediately goes on to say that the ''completely metaphysical'' distinction between deity and all else ''may be expressed under any category'' and because he subsequently speaks of ''a strong or eminent, as contrasted to a weak or ordinary, sense'' of the terms ''relative'' and ''absolute'' (32, 76; cf. 67, 75).

Such passages confirm that Hartshorne does not always say that categorial terms like ''absolute'' and ''relative,'' ''necessary'' and ''contingent,'' being matters of all or none rather than of degree, have a literal rather than an analogical meaning. It is true that the contrast he makes in the passage in which he affirms that these terms are ''analogical'' in application to deity is not with ''literal,'' but, rather, with ''univocal.'' But this difference clearly is merely verbal. For in the sense in which he uses the term ''literal'' in the other passages in which he affirms the same categorial terms to have a literal rather than either a symbolic or an analogical meaning, it means nothing other than ''univocal'' (although, as we shall see presently, this is not the only sense in which he uses the term ''literal''). Thus he argues that, whereas an analogical concept like ''feeling'' applies to the different things to which it is applicable in different senses, rather than in the same sense, the purely formal concept ''contingency'' has ''a single literal meaning applicable to all cases, the meaning of excluding some positive possibilities'' (1962, 140). Or, again, he can say of the term ''relativity,'' that ''to be 'constituted in some way by contingent relations' is simply and literally that, no more, no less, and no other'' (1970a, 154). The fact seems to be, then, that Hartshorne means as well as says that the same categorial terms both are and are not literal rather than analogical when applied to God.

Is this to say that his theory is insofar inconsistent? To the best of my knowledge, he nowhere says anything that directly addresses this question. But it seems to me that there is something he could say that would remove the apparent contradiction.

Essential to his whole metaphysical position is the claim that, in addition to ''the most general or neutral idea of reality,'' we need to make certain purely formal distinctions between realities or entities of different logical types, thereby clarifying ''metaphysical universals valid only within one type'' (1970a, 141). Thus ''reality is distinguishable categorially or *a priori* into concrete and abstract,'' and this distinction breaks down further into logical-type distinctions between ''events,'' ''individuals,'' and ''aggregates'' (or ''groups of individuals''), on the one hand, and ''qualities'' (or ''properties'') on two different levels of abstractness, ranging from ''species'' and "genera" to "metaphysical categories," on the other (90, 141, 57, 101). Moreover, there is the "unique form of logical-type distinction" between "God and other things," or, more exactly, "God and any other individual being" (144, 140). Although God as an individual is as contingent in actuality, or with respect to the events embodying the divine individuality, as any individual must be, the existence of God as the one universal, all-inclusive individual is categorially different from that of all other particular, partly exclusive individuals in being necessary (245–60). According to Hartshorne, all of these distinctions, including the unique distinction between God and all other individuals, are purely formal and, therefore, literal in that they are not matters of degree but of all or none. An entity either is or is not an event, and the same may be said about its being an individual or an aggregate, a quality at the lower level of abstractness or at the higher, or the extraordinary individual God. Consequently, while there are metaphysical categories explicative of the meaning of each of these logical types and, therefore, applicable only to entities falling within them, these categories, too, are strictly literal in that they apply to every entity within their respective types, not in different senses, but in the same sense.

Now this much Hartshorne himself clearly says or implies, and that many times over. But, then, there is something else that he very well could say that would render his apparently contradictory statements consistent— namely, that, although such terms as "absolute" and "relative," or "necessary" and "contingent," explicate the meaning of more than one logical type, and thus apply to entities within these different types in correspondingly different senses, rather than in simply the same sense, they nevertheless apply to the different entities within any single type whose meaning they in some sense explicate, not in different senses, but rather in the same sense.

Thus "relative," for example, means in the broadest sense "constituted in some way or degree by relations to the contingent." As such, it applies in some sense to entities of all logical types, except qualities at the highest level of abstractness, otherwise called "metaphysical categories." But the sense in which "relative" applies to an event, say, is systematically different from the sense in which it applies to an ordinary quality at some lower level of abstractness, whether genus or species. While an event is relative in being internally related to other entities of the same logical type, which it requires by a necessity that is "particular and definite," a species or genus is relative only in that it requires, by a necessity that is "generic or indefinite," one or more intensional classes (of individuals or of other more specific kinds), all of which are only contingently nonempty (1970a, 101f., 103, 109). Consequently, while there is a perfectly definite sense in which any ordinary quality can be said to be less relative and more absolute than any event, it can be said just as definitely that even the highest genus is infinitely more relative and less absolute than any metaphysical category, or the necessary individuality of God that is the original unity of all such categories. This means that if terms like "relative" and "absolute" are taken in their broadest meaning, without regard to distinctions of logical type, Hartshorne has sufficient reason for saying that they can be used in systematically different senses and, therefore, are analogical, not univocal, in application to deity. If, on the contrary, they are taken strictly, in any one of the senses they have when applied solely to entities within a single logical type, he is equally justified in holding that they are then used in the same sense, and, therefore, are literal, not analogical, even when applicable to God.

So much, then, for this second difficulty. Because I take my resolution of it to be firmly based in Hartshorne's own essential position, I shall proceed henceforth as though it were a proper interpretation of what he means to say, even though, to repeat, I know of no place where he actually says it.

The third difficulty that must be cleared up was already alluded to parenthetically when I remarked earlier that Hartshorne uses the term "literal," also, in more than one sense. In fact, one could say, somewhat schematically, that, if the second difficulty arises from his saying that concepts that he classifies as literal are analogical, the third difficulty arises from his saying that concepts that he classifies as analogical are literal. The difference in this case, however, is that, in speaking so, he expressly recognizes that he is using "literal" in a different sense, even though he never explains very clearly just wherein this difference lies. Thus, after a discussion of the "literalness of theism," in which he argues that it is God who loves literally, while it is we who love only metaphorically, he remarks: "If someone should say that I have been using 'literal' and 'metaphorical' in an unusual, nonliteral, and even metaphorical sense, I should reply that I have apprehensions this may perhaps be true. I should be happy to be taught how to put the matter more precisely" (1948, 38). Elsewhere, having argued that analogical concepts are "not purely formal in the same sense as the other categorial terms," he hastens to add, "And yet there is a strange sense in which the analogical concepts apply literally to deity, and analogically to creatures" (1962, 141; cf. 1970a, 155f.).

It would appear that Hartshorne is here depending, in effect, if not in so many words, upon something like the distinction made in the Thomistic theory of analogy between what is meant by an analogical term (the *res significata*) and how the term means (its *modus significandi*) (Thomas Aquinas 1964, 56–59, 66–71). By means of this distinction, one can argue that, although the primary sense of a term with respect to how it means is the sense it has as applied to a creature, or ordinary individual, the primary sense of the term with respect to what is meant by it is the sense it has as applied to the Creator, or eminent individual. Accordingly, one may hold that, even though God is the secondary analogue with respect to how an analogy means, God is nevertheless the primary analogue with respect to what is meant by the analogy.

A close reading of Hartshorne's writings confirms, I believe, that he typically reasons in much this same way, even if it is Karl Barth or Emil Brunner, instead of Aquinas, with whom he acknowledges his agreement in doing so. But if I am right about this, the third difficulty, also, can be resolved. When Hartshorne says that there is a sense in which analogical terms apply literally to God and, therefore, simply *are* literal in this application, what he means by "literal" is not that such terms apply to God in the *same* sense in which they apply to any other entity of the same logical type, this being, as we have seen, what he otherwise takes "literal" to mean. He means, rather, that with respect at least to what is meant by such terms, they apply to God in the *primary* sense in which they can be applied analogically both to God and to all other individuals, their application to such other individuals being in this respect their secondary sense.

Yet a fourth difficulty—actually, a complex of difficulties—in Hartshorne's theory has to do with his using certain terms that he classifies as analogical expressly in senses that render any such classification self-contradictory. By "analogical" here I mean in the strict sense implied by what has already been said about the meaning of "literal," namely, that terms are "literal" in the strict sense of the word when, within any single logical type, they apply in the same sense, rather than in different senses, to all the different entities belonging to the type. By contrast, terms are "analogical" in the strict sense when, even within the logical types within which alone they are applicable—which is to say, the logical types of individuals, and hence of the eminent individual God as well as of ordinary individuals—they apply in different senses, rather than in the same sense, to all the different entities within the respective types. Thus Hartshorne holds that the term "feeling," for instance, can be said to be analogical in this sense because, or insofar as, it applies to all entities of the logical type of individuals, including the unique individual God, but does so in suitably different senses to all the different kinds or levels of individuals, with its sense being infinitely different in its application to God (1962, 140).

The difficulty, however, is that it is not only, or even primarily, terms such as "feeling" or "sentience" that Hartshorne typically classifies as thus analogical when applied to God. On the contrary, because he seeks to interpret what is said or implied about God in such theistic religious phenomena as faith and worship, his preferred theological analogies involve terms like "knowledge," "love," and "will," and he likes to speak of God, as in a sentence already quoted, as "analogically conscious and loving" (1970a, 154ff.; 1962, 140; cf. 1965, 301). At one point, he goes so far as to say that "the word God . . . stands for an analogy (difficult no doubt) between the thinking animal and the cosmos conceived as animate" (1970a, 220). Considering his use elsewhere of the phrase, "thinking animal," one can only suppose that here, too, it refers to man, or a human being, in contrast to other kinds of animals who feel but cannot think, or, at any rate, cannot think that they think (1970a, 94; 1971, 208). But if this supposition is correct, any analogy between such a specific kind of animal and God is not merely difficult but quite impossible. For by Hartshorne's own criterion of the difference between an analogy and a mere symbol—namely, that the first differs from the second in not drawing a comparison between God and one concrete species of entity in contrast to all others—any comparison between God and the thinking animal cannot possibly be an analogy but only a symbol (1962, 134). Because "thinking," as Hartshorne expressly uses the word, is, in his terms, a merely "local," rather than a "cosmic," variable, if it can be applied to God at all, it has to be applied symbolically rather than analogically (1937, 111–24).

It would be tedious to show that a similar difficulty arises in connection with most, if not all, of the other terms that Hartshorne typically represents as theological analogies. In each case, the source of the difficulty is the same: in the sense that he himself expressly gives the term, it can be applied at most to entities of some specific kind or kinds and, therefore, is anything but a variable having "an *infinite* range of values" (116). Of course, he is by no means unaware of such difficulties, as is clear from the admission already cited and clearer still from his statement elsewhere, that, as compared with the traditional problem of evil, "there are other difficulties in theism" that he at least finds "more formidable." Specifically, he allows, "the old problem of analogy: how if at all to conceive an unsurpassable yet individual form of experience, volition, or love, is still with us" (1966b, 212). But as clear as Hartshorne may be that there is a problem here, he says very little, if anything, by way of solving it. In fact, in discussions of how God might be conceived as conscious or knowing, his comments range all the way from raising the question whether God is really conscious at all to speaking none too clearly of "super-linguistic consciousness" or of "the One who knows without symbol (or for whom everything whatever serves as symbol)" (1967, 4f.; 1970a, 94; 1970b, 25f.). And just as significant, I think, he nowhere seems to explain, as he clearly has to explain if "conscious" and "knowing" are analogical, how not only the greatest but even the least possible individual must in some sense be said to be conscious and to know, as well as to be aware and to feel.

So far as this fourth difficulty is concerned, then, I see no obvious way of clearing it up. If Hartshorne is to uphold his claim that terms such as "thinking" and "knowing," "loving" and "willing," are analogical in meaning when applied to God, he has to give them a sense infinitely different from the specific sense in which he expressly uses them. But in that event it is no longer clear why he or anyone else should prefer them as theological analogies to such other psychical terms as "feeling" and "experiencing," "sentient" and "aware." For, surely, the same thing must then happen to them as happens to "consciousness" when, as he himself allows, "the word means no more than 'experience' or 'awareness' in the most noncommittal meaning" (1963, 4). In other words, the dilemma in which Hartshorne appears to be caught is that he can establish the properly analogical status of his favorite theological analogies only by preserving a merely verbal connection with the primary experience and discourse to which he is concerned to do justice: the faith and worship of theistic religion, which speaks of God in the most vivid symbols, not as one who somehow senses and feels, but as one who loves and cares, judges and forgives.

As serious as this dilemma may be, however, it is still relatively minor in comparison with the other difficulties in Hartshorne's theory that we are at last in a position to discuss. Clearly, it is one question whether certain psychical terms can be coherently established as theological analogies rather than frankly accepted as only symbols, while it is another and far more serious question whether any such terms at all can be coherently classified as truly analogical rather than merely symbolic. Hartshorne explicitly recognizes this when he speaks of the terms that he distinguishes as analogical in the strict sense as "problematic," in that they are "neither unambiguously literal nor unambiguously non-literal" (1970a, 156). Even so, he attempts to show that there is indeed such a third class of terms by way of what at least appear to be two lines of argument.

At one point, he observes that "besides obviously formal and obviously material ideas about God we have descriptions whose classification depends partly upon one's philosophical beliefs" (1962, 139). As what follows makes clear, the beliefs he alludes to are those of "panpsychism," or, as he now prefers to say, "psychicalism." According to such beliefs, psychical concepts like "awareness," "feeling," "memory," and "sympathy" do not apply merely to some individuals in contrast to others, as obviously material ideas do, but, rather, are "categorial, universal in scope" (140). And yet, even for psychicalism—and this explains the qualification "partly"—psychical concepts are also different from obviously formal ideas because they are categorial, and hence universally applicable, not to entities of all logical types, but only to "concrete singulars," which is to say, individuals and events, as distinct both from aggregates, which are concrete but not singular, and all levels of qualities, which are merely abstract (141). In fact, in a parallel passage, Hartshorne even speaks of psychical terms as merely "almost categorial" because of this difference in their scope of application from "the strictly categorial notions" like "relativity" (1970a, 154).

But such a confusing, if not self-contradictory, way of speaking is uncalled for. He himself explains in an earlier chapter of the same book that "strict metaphysical generality can stop short of literally 'everything'," because "it is enough if a concept applies with complete and *a priori* universality within one logical level" (89). Moreover, as we learned from our earlier discussion, he can occasionally speak even of a purely formal concept like "relativity" as being in a broad sense analogical, because it has systematically different senses as explicative of the meaning of different logical types. But this implies that any psychical concept that is truly analogical must be just as universal in its scope of application as a purely formal term like "relativity," provided only that this term is taken, as it should be, in the sense in which it alone explicates the meaning of "concrete singular," whether event or individual. The only question, then, is whether any psychical concept is truly analogical; and Hartshorne here appears to support his affirmative answer by appealing to the philosophical beliefs peculiar to psychicalism.

But if he really does intend this as an independent line of argument, which he perhaps does not, it is open to the objection that it begs the question. Granted that psychicalism as a metaphysical position does indeed imply that at least some psychical concepts are truly analogical in their application to God, it is just as clear that psychicalism itself can be established as true only if at least some psychical terms are known to express theological analogies.

Of course, one may very well seek to support a psychicalist metaphysics by appealing, as Hartshorne does, to a direct intuition of experience or feeling other than our own insofar as "we can consciously intuit our physical plea-sures and pains as direct participations in feelings enjoyed or suffered by our bodily constituents" (1976, 71). One may then generalize this intuition and, employing the criterion of "active singularity," further argue by analogy that whatever is experienced to act as one must also feel as one, whether this be an animal or a cell, a molecule or an atom (1970a, 36, 143f.; 1979, 62). But while these arguments might well suffice to establish psychicalism as a spec-ulative scientific cosmology, and thus to show that "psychics," not "phys-ics," is the inclusive empirical science, they remain merely empirical arguments and as such are insufficient to establish psychicalism as a meta-physical position (1977). Nor can it be thus established, in my judgment, by Hartshorne's additional argument that, since nothing positive can conflict with the presence of mind in some form, it cannot even conceivably be shown to be totally absent (1953, 32f.; 1970a, 160f.). For while this argument may indeed suffice to show that psychicalism cannot be falsified, it is not sufficient to show that psychicalism is metaphysically true. This it could show only if "mind" were already known to be a concept having infinite scope of applica-tion, and this is the very thing in question.

Consequently, one is forced to conclude that, if psychicalism is to be established as indeed a matter of philosophical beliefs, and hence as true metaphysically, there is nothing to do but to appeal to a direct intuition of the one individual who is in no way merely empirical but is strictly metaphysical. Only by directly intuiting that psychical concepts apply primarily to the ex-traordinary individual God can one possibly know them to be variables with a strictly infinite range of values and, therefore, truly analogical.

Hartshorne evidently recognizes the force of this reasoning because the other line of argument by which he at least appears to support his claim for a distinct class of theological analogies is to appeal to just such a direct experi-ence of God. In fact, this may quite possibly be his only line of argument, the other apparent one not really being intended as such after all. In any event, in a closely parallel discussion of the very same question, of how problematic terms like "know" or "love" as applied to God are to be classified, he in no way appeals to psychicalism, but argues instead that, although they are "in such application not literal in the simple sense in which 'relative' can be,'' they nevertheless "may be literal if or in so far as we have religious intuition'' (1970a, 155). Recalling our earlier discussion of the different senses in which Hartshorne uses the word "literal," we can infer that what he means by saying that "know" or "love" may be literal as applied to God is not that they may apply to God in the *same* sense in which they apply to all individuals, but, rather, that they may apply to God in the *primary* sense in which they are thus applicable, their application to any other individual being secondary. Thus the point of his argument is that such terms may apply primarily to God, or that God may be their primary analogue, if or insofar as we directly experience God.

This interpretation is confirmed by Hartshorne's development of his case. "This is the question," he argues, "does our concept of 'know' come merely from intra-human experience, analogically extended to what is below and above the human, or does the concept come partly from religious experience, from some dim but direct awareness of deity?" The answer, he believes, is "that we know what 'knowledge' is partly by knowing God, and that though it is true that we form the idea of divine knowledge by analogical extension from our experience of human knowledge, this is not the whole truth, the other side of the matter being that we form our idea of human knowledge by exploiting the intuition . . . which we have of God" (155). If Hartshorne's speaking here of "religious experience" seems to refer to some special kind of experience in contrast to other kinds or to experience generally, this is not his meaning. Although he often uses the term "religion" and its cognates in a way that would require such a construction, what he intends to say here is not that where there is religious experience there is awareness of deity, but rather, conversely, that where there is awareness of deity there is religious experience. Thus he concludes by holding that experience of God is an essential moment in all human experience: "man's awareness of God is no mere contingent extension of his awareness of himself, but is rather an indispensable element of that awareness. . . . the divine-human contrast is the basic principle of all human thought, never wholly submerged, though it may often be driven rather deep into the dimly-lighted regions of experience" (156).

How successful is this line of argument? To answer this question, I first want to make sure of just what the argument has to show if it is to succeed. And for this purpose I shall cite yet another passage in which Hartshorne argues in very much the same way.

"An animal, which cannot say God," he holds, "equally cannot say I. There is no derivation of the first notion from the second; but the two are from the outset in contrast in experience. The animal feels both itself and God . . . and thinks neither; we feel and can think both. We are, indeed, likely to call the divine 'I,' 'Truth' or 'reality'; that is, we think of certain abstract aspects of the inclusive something, and do not quite realize consciously that it must be

an inclusive experience, the model of all experiences in its personal unity''
(1948, 39f.). The several parallels here I take to be clear: the same insistence
that the divine-human contrast is a priori in experience; the same denial of
one-sided derivation of the idea of one side of the contrast from the idea of the
other; and the same admission that the contrast may nevertheless not be fully
realized at the level of conscious thought.

But what is arresting in this passage, in comparison with the others cited
earlier, is the distinction Hartshorne explicitly makes between our merely
feeling "the inclusive something," only some of the abstract aspects of which
are we likely to think about when we speak of it as "truth" or "reality," and
our consciously realizing, and thus thinking instead, that this inclusive something has to be "an inclusive experience," which as such is "the model of all
experiences." It evidently follows from this distinction that, if "the inclusive
something" *must* be "an inclusive experience," it can only be this inclusive
experience that we are actually experiencing even when we merely feel something all-inclusive that we are likely to speak about only abstractly in calling it
"truth" or "reality." But it just as clearly follows that we not only do not
need to experience "the inclusive something" *as* "an inclusive experience"
but are even likely to think about it consciously without quite realizing that
this is what it has to be. It thus becomes an interesting question whether our
merely feeling "the inclusive *something*" is already an experience of "an
inclusive *experience*." Perhaps the only thing to say is that in one sense it
clearly is, while in another sense it clearly is not. At any rate, one thing is
certain: only an experience of "the inclusive something" *as* "an inclusive
experience" and hence the conscious realization that this is all it can be could
possibly warrant the claim that it is "the model of all experiences." I conclude, therefore, that if Hartshorne's argument is successful, this can only be
because it shows that we have not only a direct intuition of God but also a
direct intuition of God *as* eminently psychical, and hence also think or consciously realize that the inclusive whole of which we experience ourselves to
be parts is a universal subject of experience.

But now what does Hartshorne's argument purport to show? The question is pertinent because he seems to say different things. On the one hand, he
claims that our concept of "know" comes partly from "some dim but direct
awareness of deity," which may often be driven below the level of conscious
thought, even if it is never wholly absent there; in a word, we have a feeling
of God as distinct from thinking or knowing God (1970a, 155; cf. 1962, 110).
On the other hand, he says that "we know what 'knowledge' is partly by
knowing God," which is presumably a different and stronger claim, even
though he repeats it later in the same sentence by saying only that "we form
our idea of human knowledge by exploiting the intuition . . . which we have
of God." I am satisfied that Hartshorne's apparent vacillation here is real and
that there are good reasons for it. But however this may be, we have only to
look at his own account of such matters to learn that having a feeling of God is

one thing, and that thinking about God, or having knowledge of God, is
something quite different.

Thus, in a recent defense of psychicalism, he stresses that "on the higher levels only does it [*sc.* the psychical] include what we normally mean by
'thought' or 'consciousness.' Lower creatures feel but scarcely know or
think, and if we speak of them as conscious, . . . we stretch the sense of the
word. This can be done, but then we need another word to distinguish high-
level, thoughtful cognitive experience or feeling from mere experience or
feeling" (1977, 95). The distinction Hartshorne insists on making here as
applied to our present question can be expressed by saying that, whereas mere
experience or feeling of God can be not only direct but immediate, high-level
thought or cognition of God, being mediated, as it is, by the conscious judgment or interpretation of such feeling, is of necessity mediate. Moreover,
since, according to Hartshorne, "human consciousness is essentially linguistic," the mediation involved in any thinking or knowing of God is also a
matter of language or verbal formulation (1959, 178).

To recognize this difference, however, is to understand why Hartshorne's argument cannot possibly succeed if it claims no more than that we
have a dim but direct awareness of deity. Even if it were indeed the case that
each of us in every moment is directly and immediately aware of God,
whether any psychical concept is a true analogy would still be undecided. As
Hartshorne himself admits, we may very well have an immediate experience
of "the inclusive something" without ever consciously thinking of it, or
even, it seems, being likely to think of it, as "an inclusive experience." And
yet without so thinking of it, we could never know it to be "the model of all
experiences" and so the primary analogue of at least some of our psychical
concepts. Consequently, if Hartshorne's argument is successful, it is only
because it makes the other and much stronger claim that each of us in every
moment is not only dimly aware of God but also thinks or knows God as
eminently experiencing subject.

This claim, however, is open to the decisive objection that it could not
be true unless human culture and history were radically other than we must
suppose them to be. If the claim that God must somehow be experienced
directly and universally already appears problematic, given the sheer fact of
non- and even a-theistic religions and philosophies, how much more problematic must it be when it becomes the claim that God is everywhere consciously known! Clearly, such a claim could be true only on the absurd
supposition that every case of professed non- or a-theistic belief must involve
conscious bad faith and intent to deceive.

Not surprisingly, Hartshorne has always been careful to avoid so incredible a claim. Although he has ever insisted that God somehow has to be experienced if anything at all is experienced, he has never failed to make clear, as in
several statements already quoted, that God need not be consciously known and
may even be expressly denied without conscious insincerity. Indeed, it is

precisely the clarity with which he has thus distinguished the different levels of our experience of God that has enabled him, as I claimed earlier, to solve the problems raised by asserting the experience of God in the objective construction of this phrase. But this, of course, is exactly why I also implied that the success he enjoys in solving this set of problems explains his failure to solve the other set raised by construing this phrase subjectively. One has only to consult what he himself has consistently taught about our experience of God as object to have the very best of reasons for rejecting out of hand any claim that each of us knows and must know God as experiencing subject.

I have no hesitation, therefore, in saying that Hartshorne's attempt to establish analogy is a failure. Either the claim he makes is weak enough to seem credible, in which case it is insufficient; or else he makes a claim strong enough to seem sufficient, in which case it is incredible.

Having said this, however, I think it is important to ask whether the reasons for his failure are merely contingent, in the sense that the attempt itself might well have succeeded, or still succeed, but for inadequacies in his argument that could have been, or yet can be, avoided. My own conviction is that the reasons his attempt fails are, rather, necessary and that the same fate must overtake any other similar attempt. Because this conviction has an important bearing on the conclusion to be drawn from these reflections I now wish to explain why it seems to me to be correct.

There is a further objection that might be made to Hartshorne's argument. Even if he could establish the stronger claim that there is a universal knowledge of God as eminent subject of experience, he would have no way of ruling out the possibility that this knowledge as such, as distinct from the immediate experience of which it is the conscious mediation, is entirely a matter of, in his terms, "analogical extension," which is to say, the secondary and derivative application to God of concepts which apply primarily and originally to ourselves, and which, therefore, are not true analogies at all but mere symbols. He in effect recognizes this when he admits that "we form the idea of divine knowledge by analogical extension from our experience of human knowledge" (1970a, 155). Although he goes on to insist that this is not the whole truth, what he takes to be the other side of the matter is that we form our idea of human knowledge, not by exploiting our intuition of God as eminently knowing, but by exploiting our intuition of God—period. Thus, for all he shows to the contrary, the only thing in our concept of human knowledge that derives from our direct intuition of God is the idea of totality or all-inclusiveness, just as he himself allows that we can very well experience "the inclusive something" without experiencing it as "an inclusive experience" (1948, 39f.).

But even more than this, Hartshorne himself again and again argues in such a way as clearly to imply that the primary, or as he can say, "normal," use of all our psychical concepts is their application to ourselves rather than to God. Thus, in one essay, for instance, he first argues against the idea of

providence as a power freely determining all the details of existence by asking, "whence do we have this idea of freedom? Surely, we can conceive it
because we have some little freedom of our own. . . . we must have some
range of possibilities genuinely open to us, or we could not form any conception of God as having an infinite range of possibilities open to him" (1963–
64, 20). Employing the same reasoning, he then argues that we must also
know ourselves as causes or creators, if we are to have any conception of God
in these terms, concluding with the general comment that "we cannot simply
nullify the normal meaning of a term and still use the term as basis for an
analogical extrapolation to deity" (22). I submit that arguments of this kind
can have the force that Hartshorne takes them to have only if the whole of our
knowledge of God, beyond our unavoidable experience of "the inclusive
something," can be derived from such knowledge as we have of ourselves,
and hence is merely symbolic rather than truly analogical. If we could know
anything else about God except through the mediation of concepts primarily
applying to our own intrahuman experience, who could deny that we might
very well know God to be free or creative without also knowing this of
ourselves?

But if any knowledge of God mediated by psychical concepts would
leave open the possibility of its being merely symbolic instead of truly analogical, what could rule out this possibility? The answer, I believe, is that the
only thing that could conceivably exclude it is an immediate knowledge of
God as the primary analogue of our psychical concepts. But then, of course,
the question is whether there can conceivably be any such thing as an immediate *knowledge,* as distinct from an immediate *experience,* of God, any more
than of anything else. Certainly, on Hartshorne's presuppositions, as should
by now be clear, any knowledge of God, just as of any other thing, is by its
very nature mediate insofar as it is mediated by conscious judgment and interpretation as well as verbal formulation of what is immediately given in
experience. Nor is it otherwise on the presuppositions of philosophers generally, who concur in analyzing the phrase "immediate knowledge" as expressing a self-contradiction and hence as meaningless. But if this analysis is
sound, the reasons for Hartshorne's failure to establish analogies as a class of
terms distinct from symbols are by no means merely contingent. Because the
only condition on which any such attempt could possibly succeed is itself
impossible to meet, he was sooner or later bound to fail, as anyone else must
always be who makes the same attempt.

My conclusion from these reflections, then, is that anything like
Hartshorne's distinction between analogy and symbol, however clear it may
be in itself, can never be known to apply. If any of our psychical concepts
really is a true analogy, in that it applies primarily to God and only sec-
ondarily to ourselves, at least with respect to what is meant by it, if not with
respect to how it means, we, at any rate, neither are nor ever could be in the
position of knowing it to be so. For all we could possibly know, all our

psychical concepts apply to God not as analogies, but as symbols, in exactly the same way in which at least some of them clearly must apply if we are to do any justice at all to the faith and witness of theistic religion.

The implications of this conclusion are many and far-reaching, for my own work as a theologian as well as for what I understand by the related, but nonetheless distinct, tasks of philosophy and metaphysics. Obviously, if theological analogies cannot be established, the same is true of metaphysical analogies generally, whether those of Hartshorne's psychicalism or those of any other categorial metaphysics necessarily involving such analogies. Consequently, if metaphysics can be established at all, it is only as a transcendental metaphysics, whose concepts and assertions are all purely formal and literal, rather than analogical, in the sense that they apply to all the different things within any single logical type whose meaning they explicate, not in different senses, but rather in the same sense.

So far as I can see, the foundations for such a transcendental metaphysics—and a neoclassical transcendental metaphysics at that—are firmly laid in Hartshorne's own systematic clarifications of the strictly literal claims that are necessarily implied by any nonliteral claims about God, which is to say, his analyses of the utterly general idea of reality as such as well as of the several logical-type distinctions discussed above. Nor does the fact that these analyses, as he develops them, are not adequately distinguished from formulations that he takes to be analogical, but that I can accept only as symbolic, in any way interfere with my appreciating both kinds of formulations as having their proper places in any adequate philosophy. For if, on the one side, he has never left any doubt that they are and must be clearly distinguishable, whether or not adequately distinguished, on the other side, I have no more inclination than he does simply to identify philosophy with metaphysics. On the contrary, I fully share his own view that philosophy has "two primary responsibilities," only one of which is properly metaphysical, the other being rather practical or existential (1970a, xiv). It seems entirely fitting that, in carrying out its other responsibility of expressing effectively the meaning of ultimate reality for us, as distinct from describing metaphysically the structure of ultimate reality in itself, philosophy should in its own way make use of the same vivid symbols that religion and theology employ to this end. Thus there is very little in Hartshorne's philosophy for which I do not also find a place, even if I feel compelled to distinguish it as indeed philosophy rather than metaphysics in the proper sense of the words.

But this is not the place to pursue further these or any of the other implications of the conclusion for which I have argued. Suffice it to say, simply, that on the alternative view I have proposed, no less than on Hartshorne's own, the assertion of the experience of God that is now necessary to any adequate Christian theology can receive all the clarification and support that a natural, or philosophical, theology may be reasonably expected to provide. If, on the one hand, this assertion is construed objectively, as asserting that God is the eminent object of experience, because the only individual other than ourselves whom we experience directly and universally, it can be shown to be true both literally and necessarily, on the understanding that such immediate experience of God can become knowledge of God, or even experience of God *as* God, only through the mediation of concepts and terms. If, on the other hand, the assertion is construed subjectively, as asserting that God is the eminent subject of experience, because the only individual who experiences all things as their primal source and final end, it, too, can be shown to be true necessarily, although neither literally nor analogically, but only symbolically, on the understanding that it is nevertheless really and not merely apparently true, because its implications can all be interpreted in the concepts and assertions of a transcendental metaphysics, whose application to God, as to anything else, is strictly literal.

Those who are privileged to have Charles Hartshorne as their teacher know that not the least thing they continue to learn from him is a distinctive philosophical procedure. One of the cardinal principles of this procedure he formulates by saying, "If in philosophizing we choose one of two possible views we should always know clearly what the other view is and why we reject it" (1966a, 92). How well I may have managed to follow this principle I should not wish to say. But, since I accept it as binding even on a philosophizing theologian, I hope it is at least clear, especially to my esteemed teacher, that I have in my own way tried to be faithful to it.

Works Consulted

Hartshorne, Charles

1937	*Beyond Humanism: Essays in the New Philosophy of Nature.* Chicago: Willett, Clark.
1945	"Analogy." In *An Encyclopedia of Religion,* ed. Vergilius Ferm. New York: Philosophical Library: 19f.
1948	*The Divine Relativity: A Social Conception of God.* New Haven: Yale University Press
1953	*Reality as Social Process: Studies in Metaphysics and Religion.* Glencoe, Ill.: The Free Press
1956	"The Idea of God—Literal or Analogical?" *Christian Scholar,* 39: 131–36
1957	"Whitehead and Berdyaev: Is There Tragedy in God?" *Journal of Religion,* 37: 71–84
1959	"A Philosopher's Assessment of Christianity." In *Religion and Culture: Essays in Honor of Paul Tillich,* ed. Walter Leibrecht. New York: Harper & Brothers: 167–80
1962	*The Logic of Perfection and Other Essays in Neoclassical Metaphysics.* LaSalle, Ill.: Open Court.

1963	"Sensation in Psychology and Philosophy." *Southern Journal of Philosophy*, 1, 2: 3–14
1963–64	"Man's Fragmentariness." *Wesleyan Studies in Religion*, 56, 6: 17–28
1965	*Anselm's Discovery: A Re-examination of the Ontological Proof for God's Existence*. LaSalle, Ill.: Open Court.
1966a	"Criteria for Ideas of God." In *Insight and Vision: Essays in Philosophy in Honor of Radoslav Andrea Tsanoff*, ed. Konstantin Kolenda. San Antonio, Texas: Principia Press of Trinity University: 85–95
1966b	"A New Look at the Problem of Evil." In *Current Philosophical Issues: Essays in Honor of Curt John Ducasse*, ed. Frederick C. Dommeyer. Springfield, Ill.: Charles C. Thomas: 201–12
1967	*A Natural Theology for Our Time*. LaSalle, Ill.: Open Court.
1970a	*Creative Synthesis and Philosophic Method*. LaSalle, Ill.: Open Court.
1970b	"Equality, Freedom, and the Insufficiency of Empiricism." *Southwestern Journal of Philosophy*, 1, 3: 20–27
1971	"Can Man Transcend His Animality?" *Monist*, 55: 208–17
1976	"Why Psychicalism? Comments on Keeling's and Shepherd's Criticisms." *Process Studies*, 6: 67–72
1977	"Physics and Psychics: The Place of Mind in Nature." In *Mind and Nature: Essays on the Interface of Science and Philosophy*, ed. John B. Cobb, Jr., and David Ray Griffin. Washington, D.C.: University Press of America: 89–96
1979	"God and Nature." *Anticipation*, 25: 58–64

Thomas Aquinas

1964	*Summa Theologiae*, vol. 3: *Knowing and Naming God* (Ia. 12–13), ed. Herbert McCabe, O.P. New York: McGraw-Hill.

Response by Charles Hartshorne

Schubert M. Ogden's essay is a striking example of his vigor and courage in following arguments through to their logical conclusions. He deals with central problems in the philosophy of religion; he is aware of their history and careful to do justice to whatever author he is discussing. So central and so subtle are the matters dealt with that I cannot hope to go far here and now in clarifying the obscurities and overcoming the difficulties he finds in my writings about them. In a way, the difficulties support the position I take about the status of theological issues, which is that *the* theistic question is what, if anything, we can coherently and definitely mean by "God," not whether or not God exists. If we know, clearly and consistently, what we mean by theism then what we mean is true; if not, it is absurd and could not be true. But do we know what we mean? Ogden shows how difficult a question this is.

I have, as he says, sometimes argued that, unless we have in our own natures instantiation of concepts (say that of decision-making) which we use to conceive God, we could not have these concepts. But I have also sometimes argued that we can conceive our own form of knowing, say, by introducing qualifications into what we know of divine cognition. God knows—period; we—partially, uncertainly, vaguely; and much of what we can hardly avoid taking as knowledge is erroneous belief. The appearance of contradiction here has sometimes occurred to me.

Ogden is correct also in finding the duality, feeling and thought, or sensing and knowing, a difficulty for psychicalism. Some might contend that it is vain to replace a dualism of mind and matter by an equally baffling dualism of merely sensitive in contrast to cognitive experiencing.

The origins of language are deeply obscure. However, we have some knowledge of how children learn to speak and understand languages. It does seem that they learn how words function largely by relating them to experiences other than religious. They learn what "decide" means by attention to their own or other peoples' choosings or decidings. And there seems no doubt that the idea of God has from the beginning implied resemblance in some positive way to a human person. It has always been, in some sense, anthropomorphic. On the other hand, reading the resemblance the other way, the believer has always felt that there was something deimorphic about human beings, at least in comparison to lower animals. To think God is to think an analogue superior in principle to a human person; to think a human person is to think an individual with fallible, partly erroneous, unclear, more or less confused forms of knowledge but not the unqualified knowledge, coincident with truth, which God has. The contrast between God and the knowing animal that each of us is seems implicit in our thought about either term (as Descartes held); but the human side alone is usually explicitly attended to.

Ogden asks what is really literal, what is analogical, and what is symbolic in the foregoing. He knows my attempts to give clear meanings to these three words, and that I term "symbolic" concepts that are applied eminently to God but not at all to some sorts of creatures, for instance, "shepherd" or "light." According to my (or Whitehead's) psychicalism, "feeling" applies analogically to all concrete, singular creatures, and to God, whereas "consciousness" or "knowledge" applies only on the higher levels of reality. And discursive thought is not applicable to God. Divine *knowledge* differs infinitely from ours in at least two senses: quantitatively and qualitatively. Peirce even says that we merely "gabble" when we attribute knowledge to God.

Once more the existential theistic issue is one of meaning, not of empirical fact. And it is hardly surprising that the meaning problem is here acute. We are in this matter trying to conceive what is most unlike ourselves but superior, as in dealing with atoms and particles, we are trying to conceive what is most unlike ourselves but inferior. Difficulty is to be expected in both cases.

I agree with Whitehead in distinguishing between physical and mental aspects of feeling. Thinking and our kind of knowledge are high levels of mentality. Deity is eminent physical and eminent mental feeling; it is above our thinking, somewhat as that is above the minimal physical feeling and mentality of atoms. Mentality is sense of the future, of possibility; physical feeling is sense of the past, of concrete actuality. All physical feeling is memory in a generalized sense, prehension of the past. Whitehead implies this. No singular creature is entirely devoid either of sense of the past or of sense of the future. Nor is God without either of these. This duality is the transcendentally categorial aspect of the matter.

Eminence as superior "in principle" does not contradict the possibility of transcendentals, categories applicable to God. God feels all creatures *without negative prehensions,* that is, without loss of distinctness. My use of the idea of degrees in such contexts may not always be clear and consistent.

It is correct that we cannot experience as ours wholly unthinking, unmediated physical feelings; it is only by abstraction that we can talk about the mere feeling aspect. But I am not convinced that the abstraction is illegitimate, provided one allows for the generalized notion of mentality, of future sensing, in contrast to past sensing.

What is at least analogical in the scheme is the idea of prehension as dependence of an actuality on other actualities, or of participation, feeling *of* feeling, experience of experience, together with sense of futurity. Also the idea of creative novelty. These apply from atom to God. Moreover, all of them are directly intuited in our immediate memories of our own past, and in our experience of our own bodies. Ogden mentions this last, but wonders if it begs the question. And he thinks it is not cogent to argue that all truth must be partly positive and that the complete absence of feeling has no positive meaning but is a mere negation. I am not sure he is right about either of these points.

Just how we use the word "symbolic" is of course a secondary question. What is not secondary is the avoidance of two extremes: on the one hand the idea that we can capture deity in some verbal formulas free from obscurity or doubt, and on the other that we are totally unable to talk coherently about God. The former extreme leads to intolerance and superstition, or the idolatry of confusing God with a certain book or tradition, or a certain human concept, the latter leads to atheism, the most rational form of which is precisely the doubt whether any form of God-talk makes sense.

The dualities of feeling and thought, or of discursive thought and divine intuition above thought, seem to me less objectionable than the hard dualism of feeling, thought, and super-discursive intuition on the one hand, and mere insentient matter on the other. All of the former dualities are spanned by experience as valuational and participatory, creative and preservative, which Whitehead from one point of view characterizes as "feeling of feeling" or "sympathy," and from another point of view as creativity. It is empathic freedom on many levels, from the most trivial forms to the unsurpassable or divine form. It is freedom dealing with other freedom, tolerating or "letting it be," as Heidegger says; it is enjoyment sharing enjoyment, love or caring in a variety of kinds which is in principle infinite. There is a completeness and integrity in the view that seems to me to place it above the available rivals. Whether or not this proves it to be true, does it not give reasonable support to faith that it is true?

Concerning my reasoning that there can be no merely negative truths, and that the total absence of feeling from any part of concrete actuality is a mere negation with no positive implications, Ogden comments that perhaps this shows only that psychicalism is unfalsifiable, not that it is true. I take it to show that "unfalsifiable" here is to be taken in so strong a sense that it implies "true." Many hypotheses are unfalsifiable by humanly available means, but our capacities to know are not the measure of reality. However, the sheer absence of feeling somewhere is unobservable by any conceivable mind or any conceivable means. In contrast, the presence of feeling is in principle knowable, unless prehension as essentially "feeling of feeling" is an absurdity. I hold that in feeling pain I am intuiting feelings in my bodily constituents, feelings which are not initially mine and only become mine by participation. But what would it be like to feel the total absence somewhere of feeling other than one's own? I think that there is no way this could be done. Here again we are not discussing contingent facts but meanings, necessary or impossible combinations of basic ideas. If the combinations are necessary, they give metaphysical truth; if impossible, they give metaphysical error—in both cases with the qualification that our human understanding has only fallible powers of discernment in such matters.

Is it a "merely empirical" argument for psychicalism that nothing positive could conflict with the presence of mind in some form, or that total insentience is strictly unknowable, and the sheerly unknowable is a pseudo-concept? I think it is an argument from conceptual necessities. Similarly, the argument that psychical concepts have infinite range does not need to start from *knowing* God as psychical. It starts from whatever experiences give us the concepts of feeling and the rest, and tries to see what imaginative generalization of these concepts leads to in extending their meaning. Still, again, my argument that it will not do to attribute supreme freedom to God and no freedom at all to anything else is a conceptual argument. The analogy from us to God implies a reverse analogy from God to us. In learning the meaning of words we appear necessarily to follow the us-to-God path, but then we must be able to follow *conceptually* the reverse path to understand fully what we have done. This is a matter of logical coherence. Indeed, coherence is a basic test of metaphysical truth, and the idealists who defined truth as coherence were defining metaphysical but not empirical truth, truths of contingent fact.

I do grant to Ogden that words such as "know" or "conscious" are symbolic, not analogical, as applied to God. As the lower animals are below what we normally mean by knowing, so God is above it. These are indeed special cases, and our human knowing is a third, and the one we have to take as our primary epistemic sample. Whitehead's is by far the most brilliant attempt to generalize what is common to all three forms of the psychical by his concepts of feeling of feeling, or physical prehension, and mentality, all included in what he calls creativity.

To sum up: I still wonder why we cannot say that feeling of feeling, with the Whiteheadian characteristics of decision and the production of new definiteness (the many becoming one and increased by one), is analogically universal. And this I take to be a generalized idea of "love" as partly self-creative sympathy. Thinking or knowing, as distinguishing the human species from the lower creatures, is symbolic as applied to God, who neither knows as we do nor fails to know as the lower creatures do. But it can be argued that, while God's knowing is not our scientific or philosophical thinking, even in its most successful forms, it has all the value, and more than all the value, of that thinking. It lacks the indistinctness, fallibility, and indirectness of our discursive, inferential reasoning and perceiving. To perceive with complete distinctness is more than to perceive indistinctly while trying to make up for this by inferential reasoning, which is always capable of making a false move.

I repeat once more: the puzzle about God is not, granting that we know very well what we mean by God, does what we mean describe anything real? No, the puzzle, the mystery is, do we clearly know what we mean? How are we, who are not infallibly, all-inclusively, consistently, and with unsurpassable appropriateness loving (with a love which embraces all the value of knowledge), able to know what we mean by this description? If we can know that, we need not worry about God's existence. For this will be already included in what we will know. A nonexistent but coherently conceivable deity is not even a possibility, but only the disjunction: *either* the necessary falsity (logical absurdity) *or* the necessary truth of the idea of God. If the theistic question is, Does 'God' exist, simply and precisely, as what we think of when we use the word? then it is highly unlikely that the answer is affirmative.

For reasons of Peirce's theory of signs it might be better to say that "shepherd," "ruler," or "world soul" are metaphors for God rather than symbols, since they are not merely conventionally related to deity; a genuine resemblance is intended. Moreover, understanding that the metaphors taken from personal relations are to be supplemented and in part corrected by those from the mind-body relationship, I think the entire procedure approximates analogy in my sense. Nor, I incline to think, is it merely empirical; for in any kind of world in which the question of God or any clearly conscious question whatever could arise there would be something like minds and bodies and something like persons.

As Ogden says, I distinguish a philosophy of life, meaning human life, from metaphysics. However, I include a theory of God and psychicalism in the latter. I do not include specific religious doctrines such as the Incarnation or the special significance of any human individual. Nothing about the contingencies of human history, or the present conditions of our species, is metaphysical.

Ogden has wrestled and forced me to wrestle, however well or ill, with essential difficulties in the philosophy of religion. It was a lucky day for me when he decided to take courses with me at the University of Chicago.

R. M. Martin

3

On the Language of Theology
Hartshorne and Quine

Let me confess straightway that knowing Charles and Dorothy Hartshorne was one of the rare privileges of my youth. They are, in my opinion, one of the great couples of academe. It was my pleasure to meet them for the first time at a meeting of the Aesthetics Society of America in the early fall of 1944 at a reception in the Wade Park Manor Hotel in Cleveland. I was on my way to Chicago, more particularly to the University of Chicago, to teach in the newly formed college program in mathematics. In Dorothy I instantly recognized a woman of extraordinary intelligence, charm, and warmth. Charles's work was already known to me to some extent—he was a famous metaphysician even then—and I had heard him speak on perception at Harvard, when I was an undergraduate there, in a talk that was followed by an interesting exchange with C. I. Lewis. In Chicago, the Hartshorne home became my second home, and the kindness and warm hospitality shown me there are of the sort that one can never be sufficiently grateful for or repay. I had been a student of Whitehead's at Harvard during the very last year of his teaching there. So of course Charles and I had a close bond in our love and admiration for Whitehead. I had already read a good deal of Peirce's writings, especially his logical works, but under Charles's stimulus came to see in him a much richer and variegated philosophic mind than I had seen theretofore. The joy of talking about Peirce and Whitehead with Charles off and on during these intervening years has never ceased, even when we have not been able to see eye to eye about some niceties of detail.

It was my good fortune to be present at Charles's *rencontre* with Van Quine at Boston University the evening of October 17, 1979. What Charles and Van said that evening seems to me to provide excellent summaries of their respective overall philosophical views. My remarks today will be concerned almost wholly with this *rencontre*, subjecting it to a careful reading and ap-

From Richard M. Martin, *Metaphysics, Mereology, and Metalogic*, © copyright by Philosophia Verlag GmbH, Munich.

praisal. Although my remarks will seem largely critical, the underlying intent is constructive, to help do the job better. Philosophical theology is still in its infancy, a swaddling babe scarcely 2,000 years old, and the best is yet to come. My own view is that it cannot be brought to maturity, at this tail end of the twentieth century, without taking into intimate account the lessons the new logic has taught us.

In a very perceptive, but as yet unpublished, paper devoted to evaluation and to evaluating those who evaluate, Paul Weiss has called attention to the highly practical character of the theoretical work of logical analysis, thereby helping to verify Whitehead's famous dictum that the paradox is now fully resolved which states that our most abstract concepts are our best and most useful instruments with which to come to understand concrete matters of fact and practical affairs. In philosophical theology par excellence these three items are welded together indissolubly—abstract concepts, concrete matters of fact, practical affairs—so that Weiss's comments are of special relevance for us in our discussion at this conference. He notes that (MS, p. 13) "most of our inferences do not begin with premises known or accepted as being certainly true. Often we fail to move straightforwardly to necessitated conclusions. We begin with what is dubious, merely believed, or supposed. We backtrack and qualify to end with what is only tentatively accepted. *Rules governing the legitimate moves* [emphasis added] are today being formulated by modal, intensional, and multi-valued logicians, with the result that logic is more pertinent today to the [analysis of the] reasoning of actual men than it ever had been before. So far as what logicians have achieved is ignored, [no benefits result]."

It is interesting that Weiss mentions modal, intensional, and multi-valued logics, but not the very one that is perhaps the most suitable. What one needs is an all-inclusive logic—a "grand logic," in Peirce's phrase—in which the positive achievements of these various alternative logics can be accommodated without having to pay the high, inflationary prices they usually demand: excessive ontic commitment and involvement, "fuzzy" semantics, excessive and perhaps unsound or at least dubious axioms and rules, and failure to achieve the kind of "maximum logical candor" that should be aimed at. It has been contended elsewhere, and to some extent shown, that the approach via an *event-logic* seems to provide the kind of unified outlook required and at a reasonable price. Weiss is surely correct in thinking that logic, as construed in a sufficiently broad sense, is nowadays of greater practical, as well as philosophical, utility than ever before. The more it is used the greater its helpfulness is seen to be in assuring correctness of statement and of inference, and adequacy of assumption needed for a given purpose, in bringing to light unforeseen relationships and interconnections, in leading to new insights and new problems to be investigated.

In speaking of the burgeoning literature on evaluation, Weiss comments (MS, p. 12) that the subject "suffers from two unexamined limitations: it explicitly recognizes only a few of the methods that it actually uses, and it misconstrues the import of what it does acknowledge. It is not alone [in this]. Every practical [and, indeed, theoretical, scientific, and philosophical, it would seem] enterprise . . . suffers from the same defects, though usually in different places [and ways] and with different results.'' On one item, however, almost all types of enterprise, whether practical or theoretical, seem to share the same defect at the same place, namely, in inattention to the logical character of the basic vocabulary needed or being used, to its syntax, its semantics, its pragmatics.

The language of philosophical theology seems not to have been subjected to any very searching logical analysis in the recent literature. The reason in part is that logic itself had not yet developed to the point where this could take place fruitfully. In the past few years, however, this situation has been changing radically. Three items stand out as of especial relevance for such purposes, the systematic development of syntax, semantics, and pragmatics already mentioned, the formulation of a suitably sensitive and delicate theory of intensionality, and the articulation of the all-embracing logic governing events, states, acts, and processes, already referred to. We now seem, for the first time in history, very close to being able to examine without distortion any theological vocabulary, however subtle, and all types of reasoning, however delicate and complex, that enter into theological discussion.

A word more about the inner character of the event-theoretical framework, which consists of (1) the usual quantificational theory of first order, extended to include the theory of virtual classes and relations, (2) the theory of identity, (3) Leśniewski's mereology or calculus of individuals, (4) logical syntax in its modern form, (5) a semantics or theory of reference both extensional and intensional, (6) variant renditions of systematic pragmatics as needed, (7) the theory of events, states, acts, and processes, and, finally, (8) a theory of structural or grammatical relations of the kind needed for the analysis of natural language. Nothing short of this eightfold kind of theory would seem to be adequate, and, once available, it may be seen to provide appropriate foundations for modal, multi-valued, and other so-called ''alternative'' logics.

All criticism presupposes a background theory of some sort as a basis. The event-theoretic framework is presupposed in the following comments, where, however, the attempt has been made to keep technical matters at an absolute minimum.

Let us turn now to the formal part of this paper.

Professor Hartshorne believes that ''there are rational grounds for theism, or the assertion of the existence of God, if the word 'God' is suitably defined.''[1] Perhaps we should say here rather that theism comprises an entire theory of which statements to the effect that God exists are logical consequences of the theory's axioms, given definitions of 'God' and 'exists'. Suitable definitions of either, however, are not easy to come by, as everyone would no doubt admit. It is probably best to introduce 'God' as a logically proper name in terms of a suitable Russellian description, as Bowman Clarke has well noted.[2] Descriptions fail of their mark, however, unless postulates or theorems are forthcoming assuring the existence and uniqueness of the entity described.

Hartshorne is interested in "rational grounds" for the existence of God, or "valid reasons" or "arguments" or even "formal arguments." He never quite tells us precisely what he means by these phrases—it is very difficult to do so—but one key item about them seems to be overlooked entirely, namely, their relativity to a *system*. All such phrases are, strictly, meaningless except in terms of some system of notions or concepts. The very words 'rational' and 'valid' are delicate words that must be handled with the greatest care and precision before they yield their nectar. Also these words interanimate each other, the behavior of each contributing to the very "meaning" of the other. If separate arguments are given within separate systems, this is a significant fact to be noted. If they are all given within the same system, or some in one, some in another, this too is a circumstance of some significance. In any event, it is only by keeping "tabs on our tools" that we are able to be clear as to precisely what it is that we are saying. Philosophy, after all, needs precision of statement, more even than mathematics and natural science do.

Hartshorne lists some qualifications on theism that are to him essential: a "principle of dual transcendence" and a belief in certain "a priori" arguments (actually six of them) that are claimed to be "free from obvious fallacy" and that are suitably arranged disjunctively. Let us examine these arguments and worry a little about the kind of language-structure within which they are presumed to be formulated. Nothing is more profitable in philosophical study than worry of this sort. And nothing here looms so important as details. *Gott wohnt im Detail,* as an old German adage has it. Neglect of detail almost always leads to a sloppy vocabulary, blurred premises, inarticulate reasoning, and inconclusive conclusions.

"Dual transcendence," Hartshorne tells us, "holds that God surpasses other beings, not by being sheerly absolute, infinite, independent, necessary, eternal, immutable, but by being *both* absolute, independent, infinite, etc., *and also,* in uniquely excellent fashion, relative, dependent, finite, contingent, and temporal. This combination of traits is not contradictory, since there is a distinction of respects in which the two sets of adjectives apply to God." These interesting adjectives all need a careful analysis in their various uses in ordinary contexts as well as in the highly special ones in which they may be attributed analogically to God. It is to be feared that adequate analyses of either kind have never been given. It is one of the future tasks of logico-linguistics, on the one hand, and of logico-theology, on the other, to provide them. Nonetheless, Hartshorne is probably on the right track in holding that the notion of a "distinction of respects" is needed here. God may be said to be "absolute" in one respect but "relative" in another, "infinite" in one respect and "finite" in another, and so on. But we must immediately ask: *in what respects* is God one or the other? Without a clear articulation of the respects, dual transcendence relative to any given pair of adjectives is not very informative. Also we must worry here as to how respects are to be handled. What kind of an object are they? Are they values for variables?

In my paper "On God and Primordiality," a notion of God was put forward that turns out to be closer to that of St. Thomas Aquinas than to that of Whitehead or Hartshorne.[3] Whether the conception there is precisely that of "classical" theism remains to be considered. But in any case, it is akin to it, closer to it no doubt than that of the process theologians. However, dual transcendence—not perhaps in Hartshorne's sense but in the sense of the "six antitheses" concerning God's nature that Whitehead puts forward in *Process and Reality*—is shown to apply to it. God, in the sense of the "On God and Primordiality" paper, is explicitly shown to be both "permanent" and "fluent," "one" and "many," "actual eminently" but also actually deficient, and so on, but of course in different senses. Thus dual transcendence, in Whitehead's sense, can hold for notions of God not based on process theology, for notions more akin to that (or those) of the very "classical" theism that Hartshorne thinks is not only "false *a priori*" but also "a tragic error." I shall urge below, however, that neither of these contentions appears to be justifiable.

What view is it that opposes the principle of dual transcendence? It is to contend that deity is "in every respect absolute or infinite" and so on, and this is "either to empty the idea of any definite and consistent meaning or to make it a mere abstraction. Concrete actuality cannot be merely infinite, independent, or necessary. Hence to deny any and every sort of finitude, relativity, or contingency to God is not to exalt him." What Hartshorne refers to as "classical" theism is apparently precisely the view that denies dual transcendence in this strong sense. But does it? To establish that it does would require a considerable spelling out of the view or views. Has it really been contended that God is infinite, absolute, etc., in *every* respect? Think how strong the quantifier 'in every respect' here is. It must cover all the respects of which the language at hand can speak. Any language adequate for theology must be of a very considerable breadth and expressive power; it must include modes of expression for mathematics and science, for describing our moral behavior, our values, our hopes, fears, and loves, and so on. It is doubtful that any serious theism has ever denied the principle of dual transcendence in the very strong sense in which Hartshorne states it.

How, in a strictly logical way, are the quantifiers over respects to be handled? Hartshorne does not tell us, nor does Findlay, who makes a good deal of essentially the same notion.[4] In several recent papers attempts have been made to provide a logic of aspects using different Fregean Under-relations to allow us to say that a given object x is taken *under* a given predicate-description in a given intensional context e.[5] There are several alternative relations here to be considered. One or more of them holds every promise of providing the theologian and metaphysician with the tools for making all the distinctions concerned with aspect that will ever be needed.

Note that, in the passage just cited, Hartshorne shifts attention to "concrete actuality," which, for him, God must exhibit. The dichotomy of "concrete" and "abstract" is a tricky one, and a good deal of clarification is needed to specify the sense or senses in which any conception of God may be said to be one or the other. Additional clarification is then needed to spell out the sense or senses in which God is said analogically to be or not to be "infinite," "independent," or "necessary." Howsoever these matters be arranged, God is of course to be "exalted" above all else. This is to be done, not just by ascribing or withholding, analogically, certain adjectives of him, but rather primarily in making him the sole object of religious devotion in accord with whose will we seek to direct every act of our lives, however small, and whom we seek to love with all our heart and soul and mind and strength.

Hartshorne makes much of the a priori, as having something to do with "conceivable experiences," the *empirical* then consisting of what is not a priori. This hoary set of terms, however, has been the subject of considerable debate in recent years, and it is safe to say that the dichotomy has never been sufficiently clarified or even justified for analytical purposes.[6] At best it is a remnant of the past and probably should be buried forever. It has done its harm in contributing to philosophical confusion, and should now be allowed to rest in peace. It would seem to be a general weakness of Hartshorne's methodology that he makes so much depend on it.

The six arguments for God's existence that Hartshorne accepts are all "equally *a priori*," and against them he thinks there are no valid "empirical" reasons. One of them is a form of the ontological argument. However, no one of the six is "so evidently cogent that there can be no reasonable ground for rejecting it." This last can be said, however, without recourse to the a priori. Also it can be said of any hypothesis of theoretical science, for example, or even of mathematics. There are almost always reasonable grounds for rejecting any scientific hypothesis.

Now what is a "formal argument" for Hartshorne? It is, he tells us, "a set of options claiming to be exhaustive. If p entail q then the options are: accept q or reject p." There appears to be a category mistake here between the *semantical* notion of an *entailment* and the *pragmatic* reactions to it of *accepting* or *rejecting* its premise or conclusion. The formal argument is one, the options the other. Let us bear in mind this distinction and move on. Hartshorne's very next sentences state that "merely rejecting p is negative and rather vague as to what the rejection positively imports. Hence, in my formulation of the six arguments, the blanket negation, *not p*, where p is theism, is analyzed as a disjunction of the possible more or less positive forms the negation could take. If the disjunction is finite and exhaustive, then one must either accept the negative disjunction as a whole or accept the theistic conclusion—unless one chooses to take *no* stand, to be merely agnostic.'' These are rather obscure sentences to fathom. Let us follow the spirit if not the letter of what they are supposed to say in order to understand what the six proofs really amount to.

In the first place, a formal argument is not in any strict sense a set of options. One may *accept* the premise or premises of an argument; then, if the argument is valid, it is eminently ''rational'' to accept also the conclusion. Suppose now that sentence *a* entails the sentence *b*, i.e., that *a* is the conjunction of the premises logically implying, so to speak, the conclusion *b*. And suppose this entailment is accepted by some person. The options for such a person are then that he does *not* accept *a* or that he does accept *b*. We see this by recalling the so called *Modus Ponens* principle of pragmatics[7]

(1) $\vdash(p)\,(a)\,(b)\,(t)\,(p\ \text{Acpt}\,\ulcorner(a \supset b)\urcorner t \cdot p\ \text{Acpt}\,a,t) \supset p\ \text{Acpt}\,b,t),$

and hence

(2) $(p)\,(a)\,(b)\,(t)\,(p\ \text{Acpt}\,\ulcorner(a \supset b)\urcorner t \supset (\sim p\ \text{Acpt}\,a,t \lor p\ \text{Acpt}\,b,t)).$

Here of course '*p* Acpt *a,t*' expresses that person *p* accepts or takes-as-true the sentence *a* at time *t*. But for a person not to accept *a* is *not* the same as his *rejecting b*. To reject *a*, in the most natural sense, is to accept the negation of *a* rather than merely not to accept *a*.

Hartshorne equates these two meanings of 'rejects' uncritically. The result is that his first ''proof,'' in the form in which he presents it, is not valid. To infer from (1) or (2) that

(3) $((p\ \text{Acpt}\,\ulcorner(a \supset b)\urcorner, t \cdot \text{Sent}\,a) \supset (p\ \text{Acpt}\,\ulcorner \sim a\urcorner t \lor p\ \text{Acpt}\,b,t)$

is not valid in general. The reason is that

(4) $(p)\,(a)\,(t)\,(p\ \text{Acpt}\,a,t \supset \sim p\ \text{Acpt}\,\ulcorner \sim a\urcorner,t),$

or

(5) $(p)(a)(t)(p\ \text{Acpt}\,\ulcorner \sim a\urcorner t \supset \sim p\ \text{Acpt}\,a,t),$

but not conversely, provided *p*'s acceptances are consistent. From the *converse* of (4) or (5) we can validly infer (3), if Sent *a*, but not from (4) or (5). It is (3), however, that Hartshorne needs as a basis for his discussion of options. Nevertheless, the germ of the proof can be reconstructed without bringing in acceptance or any talk of options. To begin with, then, let us attempt to reconstruct the proof in terms of provability.

Let 'a_1' express that "there is cosmic order," 'a_2' that "there is a cosmic ordering power," and 'a_3', that "the cosmic ordering power is divine." Hartshorne assumes that the words occurring in these sentences are all suitably available either as primitives or are defined. This is a dangerous assumption which will be discussed in a moment. Let 'A'' now be '$\sim a_1$', 'A''' be '$(a_1 \cdot \sim a_2)$', and 'A'''' be '$(a_1 \cdot a_2 \cdot \sim a_3)$'. Let 'T' be '$(a_1 \cdot a_2 \cdot a_3)$'. T is thus the thesis of theism, that there is cosmic order, and an ordering power, and the power is divine. The relevant entailment is

(6)   '$(\sim(A' \text{ v } A'' \text{ v } A''') \supset T)$',

which is merely the statement of the theoremhood of the tautology

(7)   '$(\sim (\sim a_1 \text{ v } (a_1 \cdot \sim a_2) \text{ v } (a_1 \cdot a_2 \cdot \sim a_3)) \supset (a_1 \cdot a_2 \cdot a_3))$'.

If we could prove the antecedent, we would then, of course, have a proof of theism in the sense of Hartshorne's first proof.

   How could we "prove" the antecedent? By proving '$\sim A'$', '$\sim A''$', and '$\sim A'''$' separately. Presumably the system in which the proof could be carried out would be such that all of these would be forthcoming. In any case Hartshorne thinks 'A'' is "scarcely attractive to anyone," and that 'A''' is "not obviously false" for "we know that order can be at least partly brought about by an ordering power, as in political affairs." For 'A'''' Hartshorne states that he "can give reasons, cogent to . . . [him], for thinking that what gives an ordering power its capacity to order is some intrinsic merit or value. . . . In the case of cosmic order, this principle takes its supreme form."

   Hartshorne does not think of this "proof" in terms of provability, however, but in terms of acceptance, as I have already noted. His "proof" is thus really a *pragmatic* one, and moreover one relative to the person whose acceptances are under consideration. Consider a person, CH, say, whose acceptances are such that

(8) $((\sim CH \text{ Acpt } b,t \cdot \text{ Sent } b) \supset CH \text{ Acpt}^\ulcorner \sim b \urcorner t)$.

For such a person, assuming he accepts the tautology (7), and in general is "rational" with respect to his acceptance of the principles of logic, his "options" are then to accept T or to accept '$(A' \text{ v } A'' \text{ v } A''')$'. But for him to accept this last is for him to accept '$\sim a_1$' or to accept '$(a_1 \cdot \sim a_2)$' or to accept '$(a_1 \cdot a_2 \cdot \sim a_3)$'. There are just these four possibilities. One's only option, then, if one rejects these three (in either sense of 'rejects', for (8) assures that the two senses are the same for the person CH) is to accept theism. In the approach in terms of options, however, theism is not proved, but merely listed as one of the options. For a *proof,* as already noted, proofs of '$\sim A'$', '$\sim A''$', and '$\sim A'''$' must be supplied. No such proofs, however, are forthcoming. A specific person may accept them, of course, and he may have reasons, even "cogent" reasons, to do so. But such reasons do not constitute a proof. We conclude then that Hartshorne's first "proof"—even if there were no problems remaining concerning the vocabulary of its premises—is not a strict proof but merely a tautological disjunction of "options."

The problem of the analysis of the inner vocabulary of the premises remains an insistent one, however. The "logic" Hartshorne uses is merely Russell's theory of "unanalyzed propositions," an extremely narrow domain of logic that tends to shackle thought rather than to give it the freedom it needs. Note that nowhere in Hartshorne's proof is attention given to the quantifiers needed, nor is any sensitiveness shown as to how 'exists' (or some synonym) is handled. Nor does Hartshorne attempt any analysis of what "cosmic order" is, whether "approximate" or "probabilistic."[8] As to what an "ordering power" is, we are left to infer that an ordering power for the cosmos is like one shown in political affairs, on the one hand, as well as like one with which "a waking human consciousness partly orders the behavior of its human body." (Note the interesting use of the possessive 'its' here; we are allowed to infer that it is a human consciousness that "possesses" a human body.) As to 'divine', we are told that it means: "maximal in every respect logically permitting such a maximum, and in those respects of value (and there are some) that do not permit a maximum, it means *unsurpassable except by itself. . . .*"

This last "definition" cries out for a good deal of clarification. What are the values that "logically permit" a maximum? What is the logic of the scales of value presumably invoked here? Is there a single notion of *being greater than* in terms of which these scales are constructed, or are there many? How is the logic of "respects" here handled? Can this be done satisfactorily in terms of the Fregean *Art des Gegebenseins*?[9] Or in terms of the relation Under spoken of above? How is 'unsurpassable' defined? Where is the delineation of the vocabulary needed for the definiens to be found? (Some attempt has been made to deal with this last question in my paper on Anselm.[10]) Specific answers to these and many further questions must be given before any clear notion emerges from Hartshorne's definition of 'divine.' Definitions given in isolation are strictly meaningless. They must always be given in the context of a system of notions, some of which are taken as primitives. Whitehead called attention to this important fact about definitions years ago, but his warnings have been largely disregarded.

Hartshorne thinks that his argument is not empirical on the grounds that "the idea of a merely chaotic world . . . [is] a confused notion. . . . Any world in which the theistic or any other question could arise would have an order. . . . Some order or other is a presupposition of inquiry and of all thinking." (Even chaos might be thought to have its order, namely, precisely the one that, as a matter of fact, obtains.) Are these "grounds," if they be such, sufficient to maintain that Hartshorne's argument is not empirical? Both the premises and the conclusion are surely empirical, but the tautology (2) is not. The argument is thus in part empirical and in part not. Should not a kind of principle of dual transcendence be invoked here? In any case it would be a fundamental error to contend that the premises are principles of logic. Rather are they very complicated statements—those of logic are always simple— containing essential or nontrivial occurrences of such (presumably defined) words or phrases as 'cosmic order', 'ordering power', 'unsurpassable', 'divine', and so on. And concerning whatever ultimate primitives are adopted, suitable meaning postulates (or nonlogical axioms) must be assumed to enable us to prove the existence and uniqueness of some one divine, unsurpassable entity, as has already been suggested.

Hartshorne's second argument is a "revised version of the ontological argument" aimed to "discredit the idea that the theistic question is an empirical or contingent one." The argument is given a modal form. Hartshorne lets 'MT' express that 'T' is "logically possible, where 'logically' means taking into account certain meaning postulates about 'God' and about the relation between the logical and ontological modalities." However, no such meaning postulates are ever given. If 'God' is a *defined* term, the various properties God has should be forthcoming as theorems rather than as postulates. Meaning postulates are always ultimately "about" the primitives, although of course some defined terms may occur in them to shorten their length. If 'God' is a primitive, how are we to construe 'T' as stated above? The expression for which it is an abbreviation contains 'divine' but not 'God'. In any case, whatever postulates are needed to clarify what Hartshorne means by the quasi-modal 'M', they should surely be given.

Hartshorne formalizes his version of the ontological proof by taking

(9)   'MT'

and

(10)   '($\sim$ MT v $\sim$ M $\sim$ T)'

as premises, with

(11)   '$\sim$ M $\sim$ T' and hence 'T'

as conclusions. The two premises are "not derivable from logical constants [principles?] alone. . . . They are metaphysical principles." If so, are they provable from other prior metaphysical principles, or are they metaphysical axioms? Presumably the latter, for it is remarked parenthetically that "the comparison of them with axioms of set theory might be worth exploring." If they are metaphysical axioms, then of course the conclusion follows, provided

(12)   '($\sim M \sim T \supset T$)'

is also forthcoming as a logical or metaphysical axiom or theorem.

Hartshorne also states this "argument" in terms of options, but this adds nothing to the "proof" beyond what has already been said about the first one. The problems remain, however, not only of justifying the two premises, but of justifying as a whole the metaphysical system in which they may be stated.

One may perhaps construe (9) as stating that 'T' is not internally contradictory in the sense of logically entailing a contradiction. But, as Hartshorne observes, "consistency is not easily judged where, as here, the claim to have an actual case would beg the question. We know from the Russellian and other paradoxes how easily a verbal formula can conceal a contradiction." Even so, we might be able to prove that 'T' has no contradiction as a *logical* consequence without invoking an actual case. Such a proof would be elaborate and would have to take into account all the meaning postulates adopted. Hartshorne notes that "without the premise of consistency, no ontological argument can prove its conclusion." This statement is obscure, but it should be pointed out that if the premises are inconsistent, then of course all statements of the language follow from them. If the premises are inconsistent, "this does not mean that . . . [the argument] proves nothing." Quite; it rather proves too much. Hartshorne then adds that "if the argument is rejected because of the possible or actual falsity [not contradictoriness (?)] of (9), the implication is that the theistic question may, or must, be nonempirical." It is difficult to see just why this "implication" is drawn. Hartshorne explicitly takes (9) and (10) as metaphysical principles and thus presumably as nonempirical. Thus, presumably also, (11) is nonempirical—unless, of course, the meaning postulates leading up to (9) are taken as empirical, which, presumably again, they are not.

The premise (10) is said to be "implied by Aristotle's dictum" that with eternal things, to be possible and to be are the same. Hartshorne symbolizes this as

'($MT \equiv T$)'.

However, (10) does not follow from Aristotle's dictum and may obtain even if it does not. (10) can be given the equivalent form

'($MT \supset \sim M \sim T$)',

but we cannot then correctly conclude 'T' without also using (12), which neither logically implies nor is logically implied by Aristotle's dictum. Where 'N' stands for 'is necessary', (12) may of course be given the equivalent form

'($NT \supset T$)'.

Note incidentally that if Aristotle's dictum holds, together with (9), this second proof becomes trivial in the extreme.

In my paper on Anselm, an attempt was made, not only to spell out the full vocabulary needed for stating the—or at least *a*—ontological argument, but also to list in full the premises needed. The vocabulary included a predicate 'Cncv' for expressing that a person *conceives* such-and-such under a suitable linguistic description, a predicate 'Able' enabling us to express that a person has the *ability* to do so-and-so under a given description, and a predicate 'Gr' enabling us to express that one entity is *greater* than another in what is presumed to be Anselm's sense. In terms of these three predicates, together of course with suitable logical devices, a definition of 'God' mirroring the *id, quo maius cogitari non potest* can be given. Concerning these notions suitable meaning postulates were laid down. Whatever the internal inadequacies of that paper, the attempt there was apparently the first to spell out in full detail the logical structure of the ontological argument—an attempt similar to that of Jan Salamucha with respect to the *ex motu* argument of St. Thomas.[11] Hartshorne has not built upon the basis of these attempts, both of which would have helped him to see how easily a mere verbal predicate like 'M' can conceal the need for a full and careful delineation of vocabulary and for an explicit need for spelling out the postulates needed. It is to be feared that Hartshorne's version of the ontological argument has not carried the matter forward.

The notions 'possible' and 'necessary' are of course extremely troublesome ones, and Hartshorne makes the most of them. Whitehead was much clearer in construing the necessary in terms of universality, more particularly, in terms of the universality of what he took to be necessary metaphysical principles. Necessity and possibility are thus context-relative notions, on such a rendering. Hartshorne, however, seems to use these notions not only as context-free but also in a kind of epistemic sense. He wants to contend that "God could not just happen to exist, or just happen not to exist. This is an incoherent idea." Again, he states that he sees "no coherent meaning for the idea of deity as possibly existent and possibly non-existent, and . . . [he sees] no consistent way to reject theism except by rejecting its logical possibility or coherent conceivability." There is confusion in these statements between "logical possibility" and "coherent conceivability," "coherent idea," and the like. The relations between these needs to be spelled out. Hartshorne makes use not only of logical and "ontological" modalities—he nowhere tells us what these latter are—but of epistemic ones as well. But even if these could be suitably clarified somewhat, there is no getting around the fact that for any "argument" premises are needed. No argument for the existence of deity can be given in any other way.

Arguments for or against theism are very much like arguments in theoretical science, even in mathematics. If you want certain theorems to follow, make suitable assumptions. If you are hesitant about the assumptions, try your best to get along without them. If, for example, you do not like the Axiom of Choice for some reason or other, see how far you can go in the theory of functions of a real variable without it.

Hartshorne chastises those who have upheld the "traditional" version (or versions) of the ontological argument for failing to distinguish sufficiently *existence* and *actuality*. The existence of an "essence" or "coherent idea" involves that this latter is "*somehow* actualized or instantiated," the actuality of an essence involving the "*how* or in *what* concrete form, if at all" it is actualized. Most writers, it is contended, have "missed . . . [this] distinction between abstract and concrete, or mere existence of a defined essence and the concrete *how* of this existence." This is not the occasion to appraise Hartshorne's critique of his predecessors on this point. Rather we must ask him for a much fuller and more exact account of this distinction than he has given.

Hartshorne goes on to make some rather obscure observations concerning definite descriptions. "The sense in which 'the present King of France' is a definite Russellian description differs logically from that in which the definition of 'God' is such a description. Ordinarily an essence is one thing, and the existence of that essence is another and additional thing or truth. This is because ordinary beings are produced by the creative process. . . . Any production is always partly contingent, might go this way or that. The actuality is *how* it goes. In the case of God the being itself, as identified by its essence, could not be produced but is defined as eternal. This means that it is essential to the creative process rather than one of its conceivable products."

This passage and its sequel summarize the gist of Hartshorne's view better perhaps than his purported "proofs" do. It is important therefore to unearth the difficulties that lie hidden beneath the verbal surface.

In the first place, we should query the logical difference between 'the present King of France' and the Hartshornean 'the one unsurpassable [or divine] being'. That there is a nonlogical difference is undeniable. In each case the description (or essence or coherent idea) is one thing, and that of which the description is a description is another. The description is, strictly, an inscription, and neither the present King of France nor the divine unsurpassable are inscriptions. Each of these inscriptions—for the moment we may assume we are talking about just two of them, one for each of the shapes cited— functions as a proper name of (or *designates*) a given entity, provided the postulates are sufficient to guarantee the existence and uniqueness of these entities. Corresponding to each of these entities, assuming that there are such, there are corresponding concepts of them, namely, the entities taken under the respective modes of linguistic description or *Arten des Gegebenseins*.[12] The entities of course are not to be identified with these concepts. All three are *toto coelo* different in each case: the inscriptions, the entities purportedly described, and the corresponding concepts. To distinguish these three is essential, it would seem, to clear thought, and has no more to do with the contention that "ordinary beings are produced by the creative process" than with some opposing contention. Suppose we grant Hartshorne this contention, however, along with the additional one that any "production . . . might go this way or that." We would not wish to say that actuality is *how* it goes, construing 'is' in the sense of the 'is' of identity, but only that actuality is the *result* of how it goes, so to speak. There is all the difference in the world between the how and the result.

Hartshorne's ambient theory must of course contain a theory of processes of *production,* but it must also contain terms for the how of these processes as well as for their results. It must contain in addition a theory as to who or what produces what. Somewhere along the line, in his theory, a principle will be forthcoming that God is not "produced" by anything. This principle will be a "necessary" metaphysical one in the theory assuring that God is not one of the "products" of the creative process. Somewhere along the line it will obtain also that the present King of France is or is not one of those products. There is nothing at all remarkable that these two principles should obtain, the one as a metaphysical necessity, the other as a factual contingency. But God's being "defined as eternal" does not rule out that he might be one of the conceivable products in the creative process, namely, as self-producing. It is surely a "coherent idea" that an eternal entity could "produce" itself as well as all temporal entities.

"Insofar contingency does not apply," Hartshorne goes on to state, in this crucial passage. "But the noncontingency of an essence only means that there can be no such thing as the essence simply unactualized." But if contingency does not apply, neither does noncontingency. What now is the "noncontingency of an essence"? Is 'the present King of France' contingent because the statement that there is or is not such an entity is contingent? Similarly, is 'the divine unsurpassable entity' necessary because the statement that there is such an entity is a metaphysical principle? If so, very well, but this is the case, then, merely because we have formulated the metaphysics in such a way that it does obtain. In what sense now does this "mean that there can be no such thing as the essence simply unactualized"? Here of course we must distinguish existence from actuality, in accord with Hartshorne's own admonitions. But how can we legitimately pass from the statement that God exists to one that says that he is actualized? To be actualized is presumably somehow to be in the creative process, that is, *to be produced.* But no, we have been told that although God is "essential to the creative process" he is not "one of its conceivable products." Some additional "principle" is needed here to substantiate this contention. It is that "the divine is eternally somehow actualized, or the supposed idea fails to make sense and could not be actualized." This disjunction, however, is not strictly one in the metaphysical language employed thus far, but rather in a metalanguage for it, and the second disjunct we are expected to reject. To convince us that we should, Hartshorne needs to put forward a cogent theory of what "making sense" means, from which it must follow logically that nonsensical ideas cannot be actualized. The grounds for such a theory would be epistemic rather than merely metaphysical or theological. It is doubtful that such a theory will ever be forthcoming, however. The domain of what is nonsensical has no clear-cut boundaries, and varies greatly from person to person, from time to time, from one social group to another, from one language to another.

But let us go on. The "how, or in what concrete form, it [God] is actualized, can only be contingent." Let 'Actlzd' be the predicate for being actualized. Hartshorne wants then

(13)   'Actlzd God' or '$(Ee)\langle$Actlzd,God$\rangle e$'

to be a necessary metaphysical truth. Let

'e How F' or 'e In$_{\text{Manner}}$ F'

express that the process e takes place in the manner of the productions of the virtual class F (of productions). To say now that x is actualized in the manner of some F is to say that

$$(Ee)\ (\langle\text{Actlzd},x\rangle e \cdot e\ \text{In}_{\text{Manner}}\ F).$$

All statements of this form, with suitable proper names put in place of 'x', are presumably contingent or factual truths. Can we assert an analogous statement concerning God, that

(14)   '$(Ee)(\langle$Actlzd,God$\rangle e \cdot e$ In$_{\text{Manner}}$ V'

is contingent, where V is the universal class of "productions" constituting the cosmos and its history? No, this statement is presumably also a necessary metaphysical principle in the theory on a par with (13).

Hartshorne uses 'contingent' and 'non-contingent' ambiguously, as object-language words or as metalinguistic ones. It is essential, however, to be unambiguous at every point and not to shift meanings in any given context. Only thus can we avoid fallacies of equivocation.

Although (14) is presumably a necessary metaphysical truth, it contains a contingent element, we might say; namely, reference to V, the contingent cosmos consisting of all past, present, and future happenings. Hartshorne seems to think that "there can be no wholly necessary yet fully actual reality." Of course God is both necessary and actualized in view of (13), but not "fully" so perhaps in view of (14). The use of 'fully' here is not a happy one, suggesting as it does a notion of degree of actualization. It would perhaps be better to say here that God is both necessary in the theory, in the sense that (13) obtains, and also contingent in the sense that (14) does also. This would of course be in accord with the principle of dual transcendence.

Note the use of 'V' in the notation, V encompassing future happenings. The language is such that it can contain *now* a virtual-class expression denoting "future contingencies," as Hartshorne would call them. The very phrase 'the cosmos' likewise. It is difficult to see how Hartshorne could even state his metaphysical view without words or phrases of this kind. The point is an important one and I shall return to it in a moment.

Presumably because "there can be no wholly necessary yet fully actual reality," we are told that "classical theism was like belief in the class of all classes." This contention seems rather strained, however, as indeed does the earlier one that the comparison of the metaphysical principles (9) and (10) "with axioms of set theory might be worth exploring." As to this last— perhaps it would be. A very considerable difference would emerge, and what a difference it would make methodologically! Most notions of set theory are defined ultimately in terms of a relation (or relations) of set- (or class-) membership, and it is an extraordinary mathematical achievement to have shown that this is the case. Axioms of enormous mathematical power are then framed characterizing membership. By comparison, (9) and (10) do less well. They are stated in terms of an unanalyzed expression, 'M', and no attempt is made, as already noted, to analyze the constituent expressions (or ideas) contained in the sentences (or propositions) to which it is applicable. Thus there is none of the almost spectacular conceptual reducibility of the kind found in set theory. Also (9) and (10) are at best rather meager sentences, with (11) only as their one logical consequence of interest. As a consequence, (9) and (10) contain little metaphysical or theological power, so to speak, beyond what is contained in (11).

Can it justly be maintained that classical theism is like "belief in the class of all classes"? Only, it might be answered, if any formulation of it would lead to contradiction. That this is not the case has been shown to some extent elsewhere, in terms of a formulation based upon relations of *primordial valuation*.[13] In any case, Hartshorne has nowhere shown that suitable formulations of the classical theist view all lead to contradiction. What a task it would be even to attempt to show this! And anyhow, it is surely not the case. Hartshorne contends that "it was never the God of religion that classical theism defined." How can he be so sure? There is no one God of religion, and there is no one religion. There are many religions, some of them having no God or gods at all. Further, it is doubtful that there is any *one* view of classical theism. There are several, with significant family resemblances.

Hartshorne does not tell us what his third argument is, other than that it "is a revision of the old cosmological argument" and "is closely related to the ontological [one], but starts from the idea of reality in general." For this, presumably, essence, existence, and actuality must be suitably distinguished from "reality in general." But just how, we are not told, even in summary. The other three arguments are normative and "turn on ideas of value: value first as aesthetic goodness or beauty, second as ethical goodness or rightness, the third as cognitive goodness or truth." Only the ethical argument is discussed in detail. It is presented only in terms of options and not in a deductive form. However, it is easy to see what the argument in deductive form amounts to, for its structure is similar to that of the first proof. Again, the key formula needed is a tautology of essentially the same form as (7) above, but with 'a_1', 'a_2', and 'a_3' differently construed. And of course an option may be accepted or rejected or found "as obviously false as any belief I know," or "incomparably more credible to me than the . . . [others]" in true pragmatic fashion. There may well be good autobiographical reasons as to why one or more of these options appeal to one, but such reasons are not to be mistaken for metaphysical principles. That an option has certain logical consequences is also of interest but should not be mistaken for a metaphysical "argument" for deity.

Hartshorne contends that his third argument "was one of Whitehead's arguments for theism." Of course there are many ways of reading Whitehead, and one can "read into his discussions" all of the other arguments, save the ontological one, if one wishes and as Hartshorne does—but only at the price of distortion. Actually Whitehead presents no "arguments" for God at all of the Hartshornean kind. He merely presents a view in which the primordial and consequent natures play a fundamental role. God for Whitehead, it should be recalled, is the "[ultimate] limitation for which no reason can be given: for all reason flows from it. . . . His existence is the ultimate irrationality. . . . No reason can be given for the nature of God, because that nature is the ground of rationality."[14] To attempt to give "rational grounds for theism," as Hartshorne does, does violence to a most fundamental tenet of the Whiteheadean view.

Let us turn now to the matter of timeless truth, which actually turns out to be a tempest in a tea pot. Hartshorne believes "that there are new truths from moment to moment, and that the biographical truths about an individual have not always or eternally been true. This does not mean that prior to a certain time there were no truths or falsehoods. . . . With new subjects come new predicates of subjects, new possibilities of truth about the world. The idea of timeless truth about temporal things seems to me [Hartshorne] the ghost of medieval theism." Let us look at the matter closely for a moment.

Truth in the sense of the semantical truth-concept is always system-bound. It is always true in L that we must speak of, even where L is a full metaphysical or even a natural language. Let 'Tr_L' be the truth-predicate for the system L. Suppose the object-language sentences contain variables and constants for times. Let '—t—' be some such sentence or sentential form with 't' as a parameter for a time. As an example, suppose it is 'snow is white at time t'. To say that snow is white, with the 'is' construed in the present time, is to say that snow is white where t is the deictic *now*. To say that snow *was* or *will be* white is to say that snow is white at some t where now is temporally before *now* or *now* is temporally before t, respectively. This way of handling past, present, and future is to make use of the timeless form '—

t—' or 'snow is white at t'. The idea of the tense of timelessness (or the time of tenselessness, or the time of tenselessness) was first recognized by apparently both Peirce and Frege. When we turn to the truth-predicate, there is no need to construe it other than as a timeless predicate, all mention of time being now in the sentences said to be true. Thus '$Tr_L a$' is defined to state that a is true in L timelessly.

What is it precisely that Hartshorne is contending when he insists that "there are new truths from moment to moment"? What is meant here by 'new'? New to you or to me? Or to God? If this last, the word is being used analogically and must be explicated. Or cosmically? Well, of course there are "new" truths cosmically, and relative to any given now, in the sense that now is temporally before the t's involved in the statement of those truths. Wherever this obtains, the truths are new. And of course with "new subjects" come "new predicates," and "new possibilities [and actualities] of truth about the world." The doctrine of timeless truth does not deny any of this. We can go a step further. We can frame a general definition so that "snow is white' is $True_L$ now' would be defined as 'Tr_L 'snow is true now''. In this way even the truth-predicate can be tensed. Our common language does in fact condone such a form.

Here is an important point, of which Hartshorne is perhaps fully aware: however we develop the theory of tense, some timeless forms must be admitted anyhow, if only to handle mathematical principles, sentences containing only quantified time-parameters, and the like. Or consider some of Hartshorne's metaphysical statements such as 'T', a tautology, or (9) or (10) or (11) or (13). Are we not supposed to construe (9) in the tense of timelessness? Are we supposed to say rather that 'T' was logically possible, is now logically possible, or will be logically possible? Do we also have to admit iterated forms for saying that it was logically possible that 'T' will be logically possible, and so on? Such forms are not needed if 'logically possible' is taken as a timeless predicate. And similarly for 'true' itself.

Consider also the very phrase 'the cosmos'. This is a proper name, presumably, and not a description. In the meaning postulates characterizing it temporal parameters will occur. It is thus in part a temporal word, and statements containing it are in part about "temporal things." Perhaps the cosmos itself is even a temporal thing. All factual statements about the cosmos are thus in part temporal statements. According to what *seems* to be Hartshorne's view, however, there are no timeless truths to be stated about it. If so, all the statements he makes about the cosmos—as well as about order, about an ordering power, about being divine, about being unsurpassable, and so on—cannot then be given in the tense of timelessness, but all must be tensed. If this is the case, we should have to go through Hartshorne's paper, reading each sentence tensewise, in the past, present, and future, and all subsentences, dependent clauses, and so on, similarly. There are not just six proofs for God's present existence, there are proofs for his past and future existence as well. Surely at some point one will wish to call a halt. These comments, of course, do not apply to Hartshorne if statements about the cosmos are taken tenselessly.

Hartshorne's critique of timeless truth, the truth of eternity, seems ill-founded. Everything he wishes to say about truth, and about dual transcendence also, can be better said in terms of the standard kind of semantical truth-predicate. If the idea of timeless truth is "the ghost of medieval theism," let us welcome it back with open arms. We all have much to learn from it even now.

At several points Hartshorne claims that his view is in essentials that of Peirce and Whitehead. That this contention is a very considerable over-simplification of the views of those writers will be urged elsewhere.

Hartshorne comments that not "all truth can be stated in timeless terms," and he seems to attribute to Quine the view that they can be. As already noted, there are timeless truths concerning temporal things, but that this is the case is very different from what Hartshorne's comment seems to state. 'Truth' is a timeless predicate, or it can be handled as such, and it is a predicate applicable to all truths. However, this is not to contend that truth about time or times cannot be stated in timeless terms. It almost seems that Hartshorne is confusing these two contentions. "From the standpoint of eternity," he goes on, "nothing concrete or particular can be seen, only eternal necessities, and these are all abstract. Assigning dates is possible only within time. The eternal is an extreme abstraction from the temporal." It is good to be told how 'eternal' is related to 'temporal', but alas we are not told enough. And why can "nothing concrete or eternal be seen" from the standpoint of eternity? Nothing in the logic of these terms prevents this. One can "see" a temporal object without assigning a date to it; even we paltry mortals can do this. There is too much slack here in Hartshorne's use of these various words 'eternal', 'abstract', 'concrete', and 'seeing from the standpoint of eternity' for a coherent, convincing doctrine to emerge. And unfortunately it is upon this very slack that most of the diatribe against classical theism is based.

Note that the rejection of timeless truths is a special case of the rejection of the tense of timelessness. If there is no tense of timelessness there is no locution '$\mathrm{Tr}_L a$' but only 'a was true in L', 'a is now true in L', and 'a will be true in L'. Presumably one could reject the tense of timelessness in just the special case of 'Tr_L', but accept it for all other predicates. Such a position would require justification, however. Good reasons would have to be forthcoming as to why 'Tr_L' must always be tensed—at least as applied to sentences about "temporal things"—and why other predicates need not be.

In his "Comments" on Hartshorne's paper, Quine suggests that he will play the role of a "devil's advocate" and emit "an odor of sulphur, not of sanctity." One might have expected him to have played the role of a critic of Hartshorne's use of logic, logic itself being the work of the devil according to Petrus Damianus and Martin Luther. However, in this we are disappointed.

Quine is content merely to "see fairly definitely what the differences between us [him and Hartshorne] are," and to make a few remarks about them, especially as concerns freedom, truth and time, necessity, extensionalism, and the status of values. Quine does not attempt "to prove the worth" of his views on these matters nor "to disprove the worth" of Hartshorne's. The result is a rather pallid juxtaposition of Quine's form of physicalistic set-theoreticism, let us call it, with Hartshorne's six proofs and their *ambiente*.

Quine's physicalism is such as to exclude an "ordering power," in the sense of Hartshorne's first proof, let alone one that is also "divine." "Cosmic powers, or forces, there surely are," Quine says, and these are perhaps all reducible to gravitation, magnetism, and strong and weak interaction. "Taken together . . . [these forces] do constitute a cosmic ordering power in the sense that all the order there is, and all else, is an effect of them." This is of course a very strong hypothesis, transcending by far anything the physicists themselves tell us. At best it is a statement about the physical order only, and it is doubtful that all other kinds of order, let alone "all else," can be regarded as an "effect" of such forces. Quine is surely stretching 'effect' here to the breaking point. Further, a very difficult problem is concealed in the phrase 'taken together'. Physicists would like to get the four kinds of force "down to one," as Quine puts it. If this is ever achieved, taking them together will then presumably be tantamount to the one basic force. The enormous conceptual difficulties in bringing the various areas of physics into harmony with each other, let alone into a unified theory, suggests that as philosophers we should not be too hopeful in this regard. At best we can stand by the wayside and watch—and perhaps hope and pray. And even if these forces are taken together in some logically acceptable sense, there are other types of order, and perhaps also entities other than physical ones, that are left out of this extreme physicalist view. Quine relies upon physics, it would seem, much more, even, than a sophisticated philosophy of physics should condone. There are other forms of scientism also, that is, other sciences to rely on exclusively, biology, or psychophysiology, even—perish the thought—economics and sociology! That all "forces" and "order" at work in the subject-matters of these various sciences are physical forces, is a view for which there is no more evidence of a strictly scientific kind than for opposing views.

There is also mathematics, of course, in some set-theoretical garb, which is at the very center of Quine's conceptual scheme. So fundamental are sets for his view that even God, if admitted at all, has to be construed as the "unit class [set] of God." Classes or sets Quine does not object to calling 'abstract universals' and 'necessarily existing'. The divine universal for him, if there is one, must thus be a class and not an individual. This is of course a far cry from nominalism, which Quine seems to have left behind years ago. Quine's love of sets or classes, like his physicalism, arises from another facet of his scientism, this time with respect to mathematics.

The importance of set theory depends wholly upon its role in the foundations of mathematics. Just suppose set theory, however, in any of its various axiomatizations, is *not* an adequate way to found mathematics. The point is a moot one, and never more so than recently, in view of deep work done on the continuum hypothesis, on questions of consistency, and so on. Eminent mathematicians have more and more been defecting from the set-theoretic fold. The attitude seems to be developing that set theory has turned out to be an utter failure in pure mathematics, and is of no interest or help in mathematical physics (which has always used only "baby" mathematics anyhow) and other areas of application. To base a cosmology on a set theory is to cling to the past and to give hostage to future research. We see then that both strands of Quine's scientist set-theoretical physicalism do not intertwine into a viable philosophic thread. Quine thinks no doubt that he does as the scientists do, and that his view is firmly founded scientifically. Precisely the opposite, however, seems to be the case. He does not write about the sciences *ab intra,* so to speak, as Peirce, Whitehead, Carnap, and Reichenbach, for example, have done. Likewise his versions of set theory are remote from the inner workings of mathematics itself as well as from the really central problems concerning metamathematics and its foundations.

Another point Quine raises against Hartshorne concerns truth. "No difference can be drawn," he notes, "between saying that it will be true that snow is white and that it is true that snow will be white." This too is a strong contention. Of course there is a difference, but is it a significant one? Quine is saying that it is not. But is he correct in this? A good deal of grammatical theory is involved here, that far transcends anything of a technical kind that Quine has written. Even so, the gist of his contention is probably correct. Quine goes on, however, to remark that "calling a sentence true adds nothing to the sentence. The truth predicate is superfluous except for an important technical use. It is needed when we want to affirm some infinite lot of sentences that we can demarcate only by talking about the sentences." Surely; but there are other needs also. The truth predicate and its ambient theory are also useful for proving consistency, and relative consistency, for certain systems. Also, truth in the semantical sense has a most intimate connection with the ways in which language is related to the nonlinguistic world. Truth, designation, denotation, satisfaction, and determination all dance together hand in hand. Take one away and semantics collapses. It is thus not adequate to say that "calling a sentence true adds nothing to it." It adds an *interpretation,* it transforms a sentence into a statement, it leads us from mere syntax to semantics.

A word now about values. Hartshorne's fourth proof is based on values such as "meaning (or supreme purpose)," "happiness, welfare, and goodness of oneself," "welfare of some group or society, or all sentient beings (excluding God), either in this life alone, or also in some posthumous mode of existence," and meaning or purpose "as somehow permanently enriching the divine life and its happiness." For the other two normative proofs analogous values must no doubt be considered. Quine objects to Hartshorne's aesthetic and ethical values on the grounds that for him (Quine) they are human, and for Hartshorne cosmic. This difference aside, Quine is not satisfied with Hartshorne's list. "Welfare considerations [for all creatures great and small] do not exhaust the purposes we find in ourselves and regard as laudable," he notes. "There is a drive for creativity, achievement; also for social esteem and friendship." Earlier he has mentioned "our ethical standards, and . . . the degree to which other people share them and conform to them, . . . our comfort and security and . . . good fellow-feeling." Add these to Hartshorne's list, or subsume them under items in it and exclude all reference to the divine, and our two authors' lists are in virtual agreement. But what paltry lists they are, concerned with only a handful of lower values, and quite leaving out those most espoused by some of the choicest spirits in human history. A detailed comparison of these lists with that in Nicolai Hartmann's second volume of his *Ethics,* would not be without interest.[15] Also the great Pauline virtues of faith, hope, and charity are left unaccounted for—to say nothing, for example, of joy, peace, long-suffering, gentleness, meekness, humility, and temperance, or of the Vedantic *Sat, Chit,* and *Ananda.*

Hartshorne's sixth proof is based on "cognitive goodness" or truth. It would be interesting to see this proof spelled out in detail in terms of the semantical truth-concept. Any spelling out of it not taking account of this would surely be inadequate.

Here is an interesting question. Are there predicates for aesthetic and ethical goodness analogous to 'Tr_L' for cognitive goodness? If so, to what are they applicable? What principles of a logical kind govern them? Deontic logic and my "On Some Aesthetic Relations"[16] contain responses, to some extent anyhow, to these questions—or at least the beginnings of responses.

One more comment, concerning evil. Hartshorne writes, about his first proof, that "if the world is cosmically and divinely ordered, why is there suffering and evil?" His answer is in terms of dual transcendence. Also, "the creatures must have some initiative in relation to God and one another. They partly decide details of the world." All this is placed in contrast to classical theism, which "reduces the creatures . . . to nothings. They decide nothing; God decides everything." These contentions provide only a parody of the classical theist view, however, which takes account of *how* God "decides," what it means for him to "decide," in accord with what he decides, and so on. It would be interesting to compare Hartshorne's comments here with those of Maritain in his little book on evil, and with the Thomistic doctrine that *homo prima causa mali.*[17] It is rather to be feared that Hartshorne does not take account of the full complexity of the view he parodies. Also his linking together of suffering with evil seems unfortunate. Suffering is more intimately connected with goodness than with evil. He who has not learned the function of suffering in his life has lived in vain.

The foregoing is not to be construed as claiming that neither Hartshorne nor Quine subscribe to important and viable philosophical views, but only that neither seems to have stated them in a sufficiently cogent fashion to carry us forward in theology. This latter is thought to be a much more serious matter, from the logical point of view, than either is willing to concede. Now, in the closing decades of the twentieth century, logical tools are being forged which have the necessary refinement to handle these delicate theological matters adequately for perhaps the first time, as already remarked above. It is no longer philistine to lay the rude hands of logical analysis upon them—and they need not come out the worse for so doing, as Peirce noted so well in his paper ''Neglected Argument'' years back! No viable theology, however, will ever be forthcoming, on the one hand, without a very considerable logico-linguistic propaedeutic, and, on the other, within so narrow and club-footed an affair as physicalistic set-theoreticism. Like humility and good will in social intercourse—better, like profound love of God and genuine love of neighbor—adequate logical methods in philosophy have scarcely ever been tried. And wherever they have been, they have never been found wanting.

Let us close with a famous comment from Whitehead, dating back to 1936.[18] ''We must end with my first love—Symbolic Logic. When in the distant future the subject has expanded, so as to examine patterns depending on connections other than those of space, number, and quantity—when this expansion has occurred, I suggest that Symbolic Logic, that is to say, the symbolic examination of pattern with the use of real [bound] variables, will become the foundation of aesthetics. From that stage it will proceed to conquer ethics and theology.'' The distant future of which Whitehead speaks is now close upon us. In aesthetics progress is being made in the exact study of aesthetic relations, and in ethics in new and improved foundations for deontic logic. One of the high merits of Hartshorne's methodology is that he has seen this distant future approaching in theology, although he has not welcomed it with the open arms that would have been appropriate.

Notes

1. In Hartshorne's ''Grounds for Believing in God's Existence,'' presented at the Boston University Institute for Philosophy and Religion, October 17, 1979, together with ''Comments on Hartshorne on God,'' by W. V. Quine.

2. Bowman Clarke, *Language and Natural Theology* (The Hague: Mouton, 1966), p. 98.

3. In R. M. Martin, *Primordiality, Science, and Value* (Albany: State University of New York Press, 1980), pp. 3 and 10.

4. See especially the author's ''On Philosophical Ecumenism: A Dialogue,'' in *Primordiality, Science, and Value.*

5. See especially ''On Virtual-Class Designation and Intensionality,'' in *Primordiality, Science, and Value.*

6. Cf. Hilary Putnam, *Mathematics, Matter and Method, Philosophical Papers,* vol. 1 (Cambridge: Cambridge University Press, 1956), passim. See also "A Memo on Method: Hilary Putnam," in *Logico-Linguistic Papers* (Dordrecht: Foris Publications, 1981).

7. See *Toward a Systematic Pragmatics* (Amsterdam: North-Holland Publishing Co., 1959), pp. 41ff.

8. Recall R. Carnap, *Logical Foundations of Probability* (Chicago: University of Chicago Press, 1950), pp. 178ff.

9. See Gottlob Frege, "Über Sinn und Bedeutung," second paragraph, and *Begriffsschrift,* §8.

10. R. M. Martin, "On the Logical Structure of the Ontological Argument," in *Whitehead's Categoreal Scheme and Other Papers* (The Hague: Martinus Nijhoff, 1974).

11. Jan Salamucha, "Dowod 'ex Motu' na Istnienie Boga, Analiza Logiczna Argumentacji sw. Tomasza z Akwinu," *Collectanea Theologica 15,* Lwow (1934), pp. 53–92, trans. in *The New Scholasticism 32* (1958): 334–72. See also F. Rivetti-Barbò, "La Via 'Dal Divinire' per Provare l'Esistenza di Dio," *Sapienza 32* (1979): 396–419.

12. On concepts, see especially *Events, Reference, and Logical Form* (Washington, D.C.: The Catholic University of America Press, 1978), pp. 15ff.

13. In *Whitehead's Categoreal Scheme and Other Papers.*

14. A. N. Whitehead, *Science and the Modern World* (New York: Macmillan, 1925), p. 257.

15. Nicolai Hartmann, *Ethics,* vol. 2 (London: George Allen and Unwin, 1932).

16. In *Primordiality, Science, and Value,* chap. 14.

17. Cf. ibid., chap. 4.

18. A. N. Whitehead, *Essays in Science and Philosophy* (London: Rider and Co., 1948), p. 99.

Response by Charles Hartshorne

Of all the critics of my philosophy none that I can recall has been more severe philosophically, or more friendly and charming personally, than R. M. Martin. As I have written him, I find myself lucky to have such a severe critic. Most elderly people are left to die with their errors uncorrected. But, alas, and this is not without its significance as showing the nature of the philosophical task, the result of Martin's critique is not to shake my confidence in my side of the basic issue that divides us. Rather the contrary, I have been so stimulated by Martin that I have thought of new arguments supporting my position.

The basic issue is whether truths about specific historical events are timeless *or*—but only in a certain way, not just in any old way—temporal. Thinking about this, I have become aware, as never before, how isolated in space and time the belief in timeless omniscience really is. It was not in ancient Greece, unless one attributes it to the Stoics. It was not the classical Hindu position or the standard Buddhist position or, I think, the classical Judaic position. It was the medieval Christian and Islamic position, also held by some medieval Jews. The last great Western defender. of it was Leibniz, the last near-great defender Royce. Hume and Kant in different ways give reason to question it. German idealism has at most given it ambiguous support. Heidegger will have none of it, and he has German predecessors in this. French philosophers began parting company with it a century and more ago; Sartre and Merleau-Ponty reject it; Berdyaev, the Russian immigrant to Paris; scornfully rejected it in favor of a definitely changing God who acquires new truths and values endlessly from the world. Croce and Varisco in Italy reject the idea. In England, Russell and G. E. Moore of course did so. In this country, Santayana, who affirmed timeless historical truths, denied timeless knowledge of them; James and Dewey would have nothing to do with such knowledge. Peirce strongly hints at its falsity, as I take Whitehead to do. I know the texts that Martin could cite to the contrary and am satisfied that his interpretations are not valid. (What Peirce said before he adopted his tychism would not be decisive since he changed his position then, at about the age of forty. But he does say that God is not omniscient in the traditional sense, and that even a divine purpose cannot be simply immutable.) Even in Islam, the most important Islamic writer in Pakistan, Iqbal, was a Bergsonian who took a process view of God. In Hinduism a modern sect in Bengal holds that God, though in a sense perfect, yet "grows without ceasing."

None of this refutes Martin's position. Nevertheless, I hold definitely that historical considerations of this nature are not irrelevant. It seems to me implausible that all these people, and so many more, who have made a negative judgment on the medieval idea of God, were less competent than those who now wish to return essentially to the medieval perspective. In addition I am in some ways closer to Aquinas than Alston and Martin are; for I agree with Aquinas that potentiality, contingency, change, and something like temporality go together, so that if any one of these applies to God the others do also. And in this I am agreeing with Plato and Aristotle, as I interpret them.

I accept a number of logical distinctions Martin makes, but they are compatible with my position. I am disconcerted that he supposes otherwise. There are a number of dissertations that do not attribute to me the opinions in question, and I am not as yet convinced that the trouble comes merely from my lack of skill in formalization. I am not generally found hopelessly obscure.

One distinction that I make, and Martin does not see the importance of, is between eternity and everlastingness, or immortality. Objective immortality is one thing, objective eternity is another. Properly and adequately stated, all truths except mathematical, purely logical, or metaphysical ones are immortal or everlasting, but not eternal; they do come into being. Once there they cannot go out of being. Becoming is creative, but not destructive, of truth. Cumulative creation is an ultimate principle and is what Whitehead means by creativity. It is a clarification of what Bergson, G. T. Fechner, and W. P. Montague held before Whitehead, who probably knew only about Bergson.

Martin has exacting standards for method in philosophy. I, too, have some standards. I can put them in the form of maxims. One is: in debate with another thinker try at least as hard to find agreements, common ground, as to find disagreements. A related one is Popper's maxim: defend your view against rival views in their strongest and most intelligent form, not in their weakest or least intelligent. Also, when confronted with a doctrine that is logically extreme in the sense of having a polar opposite or, in the terms of propositional logic, a contrary extreme, compare the merits of each extreme not primarily with those of the opposite one, but with a moderate view sharing something of both extremes, a higher synthesis. Hegel was partly right about this. Thus, given the proposition, "all relations are internal," rather than debating the merits of this extreme against its polar contrary, "no relations are internal," look for a reasonable principle according to which some relations are internal and others are external. Martin weighs the merits of his "all truths are timeless," or can be so formulated without loss of truth, against what he takes to be my view (for no reason in my writings that I can see) that all are time-bound; he ignores the moderate or less extreme view that some (namely, truths about extremely universal and abstract, eternal and necessary things, including the essential structure of time as such) are timeless, and others (those about less universal and abstract, also noneternal and contingent things) are time-bound, but this not in every way a careless thinker might suppose but in a definite and logically intelligible way. The precedent here is Aristotle; also, less explicitly, Plato. Martin does not discuss the view in the form I give it. Again, Martin holds what I find to be an extreme form of the suspicion of ordinary language and takes me to hold an extreme form of trust in that language. Neither fits my theory or my practice. For example, I hold that expressions like "will be" or "is going to be" are loosely or ambiguously used in nonphilosophical contexts (and also in a sentence Martin quotes with mild approval from Quine) and should be precisely defined if used in philosophy. I have suggested how this is to be done. On the other hand I hold that the technical expression so many philosophers have used as though it were self-explanatory and unambiguous— "the absolute"—is viciously ambiguous and that the more nearly self-explanatory term "independent" is safer, provided one makes explicit what the entity so described is independent of, whether everything else or only some other things, and according to what principle the distinctions are made.

Martin finds a lack of system in my philosophizing. However, I do systematically test my doctrines by the above and other principles. Notably,

Martin says that his discussion is largely based on an encounter he heard me have with Quine. But can a philosopher make an entire system explicit in one talk? I do not doubt that it would have been possible for me to make references to various parts of my writings to provide the context of my statements or arguments. I am somewhat lazy about the rereading of my writings that this requires. But I almost get the impression from Martin's comments that he expects every sentence to somehow do the job of chapters or volumes.

Martin's emphasis on the all-important role of details is only partly justified, in my opinion; but this does not mean that I go to the opposite extreme. I do not. I am systematically nonextremist.

Although in my view contingent truths become true, rather than timelessly being true, this does not mean that having become true they may then cease to be true. Inadequate, elliptical formulations may be first true and then again untrue. Properly related to time, positive truths or facts remain true forever after. Thus "born in Kittanning at time t" will never cease to be true of me, but a hundred years ago it was not true. There was then no truth about me.

Quine as well as Martin misunderstands the sense in which I take (some) truths to be time-bound. First, I accept the Tarski truth definition, and therefore I agree that "no difference [or at least none of major importance] can be drawn between saying that it *will be* true that snow is white and that it is true that snow *will be* white." In both cases the meaning of "will be" is for me the point at issue, not the meaning of truth. Carnap agreed with me that the Tarski criterion is neutral to the issue between my view and the view that all truths are timeless. Second, I have long emphasized that metaphysical truths (supposing we can find them) are necessary and that the necessary is eternal. Hence all metaphysical truths are eternal; they do not become true but timelessly are true. Mathematical truths I suppose to be included; and I contrast them with metaphysical only in their being noncategorical, if-then necessities, not direct necessities, of existence. Of course logical possibilities are tenseless, if they are *purely* logical. Could a cow jump over the moon? Logic alone cannot tell us what a cow is or could do. Nor can metaphysics do this. The phrase 'logical possibility' has long seemed to me somewhat ambiguous. Among truths that are metaphysical are truths about time, but about time as such, extremely abstract truths, not truths about specific events or classes of events as actually occurring.

I hold what Arthur Prior called the Peirce view of extralogical, nonmetaphysical truths in relation to time. Such and such "*will*" *occur* has for me a strict meaning and truth if and only if the occurrence in question, call it O, is common to every real causal possibility for the future time in question. Otherwise the truth is either: some of the possibilities include O and some do not (in which case the true assertion is that O *may or may not* occur) *or else* none of the real possibilities include O, in which case O *will not* occur. The doctrine is that will, will not, and may-or-may-not form an exhaustive trichotomy; whichever one is true, the other two are false. Thus they are related as, you must do X, you must not do X, you may do X or refrain from doing it. Because of human ignorance, we must largely content ourselves with probabilities rather than with completely definite will be's, may or may not be's, or will not be's; and even God does not eternally know or temporally foreknow events in their full definiteness or concreteness.

In all this I am taking a position stated clearly enough by the Socinian theologians in the seventeenth century. They believed in a future partly indeterminate even for omniscience. If God does not know what I am going to do tomorrow it is because there neither now nor eternally are such things to be known as my tomorrow's deeds. The reality now is certain possibilities or probabilities for tomorrow. In eternity there is much less to be known. When tomorrow has become yesterday, then there will be definite deeds of mine for tomorrow's date for God to know. This is the idea of a growing knowledge and a growing world to be known. I have yet to get a clear, cogent argument from logicians against this view.

Carnap appealed here to common sense but admitted this was not a conclusive argument. It is not hard to show that common sense is less than unambiguous on the point. "What will be will be" is a tautology that either has no definite application or else begs the question as to how far the future consists of will-be's rather than of may-or-may-not-be's. Carnap no doubt had mainly in mind the argument from simplicity or convenience in semantical theory which Martin has urged. Of course this also is inconclusive. Without going all the way with Bunge in his *Myth of Simplicity* I do go part way. Simplicity is one thing, truth another. Must I give up a central tenet of my metaphysics to make things easier for logicians? I would like to encourage them in their valuable work, but the price at this point looks high. Metaphysicians, too, have their problems and conveniences, and eternal truths about specific or particular temporal facts have, in my judgment, been causing a mess in metaphysics since Aristotle made his splendid beginning in developing a semantics that takes time properly into account. The theory of timeless knowledge of temporal facts (a theory the Greeks lacked, and all the better for them) has made endless trouble for theology. Gradually since the Socinians, modern metaphysics has been struggling to develop a different theory. I am convinced that three of the greatest philosophical logicians that ever lived, Aristotle, Peirce, and Whitehead are on my side in this. Martin does not agree.

I wonder if the sense in which I affirm the time-boundedness of contingent truths would really make as much trouble in semantics as Martin fears. It would not affect mathematical or metaphysical truths, and this includes whatever is essential to worldly or divine time *as such*. If physicists assume the constancy of the laws of nature since the big bang, then these laws, if we get them right, will have been true for as long as physics seems to feel a need to talk about, say 15 billion years, and will remain true (by hypothesis) for as long as physics wants to talk about them. As for observations, they will always thereafter have occurred as they did, and they may in principle have been possible long before. I have in my article in *Mind* (74 [1965]: 46–58) discussed the relation of all this to Popper's doctrine that we falsify proposed laws rather than strictly verify them. Will and will-not statements are falsifiable, but may-or-may-not statements are unfalsifiable and are, not verifiable, but corroborated, so far as we can derive them from our assumed knowledge of laws and (never complete or infallible) knowledge of initial conditions. For many purposes not much change in semantics would be required, if the Peirce view were adopted. Peirce himself said, "Logic is not yet ready to deal with the relation of truth to time." Perhaps it is about ready now.

I agree with Martin that theistic arguments, and philosophical arguments generally, belong in a system. I have tried to put mine into a system. One of my objections to Anselm is that he seems almost to think his ontological argument could stand all by itself. My six theistic arguments are said to form a system stronger than its separate parts, and the chapter in which I expound them is imbedded in a book (*Creative Synthesis and Philosophic Method*) which attempts to give the wider context for them. For example, when I find Martin distinguishing "inscription," "concepts," and the reality conceived, I find this compatible with and partially parallel to the distinction I make in the previous chapter among formula or definition, idea, existence, and actuality, except that I think my fourfold distinction more adequate than his threefold one.

I agree that truth, designation, denotation, satisfaction, and determination belong together, though no doubt Martin has some technicalities in mind here that I am not aware of. But I suspect we differ as to how designations of particulars are possible. All designation of strictly particular or concrete realities is retrospective, on my view. Peirce regarded as a false nominalism the idea that the future consists of particular entities. The class human beings, taken as definite existents, gets new members each moment. In the sense in which there are deceased members there are no merely future members.

Martin's long paper is so densely packed with critical comments, queries, objections, that a real answer would require a large book. ("Long is art, short is life.") In some cases the relevance of Martin's comments to my position (as expounded, for example, in *Creative Synthesis and Philosophic Method,* the most philosophical of my books) seems slight. I do indeed stand on the distinction between a priori (or metaphysical) and empirical in the sense given this distinction by Popper, except that, whereas Popper defines empirical as 'conceivably falsifiable by observation' and apparently limits observation to certain forms of human perception, I sometimes include divine perception (in Whitehead's language, God's physical prehensions). It would still be true that some important propositions are nonempirical in the defined sense. Even God could not prehend anything incompatible with the existence of God, nor—in my view, as in Whitehead's—could God prehend the total nonexistence of the world, that is, prehend the total absence of nondivine beings. I heard Quine and Carnap argue about the distinction between empirical and a priori and, like many of the others at Chicago, thought Carnap more right than Quine. I do hold that all knowledge is experiential, uses experience as positive evidence. The Popperian question is, could experience conceivably show the negative? Any experience shows that experience exists, none could show a world devoid of experience.

It sometimes seems that Martin's keen eye for logical technicalities and for skill in their use is made an obstacle to communication rather than a means thereto. The fault is no doubt partly mine. If I had made more effort to meet him on his own ground through the years, he might have made more effort to really learn what my position is. Martin wonders, for example, what contradictions I could show in classical theism. One I have shown is the denial of unactualized potentiality in God (God as "pure actuality," or as the "sum of all perfections" or possible positive values) with the assertion of the contingency of the world, or the religious proposition that we should live to enhance the divine glory, to serve God. If the world could have been otherwise, then God's knowledge could have been otherwise; it is knowledge that Napoleon existed, it could have been knowledge quite lacking in this feature. If our living well and helping others to do so serves God, then, by any reasonable analogy in the use of 'serves,' God acquires a value God would otherwise lack. That God loves all creatures is similarly either unmeaning or contradictory of the total lack of dependence asserted by numerous theists of God. As Martin well says, that God is infinite, absolute, or independent in *all* respects is a very strong statement. But that a multitude of theists made such a statement, or else engaged in extreme double-talk, I stand ready to show.

In general I find Martin giving strained interpretations of philosophers. Thus he says that Whitehead gives no reasons for theism, citing a passage in which Whitehead says there are no reasons for God's nature. I see here (and in some other passages) ambiguity (Martin is austere about the need for unambiguity, and so am I). "No reasons for God's existence or nature" does not imply "no reasons for our believing in that existence." Reasons for theism are one thing, reasons for God another. Whitehead clearly gives some reasons for his belief in God, one being that otherwise (without God to objectify our experiences) "all experience would be a passing whiff of insignificance." This is not a reason for God's existing; God exists no matter what. But (for some of us) it is a reason why the idea of a Godless world is unacceptable.

To my saying that God exists necessarily because what exists contingently is produced by the creative process, which might not have produced it, Martin objects that God may be self-produced. In a sense yes, and the Whiteheadian proposition that every actuality is a "self-created creature" includes God, who is cause *and* effect, creator *and* creature, both in uniquely excellent senses. This is one corollary of the doctrine of dual transcendence.

But there is still a sense in which God is unproduced. A contingently existing being exists in that its nature is realized in actualities the first of which was produced out of a reality that previously did not actualize that nature at all. Each phase of the divine existence, on the contrary, is produced out of a previous phase of the creative process, which also involved the essential divine characteristics. Each phase is self-produced in that its subjective forms are free acts of prehending previous phases; it is produced by the previous phases in that it has to utilize them as its given data. The freedom is in the precise how of the prehending, not in *what* is prehended. The creative process might not have produced my present actuality, it might not have produced, and until 1897 did not produce, my first actuality; in the divine case there could not be a first actuality; eternally there is some divine actuality or other. This is indeed a timeless truth. Nothing in my writings implies otherwise, I believe.

I agree with Martin that it might be a good idea for me to try to state my primitive terms, as such. I say it might be, because I'm not sure. In a given exposition or explanation something is taken without explanation or definition; but I'm not clear how far this must be true of a philosophy. A philosophy is not a mere formal system. Being "better than" is close to primitive (I follow Brogan here in preferring an asymmetrical relation to a mere seemingly nonrelative term like "good"). God is such that no being could conceivably be better, except in the sense in which God can be better than God (self-surpassing is not excluded insofar as there are dimensions of value that do not logically admit of an absolute maximum). One has to take into account the distinction between being better for some extraneous purpose and being better intrinsically. On my view nothing can be better than God intrinsically, since God and God alone adequately appreciates and enjoys all actualities. Any rival to God would contribute its own value completely to God, who would also have all other actual values.

It may be that everything I have written could for some purposes be made clearer. But I am one of many who have doubts about the idea of "clearer" for all purposes. Only God knows clearly in an unqualified sense. If, as I suspect is the case, few of my readers find me as unclear as Martin seems to do, what follows? Perhaps I am not the best judge of what follows. That using formal methods as elaborate and demanding as Martin's will for some purposes be useful, I believe. Beyond that I am open to conviction.

I agree that my theistic proofs should rather be called arguments. I do not believe that philosophical questions are open to proofs, if that means that, from premises any rational person will accept, issues so vital to people as the existence of God will be rigorously decidable. I intended my "tautologies" to make clear what the issue about God's existence was, not to decide it. Martin talks of disproving all the nontheistic options. We shall see how well he or others succeed in this. I think the matter remains somewhat personal and pragmatic. What reason can do is to make as clear as possible what by implication one is rejecting if one rejects the theistic conclusion. One is accepting the disjunction of the nontheistic options. The rest is up to the individual.

True, one can set up formal arguments against the options, but one must stop somewhere.

Concerning the meaning of "order" in my cosmological argument, all that my view requires is that the order be nonstrict in such a fashion and degree as to allow for a real distinction between causally possible and causally necessary, or between the totality of necessary conditions and a strictly "sufficient" condition, and that this be true in every concrete case. It must never be so that what actually happens is the only thing that then and there could happen. This is to allow for universal creaturely freedom or genuine decision-making, implying an aspect of real chance, such as quantum theory seems now to permit. Perhaps I should say also that it must be that the higher levels of life involve greater freedom than the lower levels. With Wigner and Bohr I imagine quantum theory to be incomplete.

I do not concede that I have left the respects in which God is finite rather than infinite, or vice versa, contingent rather than necessary, and so on, in total darkness, as seems to be implied. My table of ultimate contrasts (in *Creative Synthesis and Philosophic Method*) is supposed to throw light on the matter. It is unique in the history of ideas, and is something like my substitute for the Hegelian dialectic of the unity of contraries. God, as I have explained, is absolutely infinite in potentiality but not in actuality. I have also explained that potentiality here does not mean what most have meant by omnipotence, as though God could, as it were, say "Let there be such-and-such," and there would be such-and-such. I meant that God has potentially whatever could occur or exist. This is not true of any individual being other than God. I have explained too that the divine actuality, so far as I can grasp the relevant concepts, must involve a numerically infinite number of past creatures, but the creation need not, and I think must not, be spatially infinite. Here I agree with G. E. Moore.

I concede that "abstract" has various meanings, but about this, too, I have had some distinctions to make. All concepts abstract from details, particulars; but the physicist abstracts also from ideas as universal as those of structure and quantity, which he uses, whereas the philosopher should seek ideas that are not abstract in this sense. In metaphysics the important distinctions are perhaps two. First there is the distinction between specific conceptions of kinds of actualities whose existence is contingent, as is shown by their restricting the positive possibilities for other kinds, in contrast to conceptions so generic that they do not restrict the positive possibilities. Thus Creator or Divinity, simply as such, and also creature or nondivine existent, simply as such, alone have the degree of abstractness compatible with necessary or noncompetitive existence. The second metaphysically important distinction is between any abstraction and a fully concrete actuality, the latter being one that no mere concept can fully express, and which can be given only in perception, and adequately given only in divine perception. Concrete in this complete sense are not individuals or substances but only what Whitehead calls actual entities, momentary states, of which a single human experience is a paradigm example.

Martin does not convince me that my distinction between existence and actuality is hopelessly unclear. I think it is fairly clear and immensely important. I exist, for example, so long as my individual identifying traits are *somehow* exemplified in actual entities. My actuality now is *how,* or in *just what states,* this exemplification has, up to now, occurred. I am unenlightened by the objection that the how is distinct from the result, partly because of Whitehead's principle of process, that the being is not abstractable from the becoming, and partly because of my stipulation, *how* or in *what,* in contrast to, *somehow* or in *some* actual state or other. I fail to see what is left out in this formulation. I exist now, experiencing myself typing, I could have existed now not typing. The somehow is less definite than the how or in what.

Applying the distinction even to God enables me to say that instead of the dogma that all existence is contingent, the true statement is, all actuality is contingent. God necessarily exists somehow or in some state, but the actual state is contingent, for instance, knowing me now typing, which might not have been there to be known. So the divine actuality is contingent but not the divine existence. I rather hope to be remembered for this distinction.

A serious objection to the temporal view of contingent truths is that physics seems to rule out any cosmic meaning for the present, the *now* after which various truths will continue to obtain. Both relativity and quantum theory seem relevant but no one seems to know just how the two are to be reconciled or combined. The physicist Henry Stapp has a "revised Whiteheadian" theory here which seems to solve the problem in a way I could accept, but the matter is immensely difficult, especially for one so incompetent mathematically as I am.

Martin is correct in saying that "new to God" must be analogical in meaning. I may not have said enough about the theological analogies. I do hold with Plato that God is to the cosmos as our consciousness is to our bodies, and that the other principal analogy is with person-to-person relations. If there were no difficulties here the ontological argument would indeed prove theism.

The point of "new to God" is that our decisions decide something for God, enrich the divine life, give God actual value that was *previously* unactual. I hold with Berdyaev that this means a divine kind of time. And this for me is the point of religion, that we contribute to God's consequent reality, which as Whitehead says is "always moving on or in flux." What this means without a divine analogue to time I have no idea, just as Spinoza had no idea, which is why he felt it necessary to deny the contingency of the creatures so that the whole of time could be eternal in God. With Aquinas and Aristotle I see time, becoming, potentiality, contingency as belonging together, but unlike both I put them in God as well as in creatures, and indeed, as Whitehead says, God is both creator (poet of the world) and creature. God is not temporal simply as we are but still is so in an eminent way or (as Whitehead says) "in a sense" temporal. And as for the whole of the temporal process, there is no such whole, complete once for all. There is no *the* cosmos, but a partly new creation each moment.

Creation-with-preservation is the ultimate or transcendental category, with God the eminent form of this. In God no positive truth is lost, but additional truths are gained. W. P. Montague held this view before Whitehead; doubtless both were partly influenced by Bergson. I take Peirce to point, with some hesitation, in this direction. If temporal meant that actuality and truth were being lost as well as gained, then God is "timeless." But this refers to our inferior form of temporality, supposing we can really conceive a higher form. This is the theistic question in one formulation.

For Martin's remarks about values I have only praise, except so far as they are presented as a criticism of me. Is it fair to look to my fourth theistic argument to provide my list of values, when the point of that argument was not to answer the question, What are values? or What is the good life? but rather, *for whose sake* is the good ultimately to be sought? One's own sake, the sake of people generally, animals generally, insentient beings generally, or for the sake of the imperishable and all cherishing One whose life inherits from the creatures and evermore preserves all their joys and sorrows, all the actual beauty of their experiences?

I end with a profession of faith written for another occasion than this and not as a response to Martin's criticisms.

By one interpretation Plato's absolute beauty as what ultimately inspires human love becomes acceptable. Absolutes, like other partly negative terms, are abstractions. But they have a positive aspect. In the unqualified sense, absoluteness or independence is coincident with eternity and necessity, as Aristotle saw so well. What then is the value of the absolute? It cannot have a negative value, cannot be bad, regrettable, unfortunate, or wicked. For all these terms connote the appropriateness of prevention, avoidance, alteration, replacement; and these ideas make sense only with contingent things. The eternal and necessary framework of existence cannot have a negative value. Can it have a positive value? If this meant that someone ought to have, or appropriately could have, tried to produce or preserve the absolute, then this would imply dependence, contingency, and noneternity. But positive value, unlike negative value, has an aspect that is compatible with necessity and eternity. This is beauty, that the thing is good to contemplate. There can and there must be an eternal and absolute beauty. It is the beauty of the perfect abstraction. As an abstraction it has no defect and it makes no sense to wish it had been better. Since it is an abstraction it is not the all-inclusive value. It is only the eternal standard and principle of possible achievements of value, not any actual achievement.

Plato was right that this principle cannot be love in the merely human sense of feelings and attitudes of a localized animal. It must be cosmic and superhuman in principle. What can it be if not the abstract principle of the cosmos as besouled and cherishing of all sentient actualities? And what is this but the love that "moves the sun and the other stars"? (Dante). I have believed in this, with temporary hesitations, almost as long as I can remember. This came from my pious upbringing, and also, I believe, from an early reading of Emerson's most Platonic essay, the one on love. And Emerson too was brought up in a religion of love. By that religion he lived.

No word or combination of words can be guaranteed to communicate the absolute principle. In some respects music is a superior medium for this purpose. A substantial argument could be given for the proposition that music such as one finds in Mozart's last opera, *La Clemenza di Tito,* puts one, more directly and intimately than metaphysics can do, in intuitive contact with the kind of thing which reality on its higher levels is, and, on various levels, universally manifests. Etienne Gilson was right, art is superior to metaphysics.

One reason for ending this reply to Professor Martin with the foregoing paragraph is that besides being a speculative philosopher of broad interests and a highly skilled and sophisticated logician, he is also a musician. Such a combination is remarkable and must be admired.

William P. Alston

4

Hartshorne and Aquinas
A Via Media

I

The Hartshornean conception of God has exercised a profound influence on contemporary theology and philosophy. It is recognized as a major alternative to more familiar conceptions, and its merits and demerits are vigorously debated. The conception has a number of sources, but not least among them is Hartshorne's criticism of the way of thinking about God that was brought to classic expression by St. Thomas Aquinas. In what still remains the most extended systematic presentation of his position, *Man's Vision of God,* Hartshorne develops his conception as an attempt to remedy the defects he finds in the Thomistic view. And throughout his subsequent writings this foil is there, sometimes in the foreground, sometimes in the background, but always exercising a dominant influence. It is the Thomistic conception, or the general ways of thinking about God given definitive shape by Thomas, that Hartshorne takes as his chief rival, and he takes one of the basic recommendations of his position to be that it succeeds at those points where Thomas fails.

In contrasting his view with that of Thomas, Hartshorne presents us with a choice between two complete packages. No picking and choosing of individual items is allowed. And the secondary literature has, for the most part, followed him in this. Nor is this mere sloth or heedlessness on Hartshorne's part. He explicitly propounds the view that the various elements of the Thomistic system are so tightly bound to each other that we cannot pick one or two without thereby becoming committed to the whole:

> they all belong logically together, so that there is little use in judging any of them in isolation. Either we accept them one and all, or we reject them one and all, or we merely bungle the matter. Here is the explanation of the failure of many attempts at recon-

struction in theology; they sought to pick and choose among ideas which are really inseparable aspects of one idea. Here also is seen the genius of the great theologians of the past, that they really saw the logical interrelations between a large number of affirmations (they are really and admittedly denials, negations) about God.[1]

And he often imputes an equally tight coherence to his own system. In opposition to this picture of the situation, I shall be arguing in this paper that the Thomistic theses rejected by Hartshorne are not by any means so tightly bound to each other as he supposes, and that one can, consistently and coherently, reject some and retain the rest. More specifically, I shall contend that Hartshorne's arguments against the Thomistic denials of internal relatedness, potentiality, complexity, and contingency (of some properties), arguments that I take to be wholly successful, do not, as Hartshorne seems to suppose, suffice also to dispose of the Thomistic doctrines of omnipotence, immutability, nontemporality, creation ex nihilo, and unsurpassability even by self. Nor do I find any other cogent arguments in Hartshorne against the attributes of the second group, though I will not be able to argue this last point in detail. Thus I shall be contending that the Hartshornean corpus leaves standing the possibility that a coherent, plausible, religiously adequate, and even true conception of God can be formed that combines the Hartshornean position on the attributes of the first group with a Thomistic, or at least something closer to a Thomistic, position on the attributes of the second group.

Here is a tabular presentation of the oppositions between what Hartshorne calls the "classical" position, paradigmatically represented by Aquinas, and his own, "neoclassical," position.

Classical	Neoclassical
Group 1 Attributes	
1. Absoluteness (absence of internal relatedness).	Relativity. God is internally related to creatures by way of His knowledge of them and His actions toward them.
2. Pure actuality. There is no potentiality in God for anything He is not.	Potentiality. God does not actualize everything that is possible for Him.
3. Total necessity. Every truth about God is necessarily true.	Necessity *and* contingency. God *exists* necessarily, but various things are true of God (e.g., His knowledge of what is contingent) that are contingently true of Him.
4. Absolute simplicity.	Complexity.

Classical	Neoclassical

Group 2 Attributes

5. Creation ex nihilo by a free act of will. God could have refrained from creating anything. It is a contingent fact that anything exists other than God.	Both God and the world of creatures exist necessarily, though the details are contingent.
6. Omnipotence. God has the power to do anything (logically consistent) He wills to do.	God has all the power any one agent could have, but there are metaphysical limitations on this.
7. Incorporeality.	Corporeality. The world is the body of God.
8. Nontemporality. God does not live through a series of temporal moments.	Temporality. God lives through temporal succession, but everlastingly.
9. Immutability. This follows from 8. God cannot change since there is no temporal succession in His being.	Mutability. God is continually attaining richer syntheses of experience.
10. Absolute perfection. God is, eternally, that than which no more perfect can be conceived.	Relative perfection. At any moment God is more perfect than any other individual, but He is surpassable by Himself at a later stage of development.

I shall go about my task as follows. I shall examine Hartshorne's arguments against the Thomistic attributes in the first group (absoluteness, simplicity, etc.), and show that they cut no ice against the Thomistic attributes in the second group. In order to carry this through, I will have to show that the classical attributes in the latter group are in fact consistent with the neoclassical features in the first group. In discussing the classical attributes in the second group, I shall cast a cursory glance at Hartshorne's other arguments against those attributes and suggest that they lack cogency. I would like to go on to argue for the religious adequacy of my ''mixed'' conception, but for that I will have to wait for another occasion.

Before starting on this task let me make explicit what I will not be challenging in the Hartshornean theology. First I readily and unreservedly grant that Hartshorne has made a powerful positive case for his conception of God as one that (a) is internally coherent, (b) has philosophical merit, (c) has important roots in the practice of theistic religion, and (d) nicely handles some nasty problems. Thus I allow that the full Hartshornean conception is an important alternative that must be seriously considered by contemporary theology, even though it is not my preferred alternative. Second, I acknowledge that theological thought during most of its history has been seriously hampered by the fact that the Hartshornean alternative has been almost totally ignored. Hartshorne has repeatedly shown how this neglect of an important alternative has led to bad reasoning. Finally, I grant that Hartshorne has shown the classical conception not to be required by the practice of theistic religions.

II

I now turn to a short sketch of what I take to be Hartshorne's most important arguments against the classical attributes in Group 1. Let us begin with absoluteness (in the sense of lack of internal relatedness), which is the key to the whole thing. Here I will distinguish between a very general line of argument that I do not regard as successful, and a more specific line of argument that seems to me to be completely successful.

The first argument hangs on some very general points about relations. For a given term in a relationship, the relation may be either internal or external to that term.[2] A relation is internal to a term if that term would not be exactly as it is if it were not in that relationship; if, to some extent, the term depends on the relationship for its being what it is; otherwise it is external.[3]

> But external relations are subject to two conditions. . . . First, every relation is internal to *something,* either to one at least of its terms or to some entity additional to these. Second, the entity to which the relation is internal is a *concrete* whole of which the externally related entities are *abstract* aspects. (MVG, 235)

The second point can be restated as: "The entity to which a relation is internal contains the relation and its relata as parts." We will find that this plays a major role in Hartshorne's theology.

To continue the argument:

> If the relation of the absolute to the world really fell wholly outside the absolute, then this relation would necessarily fall within some further and genuinely single entity which embraced both the absolute and the world and the relations between them—in other words within an entity greater than the absolute. Or else the world itself would possess as its property the relation-to-God, and since this relation is nothing without God, the world, in possessing it, would possess God as integral part of its own property, and thus the world would itself be the entity inclusive of itself and the absolute. On any showing, something will be *more* than an immu-

table absolute which excludes its own relations to the mutable. (MVG, 238–39)

Thus on pain of admitting something greater or more inclusive than God, we must embrace the remaining alternative, which is that the term to which the God-creature relation is internal is none other than God.

I do not find this argument impressive. Grant that every relation must be internal to something. Why should we hold that the term to which a relation is internal "contains" the relation and the relata? Or, more basically, what is meant by this thesis? In just what way does the one term "contain" the others, or in just what way, as Hartshorne says in the passage quoted above, are the relata "aspects" of that term? To focus the issue, let us consider why the second alternative in the last-quoted passage, that a God-world relation be internal to the world, is unacceptable. The reason given is that the world would "include" itself and the absolute in that case, and so would be "more" than the absolute. This reasoning shows that Hartshorne is reading more into his "containment" principle than he is entitled to. So far as I can see, the only sense in which one is entitled to say, in general, that the entity to which a relation is internal *contains* the terms, is that we have to refer to these other terms in describing that entity; that a reference to those terms *enters into* a description of that entity. But it doesn't follow from this that those terms are contained in that entity as marbles in a box, or as thoughts in a mind, or as theorems in a set of axioms, or as you and I in the universe, or as the properties in the substance of which they are properties. Thus we are not constrained to hold that the entity in question is "greater" or "more inclusive" than those entities. And obvious counterexamples to this claim are not far to seek. On Hartshornean principles, and apart from those principles, when I think about God that relationship is internal to me. Does it follow that I am "more" than God, since, on the "containment" principle, I include God as an abstract aspect?[4] Once we see the innocuousness of the "containment" that is implied by internal relatedness, the second alternative (the relation being internal to the creature) loses its repugnance, and the argument fails.

But Hartshorne also deploys a more specific argument for the same conclusion, one that depends on the character of a particular sort of relation, a relation in which God, by common consent, stands to the world. This is the cognitive relation. Hartshorne argues effectively that, in any case of knowledge, the knowledge relation is internal to the subject, external to the object,[5] and, indeed, that cognitive relations are *more* constitutive of the subject, the more certain, comprehensive, and adequate the knowledge.[6] Whenever I know something, the fact that I know it goes toward making me the concrete being I am. If at this moment I see a tree across the street, I would not be just the *concrete* being I am at this moment (though I might be the same enduring individual or substance, according to standard criteria of identity for such beings) if I were not seeing that tree in just the way I am. I would be different from what I am in a significant respect. But the tree would still be just what it is if I did not see it.

This being the case, how can we both maintain that God has complete and perfect knowledge of everything knowable, including beings other than Himself, and still hold that God is not qualified to any degree by relations to other beings? I wholeheartedly agree with Hartshorne that we cannot. Classical theology has typically responded to this difficulty by alleging that, since all things other than God depend on God for their existence, their relations to the divine knower are constitutive of them rather than of God. The usual order of dependence is reversed. But Hartshorne effectively replies that, even if finite beings depend for their existence on the creative activity of God, it still remains true that if God had created a different world then He would have been somewhat different from the way He actually is by virtue of the fact that His perfect knowledge would have been of that world rather than of this world; and so the point still holds that divine cognitive relations to the creatures are partially constitutive of God.[7]

Now for the other traditional attributes in the first group. On reflection we can see that the above argument for the internal relatedness of God as cognitive subject *presupposes* that there are alternative possibilities for God, at least with respect to what creatures, or what states of creatures, He has as objects of knowledge. For if, as both Thomas and Hartshorne hold, it is necessary that God know perfectly whatever there is to know, and if there were no alternative possibilities as to what there is to know (whether by way of alternative possibilities for divine creativity or otherwise), then there would be no possible alternatives to the actual state of knowledge. And in that case the question as to whether God would be in any way different if He did not know what He does know would not arise. It would be like asking whether God would be different if *He* were not God, or like asking if the number 6 would be different if *it* were not 3×2. But if there are alternative possibilities for divine knowledge, then this implies both that there are unrealized potentialities for God, e.g., knowing some world (as actual) that He might have created but did not, and that some of the things true of God are true of Him contingently, i.e., that there is contingency in the divine nature. Hartshorne's denial of absoluteness really presupposes the denial of pure actuality and of total necessity.

Thus there is an intimate connection between these three oppositions to the classical scheme. But in showing this we have also been exhibiting a vulnerability in the argument for relativity. For unless we are justified in the attribution of potentiality and contingency to God, the argument for relativity is lacking in cogency. Fortunately Hartshorne can, and does, argue independently for divine potentiality and contingency. Again he proceeds from premises admitted by his opponents, namely, that the world is contingent and that

God freely creates the world He creates (and, therefore, could have created some other world instead).[8] From the first premise we have the following argument.[9]

1. (A) *God knows that W exists* entails (B) *W exists*.
2. If (A) were necessary, (B) would be necessary.
3. But (B) is contingent.
4. Hence (A) is contingent.

In other words, if what God, or any other subject, knows might not have existed, then God, or the subject in question, might not have had that knowledge. For if the object had not existed, it would not have been known. Hence God's knowledge of the contingent is itself contingent. Therefore we can totally exclude contingency from God only by denying of God any knowledge of anything contingent, a step none of the classical theologians were willing to take.

From the thesis that God could have created some other world it follows that there are unrealized potentialities for God, namely, His creating worlds He does not create.[10] Thomas' distinction between active and passive potentialities[11] does nothing to invalidate this point. Of course unrealized potentialities also follow from the first argument, and contingency from the second; for these notions are strictly correlative. If it is contingent that I am in state S, then I might have been in some other state or had some other property instead (at a minimum, state non-S); that is, there are potentialities for me that I did not realize. And if there are potentialities that I might have realized but did not, then my not realizing them, and my realizing some alternative, is a contingent fact about me; it is one that might not have obtained.

Thus, starting from points insisted on by classical theology, Hartshorne has effectively shown that these points require the theologian to give up the classical attributes of nonrelativity, pure actuality, and total necessity. The final member of this group, simplicity, falls as well, since its main support was the absence of any unrealized potentialities in God.

III

Now let us turn to the classical attributes in Group 2, which I do not take Hartshorne to have succeeded in discrediting. I shall start with creation ex nihilo, since this is a fundamentally important element in classical theology, one I take to have deep roots in religious experience and practice. On this point there is a clear and sharp issue between Hartshorne and the classical tradition. For the latter not only is it the case, as Hartshorne would agree, that every finite individual owes its existence to the free creative activity of God, in the sense that apart from that creative activity *that* individual would not exist; in addition, it is wholly due to the free creative activity of God that anything other than Himself exists: it is contingent, and contingent on the will of God, that any created world at all exists. Whereas, for Hartshorne, it is a metaphysical necessity that there be a world of finite creatures, though not that there be just the one we have. This constitutes a significant difference in the area alloted to divine voluntary choice over against the area fenced round by impersonal metaphysical necessities.

Is the position of each party on this point in any way tied up with its position on the attributes of the first group? I cannot see that it is.[12] Why should we suppose that a deity with unrealized potentialities and contingent properties, and qualified by His cognitive relations with contingent objects, *must* be in relation with some world of entities other than Himself? Why should it not be one of His contingent properties that He has created beings other than Himself? Why should the fact that He *is* qualified by his relations to other beings imply the *impossibility* of there being no other beings to which He is related and thereby qualified? I cannot see that the neoclassical properties in our first group are incompatible with the correctness of the suggestions just broached. In fact, it seems that the traditional doctrine of creation is much more attractive, plausible, and coherent in Hartshornean than in Thomistic garb. When decked out in the medieval fashion, it is saddled with just those difficulties exposed so effectively by Hartshorne in the arguments canvassed in Section II. It has to struggle to combine creation by a free act of will with the absence of alternative possibilities for God, and to combine the contingency of the world with the necessity of God's act of creation and with the necessity of God's knowledge of that world. Freed from those stultifying bonds it can display its charms to best advantage. It can mean what it says by "free act of will," by "contingency," by "knowledge," and so on. I would say that in exposing the internal contradictions of classical theology Hartshorne has done it a great service and rendered its doctrine of creation much more defensible.

Indeed, to the best of my knowledge Hartshorne does not explicitly link his position on creation with his position on relativity, contingency, and potentiality, as he does link the latter with his position on temporality.[13] On the other hand, he does present other arguments against the traditional position, none of which seem to me to have any substance. For one thing, he takes that position to be committed to a temporal beginning of the world, a bringing the world into existence at some moment of time. Against this he argues that a beginning of time is self-contradictory.[14] Be this last point as it may, the doctrine need not be so construed. Classical theologians have repeatedly pointed out that creation ex nihilo does not necessarily involve a temporal beginning of the universe; though, of course, many of them believe that in fact there was such a beginning. It only requires the principle that there would be no universe at all but for the creative activity of God. This could be the case even if the universe is temporally infinite, with no beginning and no end. Whether "creation ex nihilo" is the best term for such a doctrine is not the basic issue. What is crucial is that we can combine the theses that (a) God's not having done what is required in order that there be anything other than Himself is (was) a real possibility, and (b) the universe is temporally infinite.[15]

Hartshorne also argues that if God is thought of as absolutely perfect just in Himself, apart from a created world and his relations thereto, as classical theology would have it, then there can have been no point in creation.[16] But even if this argument is sound, it does not show that the classical doctrine of creation is incompatible with the neoclassical position on relativity, contingency, and potentiality. It merely shows that in order to retain the former we must modify the classical position on perfection. And is the argument sound? Why is it not intelligible to think of God as acting purely altruistically, rather than to increase his own perfection or bliss? In response to this Hartshorne makes two points. (1) Altruism involves participation in the good or evil of another, which is incompatible with the classical doctrine of impassibility.[17] But this argument is ineffective against the position that the classical doctrine of creation is compatible with regarding God as internally related to creatures through His awareness of them and hence passible. (2) If God cannot be benefited by the creation, we cannot serve Him or contribute to Him in any way.[18] But even if God is purely altruistic vis-à-vis creation, we can serve Him precisely by furthering those altruistic purposes.

Hartshorne connects his opposition to the classical doctrine of omnipotence with his rejection of the classical doctrine of creation.[19] To be sure, one might embrace creation ex nihilo while recognizing some limits to divine power (other than logical contradiction). Nevertheless it is true that Hartshorne's position on creation, according to which it is metaphysically necessary that there be contingent finite beings, entails that it is not within divine power to bring it about that nothing exists other than God. And so Hartshorne is required by his position on creation to deny the classical doctrine of omnipotence. But does he have any independent arguments against that doctrine? There is at least one: since being is power, every being has some power just by virtue of being; but then it is metaphysically impossible that God should have all the power.[20] Or to make this an internal argument against the classical doctrine, the conclusion could be softened to read: "If there is anything other than God, God does not have all the power there is." But even thus softened the conclusion does not cut against the classical doctrine, which maintains not that God has all the power there is, but rather that God has *unlimited* power, power to do anything He wills to do. This is quite compatible with God willing to bring creatures into existence with a power suitable to their status. That is, it is quite compatible with His delegating power to creatures. And this is the way that classical theology has construed the matter, although I would admit that Thomas, for example, can be criticized for the way in which he works out the details. The basic point is that the doctrine of unlimited power that goes with the classical doctrine of creation does not imply that no being other than God has any power.

Finally, the issue over incorporeality is tied up with the issue over creation. In chapter 5 of MVG, "The Theological Analogies and the Cosmic Organism," Hartshorne argues effectively that God is related to the world in two crucial respects as a human mind is related to its body: (1) God is aware, with maximum immediacy, of what goes on in the world, and (2) God can directly affect what happens in the world. On the principle that what a mind (1) is most immediately aware of and (2) has under its direct voluntary control *is* its body, Hartshorne concludes that the world is God's body, and hence that God is not incorporeal. But this analogy can be pushed through all the way only if, as Hartshorne holds, the world (some world or other) exists by metaphysical necessity, independent of God's will. Otherwise God will not be corporeal in the strongest sense—essentially corporeal. Of course even if God brings it about by a free act of will that the world exists, we might still, in a sense, regard the world as God's body. But in that case it would be a body that He had freely provided for Himself, one that He could just as well have existed without. He would not be corporeal in the way a human being is; He would not be essentially corporeal. If we understand corporeality in this stronger sense, and Hartshorne does espouse it in this sense, it is clear that it stands or falls along with Hartshorne's position on creation. If the classical doctrine of creation is retained, one can deny essential corporeality, while still agreeing with Hartshorne on relativity, contingency, and potentiality.

IV

In the foregoing section I allowed that the classical doctrine of creation *is* in trouble if we take God to be temporal. If God is temporal we have to think of Him as infinitely extended in time. If He began to exist some finite period of time ago, that would call for some explanation outside Himself; He would not be a fundamentally underived being. His ceasing to exist is impossible for the same reason. And if the fact that there is a physical universe is due to an act of divine will, that act, if God is temporal, would have to take place at some time. But then at whatever time it takes place God would already have existed for an infinite period of time; and we would be faced with the Augustinian question of why God chose to create the universe at that time rather than at some other. Thus if we think of God as temporal the most reasonable picture is the Hartshornean one of God and the world confronting one another throughout time as equally basic metaphysically, with God's creative activity confined to bringing it about, so far as possible, that the world is in accordance with His aims. And conversely, if we are to defend the classical doctrine of creation we must think of God as nontemporal. Hence in order to hold that the classical doctrine of creation is compatible with the neoclassical doctrines of relativity, contingency, etc., I must also show that the latter are compatible with the nontemporality of God. And, indeed, apart from this necessity of doing so, I am interested in defending that position.

Now for temporality and mutability. I shall take it that these stand or fall together. God undergoes change *iff* he is in time. The possibility of existing completely unchanged through a succession of temporal moments I shall dismiss as idle. Divergence in the other direction—change, in some sense, without temporal succession—deserves more of a hearing, and I shall accord it that shortly. However, since Hartshorne is clearly thinking of the sort of change that consists of first being in one state, and then at some temporally latter moment being in a different state, I shall use the term in that way. Hence I shall be taking temporality and mutability to be coextensive.

It is a striking fact that Hartshorne considers the tie between relativity or contingency, and temporality or mutability, to be so obvious that he freely conjoins them, and treats them as equivalent, without seeming to feel any necessity for justifying the stance. Thus the conclusion of the argument for internal relatedness in God on pp. 238–239 of MVG, quoted above, is put in terms of mutability as well as relativity.

> On any showing, something will be *more* than an *immutable* absolute which excludes its own relations to the mutable. It is therefore necessary to distinguish between the *immutable* and the absolute, if by absolute is meant the "most real," inclusive, or concrete being. The *immutable* can only be an abstract aspect of God, who as a concrete whole must contain both this aspect and its relations to the novel and contingent. (Emphasis mine)

Thus Hartshorne takes the argument, which was explicitly an argument for internal relatedness, to also demonstrate mutability. Again, in the preface to DR (p.ix) Hartshorne states the basic thesis of the book in such a way as to indicate clearly his assumption of the equivalence of relativity and mutability.

> The main thesis, called Surrelativism, also Panentheism, is that the "relative" or *changeable,* that which depends upon and varies with varying relationships, includes within itself and in value exceeds the nonrelative, *immutable,* independent, or "absolute".... From this doctrine . . . it follows that God, as supremely excellent and concrete, must be conceived not as wholly absolute *or immutable,* but rather as supremely relative, "surrelative," although, or because of this superior relativity, containing an abstract character or essence in respect to which, but only in respect to which, he is indeed strictly absolute *and immutable.* (Emphasis mine)

We also get immutability assimilated to necessity. "It seems almost self-evident that a wholly necessary *and immutable* being cannot know the contingent and changing" (MVG, 242).

Although for the most part Hartshorne seems to take it as immediately evident that the relative and contingent would be mutable and temporal, there are occasional flashes of argument. At one place he simply asserts that a perfect being must change if relations to a changing world are internal to it.[21] This line of thought may indeed be the source of the impression of self-evidence. Let us try to spell it out a bit. If God is what He is partly because of the way He is related to the world, and if the world is in different states at different times, thereby entering into different relations with God at different times, it follows that God must be in different states at different times. For at one time God will have one set of relations to the world; at another time another set. Hence, if these relations are internal to God, the total concrete nature of God at the one time will be partly constituted by the relations He has to the world at that time; and so with another time. Since these relations will be different at the two times, the total concrete nature of God will be correspondingly different.

This argument involves a *petitio principii*. Of course *if* God is temporal, then He will have different relations to the changing world at different times and so will undergo change. But that is just the question. We are all prepared to grant that God changes *iff* he is temporal. We do not need the intermediate premise about relations to a changing world to derive mutability from temporality. On the other hand, if we do not *assume* divine temporality, the argument fails. If God is not in time, then the fact that relations to a changing world are internal to Him does not show that He changes. If He is not in time He is not susceptible of change. The relations in which He stands to the world as it is at various moments will qualify Him "all at once," without temporal succession between different qualifications. It will be said that this is unintelligible. I will deal with that charge below.

Hartshorne also hints at an argument for the move from contingency to temporality.

> Thus there is God in his essential, and God in his accidental functions. The only way such distinctions can be made conceivable is in terms of time; the essential being the purely eternal, and the accidental being the temporal, or changing, aspects of the divine. (MVG, 234)

I cannot see that contingency (in the sense of that which is not necessary, that the opposite of which is possible) is intelligible only for a temporal being that successively realizes various possibilities. It is true that a nontemporal being has no "open future" before it; once it exists then whatever is true of it is fixed, in a way in which that need not be the case for a temporal being. The latter can exist at a certain time, while it is yet undetermined which of various possibilities for its future will be realized. At least this is true if, as Hartshorne supposes, what is future is not yet determined. Nevertheless it can be true of a nontemporal being that although it is R it might not have been R; that, to put it in currently fashionable terms, there is a possible world in which it is not R. This is sufficient to make the fact that it is R a contingent fact. Moreover this sense or kind of contingency, there being some possible world in which it is not the case, is the basic one. Alternative possibilities for an as yet undetermined future constitute a particular sub-sense or sub-type. Its being contingent at this moment whether I shall finish writing this paper this week, is just a special case of the phenomenon of alternative states of affairs holding in different possible worlds. The additional feature in this case is that at this moment it is not yet determined which of these possible worlds is the actual world.

One who is indisposed to accept contingency without an open future should consider whether one could say that the past of a temporal being could be contingent in any respect. Is it now a contingent or a necessary truth that I went to bed at 10:15 P.M. last evening? In whatever sense we can recognize that to be a contingent truth we can also recognize various truths concerning a nontemporal being to be contingent.

Finally, let me point out that this "not true in all possible worlds" sense of contingency is the only one in which Hartshorne has given reason for supposing God to exhibit contingency without presupposing that God is temporal. Without that presupposition his argument simply amounts to the following. "The existence of the created world (or, less question-beggingly, things other than God), and any part thereof is contingent. Therefore it (they) might have been otherwise. Therefore any relation in which God stands to the world, e.g., creating it or knowing it, might have been otherwise, and so is contingent." The conclusion of this argument is simply that any relation in which God stands to the world *might have been otherwise*. There is no license for drawing the further conclusion that God exists at a succession of temporal standpoints relative to each of which there is an open future.

But, it will be said, we are still faced with the apparent unintelligibility of a nontemporal being qualified by its relations to temporal beings. Is it possible to make sense of this? I think that we can distinguish a classical, or Thomistic, and a Whiteheadian version of this possibility; and I would argue that both are intelligible, though perhaps not equally acceptable on other grounds. Let us take the Thomistic version first. Here we think of God as not involved in process or becoming of any sort. The best temporal analogy would be an unextended instant, an "eternal now." This does not commit us to the standard caricature of a "static" or "passive" deity, "frozen" in eternal immobility. On the contrary, God is thought of in this conception as being preeminently active, but active in ways that do not require temporal succession. The idea is that such acts as acts of will and acts of knowledge can be complete in an instant. Can we think of such a God as being internally related to the world in the ways we have been envisaging?

As for as knowledge is concerned, it seems to me that the psychological concept of the specious present provides an intelligible model for a nontemporal knowledge of a temporal world. In using the concept of the specious present to think about human perception, one thinks of a human being as perceiving some temporally extended stretch of a process in one temporally indivisible act. If my specious present lasts for, e.g., one-twentieth of a second, then I perceive a full one-twentieth of a second of, e.g., the flight of a bee "all at once." I don't *first* perceive the first half of that stretch of the flight, *and then* perceive the second. My perception, though not its object, is without temporal succession. It does not unfold successively. It is a single unified act. Now just expand the specious present to cover all of time, and you have a model for God's awareness of the world. Even though I perceive one-twentieth of a second all at once, I, and my awareness, are still in time, because my specious present is of only finite duration, and, in fact, of much shorter duration than I. A number of such acts of awareness succeed each other in time. But a being with an infinite specious present would not, so far as his awareness is concerned, be subject to temporal succession at all. There would be no further awareness to succeed the awareness in question. *Everything* would be grasped in one temporally unextended awareness.

In presenting this model, I have said nothing about internal relatedness, but I cannot see that the intelligibility of the model depends on excluding that. Let us say that God would not be exactly what He is if the objects of His awareness were different. How does that make the concept of an infinite specious present less intelligible?

Volitional relations to the world can be handled in the same way. Of course, if we are strictly Thomistic and hold that God determines every detail of the world, then we can simply think of a single act of will that handles the whole thing and does not require temporal successiveness. But suppose we hold that God has endowed some or all of His creatures with the capacity to choose between alternative possibilities left open by the divine will. In that case many of God's volitions and actions will be responses to choices by creatures the exact character of which God did not determine. Even so, if within a specious present we can have nonsuccessive awareness of a succession, why should we not have nonsuccessive responses to stages of that succession?

The concept of nonsuccessive responses to stages of a temporal succession of events may seem too much to swallow, even to those who are prepared to admit the intelligibility of the specious present for cognitive phenomena. Rather than stay and slug it out on this point, I prefer to give ground and switch at this point to the Whiteheadian concept of a nontemporal deity. This decision is prompted not only by cowardice, but also by the conviction that the Thomistic conception, excluding any sort of divine process or becoming, does run into trouble with divine-human *interaction*. It is surely central to the religious life to enter into commerce with God, to speak to Him and be answered, to have God respond to one's situation, to have God act on and in us at certain crucial moments. These back-and-forth transactions are not felicitously represented in the classical scheme, especially when we recognize that

God is not determining every detail of what happens. Let us see if Whitehead enables us to tell this part of the story better.

The Whiteheadian concept that would seem to offer some hope here is that of the *concrescence* of an actual entity, the process by which an actual entity comes to be. Let us first see how Whitehead develops this notion for finite actual entities, and then look at the application to God.

An actual entity consists of the process by which it comes to be.[22] Without trying to go into the details of this, let us note that the process is one of developing and unifying a set of initial "prehensions"[23] into a more or less satisfying experiential whole. The particular feature of concrescence that we are interested in at this moment is the fact that it does not involve temporal succession. Whitehead was convinced by Zeno-like paradoxes that process must be made up of indivisible units, "drops" or "bits" of becoming that do not themselves consist of earlier and later becomings.[24] These quanta of becoming are called "actual entities." A finite actual entity occupies a certain position in the spatio-temporal matrix. It prehends the world from a certain perspective, one that can be determined from the relative fullness with which it objectifies the other actual entities it takes as its data. This position will involve temporal as well as spatial extension.[25] But though it occupies a temporal duration, it does not come into being by *successively* occupying the parts of this duration. It happens "all at once."

> In every act of becoming there is the becoming of something with temporal extension; but the act itself is not extensive, in the sense that it is divisible into earlier and later acts of becoming which correspond to the extensive divisibility of what has become. (PR, 107)

> There is a becoming of continuity, but no continuity of becoming. (PR, 53)

> The epochal duration is not realized via its successive divisible parts, but is given with its parts. (SMW, 183)

Hence all the parts of an actual entity are present to each other in a felt immediacy. The goal of the process, the final unity of feeling, is present throughout the process, shaping its course toward itself. Using the term 'superject' for the final upshot of the concrescence, that which will be taken as datum for later concrescences, Whitehead writes: "Thus the superject is also present as a condition, determining how each feeling conducts its own process" (PR, 341). Again: "The ideal, itself felt, defines what 'self' shall arise from the datum; and the ideal is also an element in the self which arises" (PR, 228).

In expounding this doctrine Whitehead appeals to James' concept of the specious present, but it is clear that he is going beyond that concept. The psychological concept of the specious present is intended to embody the possibility that one might be aware of a process without successively being aware of its temporal parts. But this does not imply that the awareness itself is *a process* without succession. The concept of the specious present provides for process in the object and lack of succession in the awareness; it does not provide for the joint exemplification of these by the same entity. But that is just what Whitehead is claiming. Not only is an actual entity nonsuccessively *aware of* a process; it *undergoes* the process of its own development nonsuccessively. Thus the Whiteheadian notion of concrescence is more radical, more paradoxical than James' notion of the specious present. It is not entirely clear to me whether we can form an intelligible conception of process without temporal succession. This will obviously depend on our conception of time, and it is clear that the intelligibility of Whiteheadian concrescence hangs on the intelligibility of an atomic or "epochal" conception of time, one that is very different from our usual way of thinking of these matters. But I will not be able to go into all that in this paper. Assuming that the Whiteheadian conception is intelligible, let us see how it could be used to form a conception of process without temporal succession in the divine life.

The answer to that "how" question is very simple, in outline. We simply think of God as a single infinite actual entity, whose "extensive standpoint" is unlimited in space and time. As an actual entity, God will undergo concrescence, a development of Himself, His distinctive unity of experience, out of His prehensions of the other actual entities. And since He is a single actual entity, not a "society" of temporally successive actual entities, like you or me, the various stages of His life will not occur successively in time but will occur or "be given" in one unity of felt immediacy. A finite actual entity, though enjoying the common privilege of all actual entities—of concrescence without temporal succession—nevertheless occupies a particular finite position in the spatio-temporal continuum. But since God's concrescence is unlimited, His "position," if we may use that term, is the whole of time and space. He is subject only to the kind of process involved in concrescence, not to the temporally successive process involved in "transition" from one actual entity to its successors.

On my reading, this is just Whitehead's own conception of God. Throughout *Process and Reality* he refers to God as *an* actual entity. But then, unless Whitehead is going to "treat God as an exception to all metaphysical principles, invoked to save their collapse" (PR, 521), he must hold that there is no temporal succession in the divine life, just as there is none in the concrescence of any other actual entity. This is, indeed, a controversial point in Whitehead exegesis,[26] but I can see no other plausible way of reading the text. Let me mention two other points in support of my reading. (1) Whitehead repeatedly makes the point that the divine concrescence differs from the concrescence of finite actual entities in taking its start not from "physical" prehensions of other actual entities but from a "conceptual" prehension, the "unconditioned complete valuation" of all eternal objects.[27] But, by the nature of the case, there can be only one such *unconditioned* valuation. Hence

God can only undergo a single concresence. (2) The world is objectified in God's "consequent nature" without loss of immediacy.

> The perfection of God's subjective aim, derived from the completeness of His primordial nature, issues into the character of His consequent nature. In it there is no loss, no obstruction. The world is felt in a unison of immediacy. The property of combining creative advance with the retention of mutual immediacy is what . . . is meant by the term 'everlasting'. (PR 524–25)

But mutual immediacy is retained only within a single concresence, not in the transition from one concresence to another. Again, we get the conclusion that the divine life consists in a single concresence.

When one reflects on Boethius' formula for the eternity of God, quoted with approval by Aquinas,[28] "the simultaneously whole and perfect possession of interminable life," one may well be struck by its affinity to the Whiteheadian concept of an infinite concresence. I would say that one of Whitehead's signal achievements was to develop a conceptual scheme for handling this classical notion of divine eternity, a scheme that does the job much better than any used by the classical theologians themselves.

It must be admitted that Whitehead's view of God as a single infinite actual entity is incompatible with his principle that there is no prehension of contemporaries. Since God, on this view, is contemporary with every finite actual entity, being neither in the past nor in the future of any other actual entity, God, on the principle in question, would be able neither to prehend nor to be prehended by any other actual entity, a conclusion more radically at variance with religious experience and practice than the doctrine Whitehead was invoked to repair. In addition, such a windowless monad of a God would fail to perform His basic metaphysical functions in the Whiteheadian system. Hence God would somehow have to be made an exception to this principle, as Whitehead explicitly makes Him an exception to the principle that the concresence of an actual entity begins from physical prehensions. In this paper I am not concerned with how, or how successfully, this modification might be carried out. It is not my job here to develop or defend Whitehead's metaphysics. I have merely sought to point out a way in which we might think of a nontemporal God as undergoing process, thereby reinforcing the point that the Hartshornean position on divine relativity, potentiality, and contingency does not necessarily carry with it the Hartshornean position on divine temporality.

Finally, the issue over temporality is intimately bound up with the issue over how to understand divine perfection. Hartshorne took this issue as the opening wedge of his battle with Thomism in MVG. In chapter 1 of that work Hartshorne distinguishes between *absolute* unsurpassability, impossibility of being surpassed by anyone, even oneself, and *relative* unsurpassability, impossibility of being surpassed by anyone else, but leaving open the possibility of being surpassed by oneself.[29] This distinction has a point only for a tem-

poral being. A being that does not successively assume different states could
not possibly surpass itself, i.e., come to be in a state superior to its present
state. The concept of surpassing oneself has application only to a being that is
in different states at different times. Not surprisingly, Hartshorne takes advantage of the possibilities opened up by a temporal conception of God, and
plumps for *relative* unsurpassability. At a later stage of his thought this becomes the notion of perfection as "modal coincidence"—God, at any moment, actually is everything that is actual at that time (through his perfect
"objectification" of everything in the world), and potentially is everything
that is possible as of that moment.[30] God's actuality includes all actuality, and
his possibilities include all possibilities. But if we are correct in holding that
the Hartshornean position on relativity, contingency, and potentiality is compatible with a nontemporal conception of God, then it follows that the
Hartshornean position on those Group 1 attributes is compatible with taking
God to be absolutely unsurpassable, since, as we have seen, relative unsurpassability differs from the absolute variety only for a temporal being. The
Thomistic, as well as the Whiteheadian, God cannot surpass himself at a later
time, for he does not move from one time to another. He simply is what he is
in one eternal now (Thomas), or in one indivisible process of becoming
(Whitehead).

There is, to be sure, Hartshorne's often repeated argument that since the
simultaneous actualization of all possibilities is logically impossible (since
some logically exclude others), the notion of a unique maximum of perfection
makes no sense.[31] But this argument construes perfection in a crude, quantitative way that is, to say the least, not inevitable. Absolute unsurpassability
need not be so construed that to be absolutely perfect a being would have to be
both in Paris and not in Paris at a given time (since these are both possibilities), and so on. Nor have the main classical theologians done so. Sometimes they say things that are not clearly enough distinguishable from this, as
when Thomas speaks of the perfections of all things as being in God,[32] but
there is really no warrant for reading him as holding the absurd view that God
actualizes every possibility. And Anselm's idea that "God is whatever it is
better to be than not to be"[33] is poles apart from the notion of the actualization
of all possibilities. Thinking of the perfection of God along Anselmian lines,
it remains to be shown that there is any logical impossibility in this being
exemplified in a single state of a being.

V

I began this paper by contesting Hartshorne's claim that the classical and
neoclassical conceptions of God must each be accepted or rejected as a whole,
that each is so tightly unified as to make it impossible to accept or reject one
component without thereby accepting or rejecting the whole package. I have
opposed this claim in the most direct way possible—by doing what is claimed

to be impossible. Actuality is the most compelling proof of possibility. More specifically and more soberly, I have presented strong reasons for viewing the matter in the following way. The points on which the two conceptions differ (and I have said nothing about the many points of agreement) can be divided into two groups. Group 1 contains such classical attributes as absoluteness (construed as absence of internal relatedness), total necessity, pure actuality, and simplicity—along with their neoclassical counterparts, relativity, contingency, etc. Group 2 contains such classical attributes as creation ex nihilo, omnipotence, incorporeality, nontemporality, and absolute unsurpassability, along with their neoclassical counterparts. The neoclassical position on Group 1 does not entail the neoclassical position on Group 2, though it is, of course, consistent with it. On the contrary, the neoclassical Group 1 attributes can be combined with the classical Group 2 attributes into a consistent and coherent conception that captures the experience, belief, and practice of the high theistic religions better than either of Hartshorne's total packages. (I have not argued for that latter claim in this paper.) Thus there is a rent in these supposedly seamless fabrics along the lines indicated by my division of the attributes into two groups. To be sure, this rent is not as extensive as it might conceivably be; I have not argued, nor does it seem to be the case, that one group of attributes in one conception *implies* the other group of attributes in the other conception. Indeed, I have not even suggested that the classical Group 1 attributes are consistent with the neoclassical Group 2 attributes, and it is pretty clear that they are not. How could an absolutely simple, purely actual deity be mutable and temporal? Nevertheless the rent is sufficiently serious to be worth our notice. Because of it we are faced with a much more complex choice than Hartshorne would have us believe.

Notes

The titles of certain works will be abbreviated as follows:

DR   Charles Hartshorne, *The Divine Relativity*. New Haven, Conn.: Yale University Press, 1948.

LP   Charles Hartshorne, *The Logic of Perfection*. LaSalle, Ill.: Open Court, 1962.

MVG   Charles Hartshorne, *Man's Vision of God* (originally published 1941). Hamden, Conn.: Archon Books, 1964.

PR   Alfred North Whitehead, *Process and Reality*. New York: Macmillan, 1929.

SMW   Alfred North Whitehead, *Science and the Modern World*. New York: Macmillan, 1925.

    1. MVG, 95. This view sorts ill with Hartshorne's frequent assertion that the position contains internal contradictions. If each of the basic theses of

the Thomistic theology entails all the rest, and if the whole set is contradictory, then each of the theses individually is contradictory, a most implausible conclusion.

We should also note that Hartshorne must be very careful as to just what set of propositions he alleges to have this tight logical interconnection. Otherwise he will be saddled with the unwelcome conclusion that one cannot attribute knowledge to God without accepting the whole Thomistic system.

2. MVG, 235; DR, 6–8.

3. DR, 6–7.

4. Hartshorne will reply that I am aware of God only in a dim, inadequate, incomplete, and abstract way when I think of Him, whereas God's awareness of me is quite the opposite in these respects. I grant the point. The fact remains that when I am aware of God in any way, I am thereby related to God in a certain manner, and apart from that relationship I would not be exactly as I am. (You may substitute the solar system for God without affecting the argument.)

5. DR, 7; 17.

6. DR, 8–10.

7. DR, 11. The matter is further complicated by the Thomistic principle that there is no distinction between God's knowing and willing. However even if that extraordinary claim were accepted it is not clear that it would negate the point that God would be different from what He is, in his concrete reality, if He did not know what He knows.

8. And, as the classical theologian would add, could have refrained from creating any world at all. Hartshorne does not accept this addition; I will deal with that issue below. For now I am exploring implications of the common ground—that God could have created a world different from the one He did create.

9. DR, 13ff.

10. DR, 118; LP, 37; MVG, 108.

11. *Summa Theologica,* Iae, Q. 45, Art. 1.

12. A crucial part of my support for this is contained in the next section, where I argue that temporality is not required by relativity, potentiality, etc. For if God is temporal, creation ex nihilo is difficult to maintain.

13. See below.

14. MVG, 233.

15. This may be contested on the grounds that an act of will must take place at a time and, hence, that a temporally infinite universe could not depend for its existence on an act of will. For whenever that act of will took place, the universe was already in existence. But this last claim is acceptable only if the Creator is in time.

16. MVG, 115–20; DR, 19.

17. MVG, 115–17.

18. MVG, 117–20.

19. MVG, 105–9.

20. MVG, 14.

21. DR, 19.

22. "How an actual entity *becomes* constitutes *what* that actual entity *is*. . . .Its 'being' is constituted by its 'becoming' " (PR 34–35).

23. A "prehension" is an apprehension without the "ap." That is, an awareness that may or may not be conscious.

24. PR, 105–7; SMW, 183–85.

25. The spatial dimension can be determined by tracing out simultaneity relations between actual entities.

26. See, e.g., Charles Hartshorne, "Whitehead's Idea of God," in *The Philosophy of Alfred North Whitehead*, ed. P. A. Schilpp (New York: Tudor, 1941); John B. Cobb, Jr., *A Christian Natural Theology* (Philadelphia: Westminster, 1965), pp. 176–92; Lewis S. Ford, "The Non-Temporality of Whitehead's God," *International, Philosophical Quarterly,* March, 1974.

27. PR, 134, 528.

28. *Summa Theologica,* Iae, Q. X, Art. 1.

29. He also distinguishes between being surpassable in all, some, or no respects, but we will not need to attend to this and other distinctions that he draws in that chapter.

30. LP, 34–40.

31. MVG, 22, 37; DR, 144; LP, 36.

32. *Summa Theologica,* Iae, Q. 4, Art. 2.

33. *Proslogium,* chap. 5.

Response by Charles Hartshorne

I think I am entitled to be proud of my one-time student, William P. Alston. He has written a lucid essay which shows fine understanding of some aspects of my thought. I am encouraged by his acceptance of a substantial part of my criticism of classical theism as found in Aquinas; however, he sides with Aquinas and against me on some issues. He defends this partial disagreement with remarkable fairness. It is a privilege to defend oneself against such a critic.

The departures from Aquinas which Alston accepts are, I agree, the ones for which my argumentation is the most adequate and manifestly cogent. Nor is Alston the only one who has gone this far with me but parted company on some other issues. But he has made the case most lucidly for this half agreement, or half disagreement, with neoclassical theism.

My critic does not refer to *Creative Synthesis and Philosophic Method*, my most philosophical book and the one coming closest to summing up my system. If he has read that book, he knows that I have come to state my position in philosophical theology in terms of the doctrine of "dual transcendence." Theists have tended to agree that deity contrasts with other forms of reality as the independent or absolute contrasts with the dependent or relative, also as infinite contrasts with finite, impassible with passible, necessary with contingent. The neoclassical view is that, while this traditional contrast is valid, it is only half of the story. Deity is indeed to be thought of as uniquely independent, infinite, impassible, and necessary. But, as Alston concedes, it will not do to suppose God exclusively necessary and in every way absolute or immune to influence. For this implies, to note only the most obvious objection, that God could not in any intelligible sense know a contingent world, whereas Aquinas and all the scholastics held that God does know such a world. So dual transcendence must be accepted, at least so far as necessity and contingency are concerned. There must be a supremely excellent way of being contingent. Otherwise, we have the Spinozistic doctrine, which few theists have been able to accept, that God, being wholly necessary, knows an equally necessary creation. For similar reasons, which Alston grants, there must be what the title of one of my books implies, a divine relativity or dependence. Thus the famous "negative theology" is not the whole story. But whereas, with Aristotle and much of the tradition, I hold that contingency and change belong together, as do necessity and eternity, my critic wants to separate contingency and change sharply in application to God. I hold that Aristotle was right: in my words, accidents do not happen in eternity. In Aristotle's words, "With eternal things to be possible and to be are the same." Seldom has a philosopher stated so much truth in so few words. It follows that any contingent aspects of deity must be noneternal, and vice versa. This is one of the two main reasons why Aquinas denied change of deity; he wanted to deny any contingent aspect of God. (The other reason is that an absolutely perfect being could have no reason to change, improvement being contradictory in this case, and capacity for degeneration being manifestly an imperfection.)

For me, Aristotle's dictum, quoted above, is about as intuitively convincing as anything so fundamental can be. I believe that our understanding of contingency is inseparable from our intuition that, whereas past events are settled and definite, future events are not settled or definite. Indeed, as Whitehead says, there are no such entities as future events. There are only the *more or less definite possibilities* or probabilities constituting the future so long as it is future. Futurity and real possibility are one. Here Alston, somewhat to my surprise, argues that it would follow that there could have been no possibility of yesterday having been otherwise than it has been. He seems to forget that yesterday was once tomorrow. To say that yesterday might have been otherwise is to imply that, as things were the day before yesterday, or a year or a century ago, or at the big bang, or . . . , it was not entirely settled what yesterday was to be. Perhaps the day before yesterday someone made a free decision, not settled in advance, which influenced yesterday in a manner different from the way it would have been influenced if the decision had not been made. I think any pragmatist would see that my doctrine makes sense here. Each day we are deciding just what new items are to go into the ever-growing total past. The items are contingent in that the decisions are free. But the decisions once made, the possibility of making some alternative decision is gone forever. It remains true that there was such a possibility. To fully generalize the foregoing view, even the laws of nature, so far as contingent, are to be attributed to divine decisions made, not in eternity or for all time, but at a finite time in the past. I incline to Whitehead's view of cosmic epochs, each with its own laws.

Alston quotes a passage from *Man's Vision of God* which he takes to imply that if one rejects any of the propositions of classical theism one must reject them all, since they are "inseparable aspects of one idea." With this interpretation, the passage *is* mistaken. But it is not what I meant. I do not regard any philosopher's system as so "tightly coherent." However, the passage as I read it does not quite say what my critic here takes it to say. Rather it says that a certain set of theses affirmed by Aquinas and other classical theologians, theses listed in the paragraph from which the passage is quoted, are inseparable. They are precisely those theses which are used to affirm nondual as distinct from dual transcendence. Propositions which the two theories of transcendence have in common are of course among those which I accept, rejecting only what restricts transcendence to the nondual form. Alston goes partway with me in this, but makes some exemptions that I do not make. Thus he accepts both sides of the dependent-independent and contingent-necessary contrasts as applicable to deity, but not changeable-unchangeable, embodied and bodiless, self-surpassable and self-unsurpassable. (He holds that God is at most *contingently* embodied, in case there is a world.) I agree that if one makes any of these three exceptions one should make them all, but I see no sufficient reason for making any.

To say that God is contingently such-and-such is to imply a genuine possibility of God's not having been such-and-such. How is the actual divine state to be distinguished from and related to the merely possible one? I see no way other than that of some sort of time or sequential becoming. Curiously, Karl Barth tells us that there is "holy change" in God but "no potentiality." I hold with Aristotle, Aquinas, Lequier, and others, including Berdyaev, that contingency, potentiality, and some sort of change or temporality belong together. Whitehead finesses the issue, saying that God is "in a sense temporal." I prefer Berdyaev's "divine kind of time."

As for self-surpassability I take this to be an essential religious value. As Fechner was the first to say, by knowing each new creature God surpasses God. This is for me the meaning of life, serving God by contributing (in ideal, optimally) to the divine life, "enriching it," as Berdyaev says, and as Tillich says after him. Otherwise the old saying, "The aim of life is the service of God," lacks a clear meaning. Moreover, though Alston concedes that we influence God, he denies that this benefits God, who is absolutely perfect with or without us. My argument that absolute perfection, taken as fully concrete, is contradictory since there are incompatible possible goods, so that even God cannot exhaustively actualize them, Alston rejects, arguing that this is not what absolute perfection, taken as more than an abstraction, means. What then does it mean? I think that Alston does not know and that nobody knows.

If God's awareness of us contributes no value to God, then our existence is idle. The glory of God is the inclusive value; if we add nothing to it, then our existence adds nothing to reality as a whole. Value to God is the measure, not value to us. To be is to be for God. Alston says that we serve God by cooperating with the divine purpose. But then, by implication, he implies that how well we do so does not benefit God (for nothing does).

The twentieth century is not the thirteenth, and there is a whole set of questions which, in that earlier time, were all answered almost automatically in the same way, the way of the negative theology; but we have come to see these answers as highly controversial. Dozens of thinkers, especially in recent centuries, have been making the movement from nondual to dual transcendence. Whitehead's "two natures of God" crystallizes a long development. Alston's via media seems a somewhat arbitrary compromise, from this standpoint.

Taking God to be absolutely perfect in all respects (yet relative to the world!), my critic, with a certain partial consistency, also holds (with classical theism) that God does not *necessarily* create at all and might have existed solus. He expresses this by the old formula *creatio ex nihilo*. Such a "freedom" not to create at all would be freedom to be only potentially a creator, only potentially making any positive use of freedom. I see no enhancing of freedom in this wholly negative option, and no limitation in being essentially, rather than contingently, creative, or embodied in a cosmos, some cosmos or other.

We are offered the old argument that perfect love must be purely altruistic, must gain no benefit for self. I argue, on the contrary, that it is we, not God, who must act to produce values from some of which we cannot benefit ourselves, since we may not survive to know these values or, being incurably more or less ignorant, may not know the results of our actions, whereas God will survive and know what results from no matter whose actions. It is God who can and will vicariously rejoice in all joys and suffer with all sufferings. God has no motive that *makes against creaturely good,* hence no motive that is selfish in the proper sense. Rather, entirely the contrary, the divine love is the only pure love there is. This is my deepest conviction. Classical theism did not really conceptualize the idea of a God who "is love."

A subtle issue concerns my doctrine that a relative or dependent term includes the term (or terms) on which it is dependent. Or, the term for which a relation is internal includes the relation and the other term (or terms). Thus my relation to my ancestors is internal to me but not to them. I was not in their world but they are in mine. In the dim recesses of my largely unconscious perceptions and memories they are present; but I was not present in even the dimmest of the recesses of their memories or perceptions. In this sense each of us also includes the divine life, without for the most part consciously knowing it. However, God fully knows us with no limitations of dimness or unconsciousness. If Alston thinks this a difficult doctrine, I agree with him. But perhaps reality is difficult to comprehend. In any case, the doctrine that the divine reality is all-inclusive is meant in the sense that to know something unqualifiedly is to possess it entirely, to have it within one's own reality. To know something in a qualified way, the creaturely way, is to have it in a qualified sense, below the level of distinct consciousness. I cannot detect my ancestors in myself, but God can detect them there. This is akin to Spinoza's doctrine of clear and unclear ideas. At this point I, like Whitehead, am a Spinozist. And on this point Leibniz did not differ from Spinoza.

Although I shall not spell out the argument here, I think that there is an implicit contradiction in holding that we depend on God, who timelessly knows all our acts, past or future as they may be for us now, and yet our present reality does not necessitate our future acts. I here agree with Jules Lequier's careful analysis of this problem. The classical doctrine is that God knows our acts not before they occur but timelessly. But what is true timelessly cannot be untrue at any time. If what I do tomorrow is not wholly definite now, still less is it definite eternally. Aquinas makes it as clear as possible that he is indeed "spatializing time" and thus, from the process point of view, falsifying it. In eternity there are only symmetrical dependencies. Only through becoming as creation of new presents, i.e., new items in a partly new total past which is adequately preserved for all the future, in God, can there be the mixture of contingency and conditional necessity (necessary conditions but no fully necessary consequences) which is reality.

As W. P. Montague saw so clearly (with no doubt some help from Peirce and Bergson), becoming as sheer growth, increase without loss, is the concrete reality and the secret of both being and becoming.

One last question. Can God do what God wills to do? Of course, but what does God will to do? Alston (departing from Aquinas who, and not alone in my opinion, is terribly equivocal on this issue) says that God wills that creatures shall have freedom, so that their decisions are made possible, but not fully determined, by God. I agree but add: God had no alternative to willing that there be some free creatures, first because (pace Alston) the idea of not creating at all could occur (if I may say so) only to a confused creature, second because, as Peirce, Bergson, and Whitehead have seen, by a "creature" we can consistently mean only a lesser form of the freedom or creativity which in eminent form is deity. Divine freedom is correlative to nondivine freedom in some form; both as such are necessarily and eternally existent, that is, with some instances or other. An actually creating, loving creator is the only unqualified necessity; all else more specific or particular than this abstract essence is contingent, the play of divine-creaturely freedom.

My warm thanks to Alston for his interesting and challenging essay.

John E. Smith

5

Some Aspects of Hartshorne's Treatment of Anselm

This symposium devoted to critical discussion of the thought of Charles Hartshorne provides an opportunity for me to press further some points I raised earlier in reviews of two of his books, *The Logic of Perfection* (1962) and *Anselm's Discovery* (1965), both of which had to do with the original ontological argument and the import of Anselm's meditations. I confess that I have always found myself ambivalent as regards that famous argument. That is to say, I am not confident in giving an unambiguous answer to the question, Is the Argument valid? By contrast, for example, I do not hesitate to say that Hume's claim "whatever is distinguishable is separable," is wrong, but in the face of the ontological argument, I hesitate. On the one hand, the argument, understood in its proper setting, is not just so much nonsense or empty verbiage, for it contains a crucial logical transition pointing to a necessary relation between concepts, which, at the very least, can be argued about. And, as Hartshorne has pointed out, many of the "refutations" of the argument have been based on faulty apprehensions of its meaning or upon dogmatic assumptions such as the thesis that no existence can be derived from "mere" ideas or that existence is not a predicate. On the other hand, like Royce's argument for the absolute from the possibility of error, one has the sense that the ontological argument establishes something, except that it is difficult to say exactly what that something is. It has always seemed to me that, on any interpretation of the argument, it enjoys an element of superiority over the cosmological arguments in its starting with the idea of God and of perfection rather than with an other. For the approach to God through the other must be limited by the fact that one reaches only so much, so to speak, of God as can be manifested in the nature of that other.

Generally speaking, I regard Hartshorne's treatment of the argument and his tracing of its subsequent history as making at least three distinctive contributions to this philosophico-theological topic. There was first his return to the original argument without, we may say, benefit of Descartes, who confused the issue by asking for the *cause* of the idea of God. This return was accompanied by a new emphasis on the importance of the *nature* of God achieved by a reinterpretation of the "that than which nothing greater . . ." formula. The question of the divine nature was often thrust into the background because of exclusive concern with the divine *existence*. Hartshorne rightly redressed the balance in calling attention to the abstract character of existence taken by itself. Second, Hartshorne, with the aid of his neoclassical metaphysics, was able to show the need for real modes of Being in which the distinctive type of Being in question makes a real difference, especially in relation to divinity, in opposition to Kant, for instance, who thoroughly disconnected modality from the content of the concept, and thus found himself left with but one mode, that of spatio-temporal existence, as the matter for knowledge. Third, Hartshorne's critical review of the assessments made by later philosophers of Anselm's argument opens the way for a reversal of the usual procedure. Instead of attending only to a given philosopher's verdict on the validity or invalidity of the argument, we are led to inquire into the validity of the standpoint from which the judgment was made. In short, the ontological argument can be made to stand as a touchstone for philosophical positions; what does the verdict of a given philosophy on the argument tell us about the assumptions and the viability of that philosophy itself? This reversal, in which Anselm and his followers no longer automatically stand in the dock but instead assume the role of prosecuting attorney, provides a new perspective on the entire discussion of the ontological argument, a perspective badly needed in view of the sorry record set by a host of past philosophers who, for the most part, failed to penetrate the substance of the argument because they already knew by heart the litany whose refrain is "Existence is not a predicate."

Turning now to matters of detail, I would like to press the point I raised in my review of *The Logic of Perfection* concerning the status of logic; my contention is that unless, as Hegel, Peirce and others have held, logic has an ontological reach especially as regards the modal categories the sort of reasoning represented by the argument must fail. This holds true for other metaphysical doctrines, including the basic one set forth by Hartshorne in his paper "Some Empty Though Important Truths." The underlying problem concerns the status accorded formal logic, especially since it has assumed symbolic, mathematical form. Does it reflect the nature of reality, or is it a merely formal structure governing the use of language? In short, are we to have no more than "logic without ontology"? I believe that Hartshorne takes too lightly the force of the view according to which logic marks out the domain of the "necessary"—sometimes construed as the tautological—while the "real" coincides with contingent existence in the domain of fact. The consequence of this juxtaposition is that the "real" and the necessary are mutually exclusive.

Hartshorne appears to accept the formal/factual dichotomy,[1] thinking of God as belonging to the domain of necessary truth rather than to the side of fact. I do not, however, understand how Hartshorne's philosophical theology can succeed unless based on a logic with ontological import. His principle of "modal coincidence" is, I presume, intended to resolve the problem, but if it does, it is only because the modes are real and not only logical or linguistic. Hartshorne suggests that Carnap's "meaning postulates" allow for the introduction of analytic judgments other than those that are merely logical, and presumably assertions about God belong to this class. He goes on to say that "it may be" that Carnap's proposal is the key to reconciling the logical meaning of necessity with the ontological. This seems to me the central matter and one cannot take it too lightly especially in view of the fact that, in Carnap's treatment of modalities, only the modal property "contingent" correlates with the "factual" taken as a semantical property; all other modal properties correlate merely with L-forms.

I do not overlook the fact that there has been much discussion in the intervening years—the shaking of the foundations of the analytic-synthetic distinction, for example—which surely does not leave the situation unchanged. As regards the dominant climate of philosophical opinion, however, despite all the disclaimers that have been made concerning classical empiricism and positivism, the old dichotomy between a domain of sensible fact on the one hand, and sets of logical forms on the other, seems to persist and behind it the old dogma that where we have necessity we have merely tautology, and where we have fact or "experience" there is no necessity. The reason I addressed the problem to Hartshorne initially is that, from one end of his thought to the other, he has made strong claims in behalf of his use, presumably in contrast to that of some other speculative philosophers, of modern formal logic, and I wanted to assure myself that he was under no illusion concerning the status accorded formal logic by many logicians and the force of the attempts to have, in Ernest Nagel's expression, "logic without ontology."

I can express my point through an example, almost certain to be unfamiliar to most, taken from Royce, a thinker studied by both Hartshorne and myself, and, I should add, a philosopher who had his own somewhat transcendentally colored ontological argument for God. In 1908, at the International Congress of Philosophy in Heidelberg, Royce delivered a paper entitled "The Problem of Truth in the Light of Recent Discussion." The interesting and quite surprising substance of this paper is an enthusiastic endorsement of the then new mathematical logic and studies in the logic of mathematics associated with such thinkers as Russell, Frege and Dedekind. Royce fully accepted Russell's logicist thesis—the voluntaristic twist given to it by Royce we need not consider here—that there are "absolutely true propositions" in pure mathematics which are, in turn, based on absolute truths of pure logic. The point germane to this discussion is that Royce was not only heralding the new logic for its concept of truth, which he regarded as far superior to that of pragmatism, but he was also assuming that this same logic could be used for the development of an exact metaphysics of the sort exemplified in the Supplementary Essay to *The World and the Individual*. Royce did not live to see the fulfillment of his high hopes and the development of this logic by some logicians not only into an instrument for the elimination of metaphysics but into a formalism and conventionalism in which truth in Royce's sense no longer figured. Since Hartshorne's knowledge of the developments that have taken place in logic over the past few decades is far superior to my own, I would be most interested in having his opinion about the general issue of the status of logic vis-à-vis metaphysical argument, especially in relation to recent discussion. And, in inviting him to respond to this query, I am not unaware, as Hartshorne himself has noted, that we must not take it for granted that the house of logic is in simple and good order, another indication, in my view, of the impossibility of disconnecting purportedly formal instruments from basic philosophical issues.

To begin with, I believe as I indicated earlier, that Hartshorne has done a great service to the odyssey of the ontological argument in the careful way in which he returned to the original text with its quite remarkable combination of meditative experience and rational articulation, as the basis for assessing the treatment accorded Anselm's reasoning by subsequent thinkers. I would reaffirm my agreement with Hartshorne on the absolutely essential point that the ontological argument, properly understood, asserts that God's existence is either necessary or impossible and, since there are no other alternatives, the argument cannot be discussed as if it involved merely the alternative of existence or nonexistence. This mistake has been the one most frequently made, and it finds its roots in Gaunilo's example of the island; this line of thought received further support from the nominalist strain in modern philosophy wherein all real modes were denied with the exception of sensible existence. I believe that this criticism holds quite apart from the resolution of the question whether it is legitimate to speak of the presence of two arguments in the *Proslogium*. The reason is clear: the discussion about existence as a perfection, as if that were all that is involved, does not make explicit the far more important point that, in the case of "God," properly understood, nonexistence was never a real possibility, a consideration entirely overlooked by those who blithely say that, of course, we all know that no existence can be derived from "mere" ideas. The latter point brings us to what I take to be a novel and illuminating idea in *Anselm's Discovery,* namely, Hartshorne's answer to the question of exactly what Anselm discovered.

According to Hartshorne, Anselm was engaged in a meditative analysis of what it means to believe in God from within, as it were, since the believer is involved in a self-examination. From this starting point, Anselm is said to have shown that if believers understand their faith, they "are the only ones who do understand it" (p. 22), from which it would follow that it is only lack of understanding which leads a person to reject theistic belief. The positivist, according to this account, can avoid this conclusion only if he can consistently make good the claim that the term "God" is meaningless, which is a way of saying that God's purported existence is not a logical possibility in any sense. In addition, Hartshorne claims that one who denies the existence of God explicitly cannot avoid Anselm's conclusion under any circumstances, since his finding meaning in the central religious question at once prevents him from denying the necessity of the affirmative answer. On his own terms, Anselm is said to have shown that as long as "the fool" continues to conceive God he cannot consistently withhold assent to the necessity of the divine existence, *unless* he is using the term "God" in a sense different from what the self-understanding believer means by the term.

This, I believe, is an accurate representation of what Anselm intended by his meditation on the grounds of faith seeking understanding, and Hartshorne's account clearly expresses the situation of the believer in relation to the two opponents. There is a question, however, about what limitation Hartshorne believes is imposed by the initial dependence of the argument on the idea of God derived from the faith and the self-understanding of the believer. In short, exactly what role is played by the faith from which the argument sets out? This question is not easy to answer, and it must arise ever again in any attempt to explain the approach through "faith seeking understanding." Hartshorne claims that, since all proofs have premises, Anselm's argument must be based on the assumptions that faith is a real possibility and that the idea of God is free of inconsistencies. But these assumptions ("meaning-postulates") do not coincide with "faith" in the sense of the *fides* that stands in need of understanding. Meaning-postulates may indeed be required, but they do not furnish the appropriate religious meaning with which Anselm began the argument. I would agree with Hartshorne when he says that the argument is more subtle than the derivation of God's existence from the premise supplied by the initial faith that God exists. If this is so, then the question arises as to what meaning is to be attached to the term "God" and how this meaning is to be circumscribed by faith. Moreover, did Anselm propose in the *Proslogium,* as he did in the case of the Incarnation in *Cur Deus Homo,* to demonstrate a doctrine to anyone regardless of their assumptions, or is the demonstration of God's existence directed only to those "believers" who understand what is meant by "God" in a certain way? If the latter, how shall we know when we have started with the premises actually meant by a "believer"? Hartshorne does not pay sufficient attention to this problem because, in my view, he does not take seriously enough the historical, Judeo-Christian content underlying Anselm's formula. Hartshorne does ask why Anselm chose his formula, "That than which nothing greater . . ." and answers, "I suppose because he takes it for granted that by 'God' is meant the universal object of worship, and if God could have a superior, then only the ignorant or superstitious would worship Him" (p. 26). Does this mean that Anselm was reflecting what "believers" mean, any believers, or rather what a "rational" believer *must* mean if he is really to talk about God? I find

Hartshorne's answer somewhat curious in that it envisages Anselm as having in his possession some generic category called "the universal object of worship" which determined the formula at the heart of the argument. While I would insist that "God" expresses a concept and is not only a proper name within a certain historical tradition, I believe that Hartshorne pays insufficient attention to the force of that tradition in shaping Anselm's meditation. The "that than which nothing greater . . ." formula is Anselm's attempt to express the perfection, majesty, and transcendence associated with the thought of God throughout the fabric of biblical religion—"Thou shalt have no other gods before me."

The term "God" was obviously in use in the Christian communities long before Anselm commenced his meditations. While he couched the meaning of deity in his own formula, it is scarcely imaginable that he meant to do anything else but express what Christians mean by "God." Hartshorne admits that Anselm may not have succeeded in expressing the Christian understanding accurately. Unless, however, there were a faith *content* for "God" existing prior to Anselm's formula, how would Hartshorne (or anyone else) know that interpreting "none greater can be conceived" to mean the "Perfect which cannot change" is "merely Greek" doctrine and not faith? Hartshorne in fact claims (p. 29) that Anselm adopted the Greek view and consequently that he sacrificed his right to say that his formula expresses faith. Such a claim, however, could be made only on the supposition that for "faith" or for the "believer" there is a meaning for the term "God" which Anselm may not have articulated correctly. The question then is, What is this meaning and how do we have access to it?

Since I would still urge the same line of argument on this point set forth in my review of *Anselm's Discovery,* I shall quote one paragraph from that review.

> The point is of the utmost importance because it concerns the meaning which the term "God" has for "faith" prior to its identification with Anselm's formula. And indeed the term must have such a prior meaning if (a) we can significantly discuss, as Hartshorne claims, whether Anselm's formula does express "Greek doctrine" or faith and (b) we can decide whether Anselm's formula adequately expresses faith. The first point to be noticed is that the formula does *not* purport to express a convention—let "p ⊃ q" mean "it is not the case that p is true and q is false"—but rather what is actually meant by the term "God" in the thought of a believer. "Faith" in the sense in which it figures in Anselm's proof does *not* mean faith in the existence of God; it means instead the content which expresses the nature of God. If faith meant no more than the former, Hartshorne would be correct in saying that the Argument is merely the deduction that God exists from the premise "God exists." But Anselm's premise is not that "God exists" but, rather, that the term "God" or "that

than which nothing greater . . . ,'' when properly understood, leads to a contradiction when one and the same person claims to understand this term without being bound to acknowledge the impossibility of the divine non-existence. Anselm's proof is dependent upon ''faith,'' but not faith in the divine *existence;* instead, ''faith'' means the content of the idea of ''God.''[2]

I am inclined to think that Hartshorne's reinterpretation of perfection in terms of the self-surpassing individual has the merit of overcoming the static connotation invariably associated with the perfect and of recovering the ideas of life and spirit within the divine nature. It is, however, necessary to see how this concept is related to ''faith.'' It seems to me that Hartshorne has three options: (1) he may claim that his conception is what Christian believers *do* mean by ''God,'' or (2) what they *would* mean if they properly understood their faith, or (3) what ''God'' *must* mean if the argument is to succeed. I believe that Hartshorne can bypass option (1) because the issue turns in the end on a matter of principle, but I see him as committed to (2) and (3), but then he must maintain that the meaning in both these cases is coincident.

There need be no problem in calling attention to the dependence of the argument on faith and to the fact that faith is the source of at least one of its premises. This dependence of itself does not serve to show that there is no logical transition in the argument. The validity of the argument must turn on how the premise is *understood* and not upon its *source.* In this connection I would say that Anselm's ''discovery''—he may have made more than one— is that the divine nonexistence is not a *real* possibility because it contradicts the meaning of ''God'' properly understood.

Notes

1. *The Logic of Perfection,* p. 54.
2. *''Anselm's Discovery: A Re-examination of the Ontological Proof for God's Existence,'' The Journal of Religion* 47, no. 4 (1967): 365.

Response by Charles Hartshorne

In reading a book or essay I often write *y* for ''yes'' in margins. No's are less frequent. I put only one *no* in reading Smith's essay, and I suspect it is less a disagreement than a slight forgetting on his part, when he wrote that I assign God ''to the domain of formal, pure, or necessary truth rather than to the side of fact." I assign only the bare, abstract truth *that* God exists to the nonfactual domain, but not the full concreteness of the divine life, which I call the divine "actuality." I never say that God is purely formal or necessary, only that the divine existence is so. The divine actuality, which is *how,* or in what state or states, the essence is actualized, is definitely contingent or factual. This is an aspect of what I call "dual transcendence." Smith says that my principle of "modal coincidence" (to be possible is to be possible for God, to be actual is to be actual for God) is addressed to the problem of the factual side, but that my ontological argument must appeal to modal logic as expressive of *real* possibility and necessity, and that logicians express doubts about these. I agree that my argument must so appeal, and that many logicians do express such doubts.

Against such logicians I appeal to a number of considerations. One is that my theory of real possibility and necessity has much in common with views of three great logicians of the past, Aristotle, Peirce, and Whitehead. With them I take seriously the apparent asymmetry of becoming, time's arrow, according to which the past is (in Peirce's words) "the sum of accomplished facts," of definite particulars, whereas the future is *exclusively* constituted by real Thirds, that is, not fully particularized generals, which will be *somehow* particularized as the future becomes past but are not particularized in advance or eternally. The eternal necessity of some actualization of divinity, God's existence, is what all possible futures have in common. It is infinitely less particular than any *given* real possibility or actuality.

This theory is between the extremes, sheer denial of objective or ontological modality and the Leibnizian type of "possible worlds" theory which seems to have some vogue among recent logicians. Aristotle, Peirce, and Whitehead do not use the concept of possible world; I also avoid it, except sometimes as shorthand. There are always contrasting possible future states of the actual world. Thus there may now be a real possibility of Reagan's being reelected and also a possibility of his not running for a second term or of being defeated. Some logicians take this tack. According to it there may be possible states of given *individuals* but there are no merely possible, yet fully definite, particulars. Unqualified definiteness, particularity, and actuality are coincident. And Peirce says flatly, "It is the past which is actual." Real possibility is real futurity. Becoming is creation of definiteness, *new* Firsts, Seconds, and Thirds added to the already accomplished ones.

I give several criteria for the contingent as distinguished from the strictly necessary. Any *positive* conception whose instantiation restricts that of some other positive conceptions (for example as red-here-now restricts the occurrence of green-here-now) refers to a contingent aspect of reality. Incompatibility, not merely between P and not-P, but between P and Q, as two equally affirmative propositions, indicates contingency. I argue that the bare existence of God restricts no positive possibility whatever. God could coexist with anything else capable of existing. This is why theism cannot be observationally falsified, or in the proper sense empirically tested. As Popper says, observation is always of the presence, never of the mere absence, of something positive. Even black holes are not mere nothings.

George L. Goodman has discussed the relation of my ontological argu- *Lwin* ment to formal logic in his book on that subject. William Lucas has proposed, in a dissertation completed in Austin, a formal system in which the problems can be discussed.

It still seems to me that "meaning-postulates" (Carnap's phrase) must be given for general ideas beyond the recognized logical constants; one cannot define theism by these constants alone. But the ideas are no less universal in the metaphysical sense than are the logical constants. Whatever is implied by the mere meanings of Plato's idea of Good, or of value, and "better than," or of Whitehead's creativity, the ideas of dependence, independence, and still others (coherently combined) is metaphysically necessary and eternally true. Not only the divine existence but the actuality of some nondivine existence, is thus ontologically necessary. The bare idea of world-as-such is as ultimate as that of God, the ground being the equal tolerance for the positive coexistence of whatever you please. A worldless God is on the same footing of absurdity as a Godless world. But our actual world is purely factual, with no necessity requiring it.

I largely agree with what Smith says about the religious meaning of the term "God." I argue that, the world over, there has been some idea of a transcendent reality appropriate to the first "great" commandment, "Love the Lord thy God with all thy mind and heart and strength." I take this to imply that the transcendent reality must be somehow all-inclusive; that it must itself love all other realities and be related to them analogously to the way a human soul, that is, a personally ordered society of human experiences, is related to its body; also as a parent is related to its child, or as a ruler is to the subjects. Divine right of kings has always been fictitious, but deity is indeed, by eternal right, Lord or ruler of all—not, however, by making decisions determining all that happens, leaving nothing for others to decide. Whoever seeks to do that is a tyrant, not a proper ruler. The word "omnipotent" stands for a human mistake, among the greatest of all such mistakes. It does not describe the one we are to love with all our being. In this contention process theism is not merely Western; Sri Jiva Goswami of Bengal was such a theist; so was Iqbal, the Islamic thinker and poet of Pakistan. But they were not classical theists of the medieval Western type. They were closer to the theologians of the Socinian sect in the seventeenth century.

Since the publication of my two books focusing on the ontological argument, the most important things I have done have been little noticed. One is to sketch a logic of "ultimate contrasts," with some analogy to the Hegelian dialectic; the other is to work out a new form of theistic arguments, some six of them, the ontological being only one, but the others being equally a priori. Both topics are the subjects of chapters in my *Creative Synthesis and Philosophic*

Method. The scarcity of responses to these chapters illustrates my contention that it is possible to publish important ideas, reasonably well stated, virtually without attracting the attention of those concerned with the subject. The world, including the scholarly world, is always busy, always prejudiced. Various factors, in addition to good writing, must combine to gain its attention.

The real argument for God is the total context in which about six arguments, encapsulated in what I call the global argument, need to be placed. The chief contribution of the ontological argument is to make explicit the logical status of the theistic question, its transcendence of observational falsification. For the believer "the heavens declare the glory of God," but not even for the atheist can the heavens, or any observed realities, declare the divine nonexistence. To suppose that they could violates the logic of the idea of deity. Nontheism must argue on logical grounds, using "logical" here more broadly than some logicians would, not on observational grounds. This was Anselm's discovery, but Aristotle already knew it. "With eternal things, to be possible and to be are the same."

Formalization of a theistic argument is only as convincing as the intuitions supporting its premises. But formalization helps to articulate the extralogical premises, the intuitive content, of a belief. Anselm's premises (as I revise his procedure) were two: there is a coherent idea of God, as all-surpassing, rivalry-excluding; this idea entails its own actualization, not *how,* or in what concrete actuality, it is actualized, but *that* it is *somehow* actualized, in *some* concrete form. The being "somehow actualized" of an essence or property is *existence,* as I use the word; the how or in what it is actualized is *actuality.* The latter is always contingent, even in the divine case; the former is contingent except in the divine case and whatever is implied by the bare idea of nondivine reality, some world or other.

Paul Weiss

6

Nature, God, and Man

I

In "Man in Nature,"[1] Charles Hartshorne stated that his interests are "nature, God, and man, in about that order" (in *Experience, Existence, and the Good,* ed. Irwin C. Lieb [Carbondale, Ill.: Southern Illinois University Press, 1961], p. 89).

It would be hard to find a more succinct statement which conveyed, not only the extraordinary range of Hartshorne's thought, but his abiding concern with the most basic questions of mankind and philosophy, his concentration on pivotal issues, and his readiness to affirm just where he stands. These virtues characterize his entire career, a career which I have been privileged to grow with and to benefit from almost over its entire course. I am grateful for this opportunity to do honor to a philosopher who has signally occupied himself with illuminating and communicating independently, honestly, and courageously matters that are of importance to every one of us.

The originality of Hartshorne's discussions about the nature of God, and particularly his daring and novel defense of the ontological argument, have led some to overlook the fact that, as he himself says, his primary interest lies elsewhere. It is good that this is so for, with Whitehead and most other process philosophers, the God about which he writes is pertinent primarily to the beliefs of Christians, particularly low-church Protestants. Little regard is paid by him or his colleagues to Judaism, and none at all to Islam or Shinto, although these take themselves to have beliefs, theologies, histories, and tasks quite different from those characteristic of Christianity. It is, moreover, rather difficult to tie a process account in with some of its current acceptances of pivotal Buddhist views, since the Buddhists take themselves to have a single coherent position in which there seems to be no room for anything like the

God of the Western religions. However, when his discussions of God are freed from their religious trappings, it becomes apparent that what is being attended to is an irreducible reality, standing apart from but in vital interplay with actual entities. Once it is noted that his God has at least that status, that it is irreducible and final, the way is open for the acknowledgment (with both Plato and Aristotle) of a number of other equally basic realities. These, together with finite, transient, actual entities, determine the character and course of the cosmos. They allow us, also, to point up two unexplored topics, the examination of which should help us move to a new stage in philosophic understanding.

1. If God is a primal reality, existing outside the limits of religious interest or grasp, he can provide a locus for the referents of any and every possible religion. Different revelations, prophets, miracles, and expressions of faith—for those who are able to make use of them—provide agencies by means of which the transcendental majesty of the divine can be shown to be pertinent to men. More boldly, by acknowledging that there are other final realities on a footing with such a God, one is able to find a place for many different religions, even for those which pivot about things, animals, or signal events in nature. These religions can be viewed as specializing some ultimate reality other than the God on which Westerners fasten. Finally, if one envisages all final realities as being together only as merged, with all distinctness and determinateness lost, one will have a base toward which the religious interests of the East are directed. Better, by taking different Eastern religions to be occupied with reaching the still center of different final realities, where no diversity is to be found, and where there is no way of referring to anything else, one can come to see how Taoism, Hinduism, Buddhism, and the mysticisms based on other religions can differ while being equally well grounded.

2. The ontological argument, so brilliantly and illuminatingly opened up again by Hartshorne, refers to God, not in his full concreteness and as involved with what is beyond him, but as he is by himself, forever, in his self-sufficiency. Might not the argument also be used to justify the acknowledgment of other ultimate realities as they stand apart from all else? Or is the ontological argument to be restricted to God, with the other ultimate realities "proven" in quite different ways? Or does the ontological argument perhaps apply to no one of them, but only to them together, with each having the status of what Hartshorne calls an "accident"? Or does this and similar arguments deal only with the centers of final realities, each of interest only to those who share a particular commitment?

The catholicity and the neutrality of philosophy, I think, requires one to accept the options that the first question offers us. We then can make provision for the insights of the most disparate religions, taking them to be occupied with different specializations of different ultimate realities. In this way it is possible to avoid disparaging the great events, myths, and central figures cherished by others, without being forced to subscribe to the claims of any one of them.

The second question is more difficult to deal with. To know whether ultimate realities can be proven to exist, by repeating the ontological argument or by tailoring it so that it is pertinent to their different natures, powers, and roles—and this apart from any commitment to a particular religion—requires one to do no less than produce the argument. Hartshorne's "proof," unfortunately, is so closely tied to the questionable views of certain modal logicians that it is hard to know whether it can apply only to God or can also be extended to other ultimate realities. I think it gets and can get no further than the affirmation that the idea of God is the idea of an existent God. Surely, no argument can ever take one from an idea to a reality. And then one must face the question whether the ontological and cognate arguments may have to do, not with what is in fact real, but with what, as Hartshorne sometimes says, is an abstract aspect of this. And if the arguments are to have any pertinence to what concerns religious men, they will of course have to refer not to something abstract, or to what is common to all fundamental realities, but to just one of those realities, approached from a distinctive position. But whether one supposes that the ontological argument, or any others, deal with what is merely abstract, with what is common to all ultimate realities, or with the unspecified center of some final reality (the most promising I think of the alternatives), one will have to supplement the argument by what is known or acknowledged by religious men. Otherwise, what one "proves" will not be pertinent to what these call "God."

The topic should not be dropped before it is remarked that there are radical differences between Whitehead's and Hartshorne's views of God. Hartshorne deviates from his master, not always to his advantage, in holding that God exists moment after moment; that he is a kind of society, is not occupied with eternal objects, has an abstract and an accidental dimension, does not contrast with the world as a one for its many and a many for its one, is not a creature of a primary creativity, suffers with and loves men, and is getting better and better. Neither Whitehead nor Hartshorne has room for a God who is angry, who is not the only finality, or who creates. Neither, therefore, can do full justice either to the demands of the followers of Western religions or to the implications of a dispassionate metaphysic.

II

Most current defenders of the process view seem to be theologians. Hartshorne, instead, is primarily a philosopher. As he said, he has other interests. But it is not altogether clear whether his triad of interests—"nature, God, and man, in about that order"—is to be read as ascending or descending. If we are not to lose the benefit of his thought, it is necessary to put both man and nature in the foreground and keep God and other ultimate realities in the background. But it will then be necessary both to correct some excesses of the process view and to enrich it so that it makes provision for the fact that men are unitary, complex, living beings with distinctive privacies, persistent and responsible. It will also allow one to acknowledge a nature where such men can be together with other irreducible living beings, with the ultimate units they encompass, and with combinations of all of these.

Much of what we seek to know about nature and man is caught up in the question: If there is a cosmos of ultimate units, interplaying with final realities; are men and nature part of it? Every one, with the exception of scientists and philosophers, seems ready to answer this with a strong affirmative. We should join them, but with the qualifications which accrue when the answer is won by taking account of the views of those who reject it.

Existentialists, personalists, and phenomenologists have today been suddenly joined by linguistic analysts. None of them, confessedly, can find warrant for the claim that there is a world existing independently of man. Science, incidentally mathematics, philosophy of course, and surely religion are viewed by these different thinkers as having only conventional, social, or historic warrants. None, it is held, can be shown to be related to anything existing apart from man's intentions, language, desires, concerns, talk, or presence. They inevitably cancel out the possibility of prehistory, natural cataclysms, birth and death (and, of course, the men who are able to be existentialists, or analysts, or whatever, maintaining that there could or could not be a world they did not constitute).

A philosophy which cannot get beyond personal commitments or a common language, no matter how carefully it speaks or how closely it adheres to current theories, is radically defective. And it will remain so, I think, if it is unable to allow one to affirm that there are animals, birds, trees, hills, rivers, a sun and moon, even when there are no men, or when they say nothing about these.

If it be allowed that science makes some kind of contact with more than theories, formulas, variables, formally defined values and constants, it must be added that any units with which it might rest will be publicly related entities with extensions conceivably divisible into smaller units. A cosmology dealing with irreducible unit-occurrences, interplaying with universally pertinent and irreducible powers, will then be outside its provenance. That fact, instead of showing the impossibility or uselessness of a cosmology, points up the inadequacy of a merely scientifically expressed account.

Whitehead and Hartshorne are in agreement with almost everyone else, and particularly with the classical atomists, in holding that the cosmos existed before there were men, that it will exist after men no longer do, and that both when there are men and when there are not, ultimate units exist and act more or less as they had always done. With the ancient atomists, they hold also that the cosmos embraces only ultimate unit-entities, all subject to the same universal conditioning powers. Although it is not altogether clear just how the atoms are known to be, it is quite clear that these atoms are not identifiable with the particles or waves with which current scientists have come to rest. Nor are they units which experiments have forced one to acknowledge. Rather, they are what such experiments and their objects are assumed to presuppose.

Process atomism improves on the classic in two important respects: It rejects the cosmic determinism that characterized the earlier view, and it denies that the ultimate units are static, public, and forever.

Though there seems hardly anyone today who explicitly accepts a cosmic determinism, the idea is implicit in the views of those contemporaries who, taking computers as their guide, seek to understand life and thought, and all their works, as summations of the moves of a multiplicity of units acting mechanically in the same ways always. The position is radically speculative and lacks supporting evidence. It also has the paradoxical consequence that it allows no place for the novel thoughts or minds of its proponents, or for the invention, making, use, sale, or understanding of the computers on which they ground their analogies. Because process atomism is not deterministic, implicitly or explicitly, it is able to make room for novelties, transience, diversity, and growth. That is enough to justify contemporary atomists in accepting it, and in rejecting the old form.

The second signal difference between process and classical atomism is perhaps the most widely known and most emphasized. Instead of taking ultimate units to be just filled-in regions of space, each substantial, persistent, and inert, Whitehead and Hartshorne hold instead that they have privacies and in effect are "living" units, coming into being and passing away, moment after moment, but not without preserving and transmitting what had already been achieved. It is hard to exaggerate the brilliance and daring exhibited in Whitehead's account of the way in which unit actual occasions combine both a past and future, and a universal guidance and individual self-determination. Unfortunately, the achievement has been allowed, both by its defenders and by its critics, to get in the way of an adequate consideration of the question as to whether complex living beings, encompassing a number of parts and, of course, a number of ultimate units, are not more than sequences, societies, devoid of the power, and lacking the concreteness, the self-creativity, the retentiveness, projectiveness, and involvement with final conditions that is characteristic of the ultimate units.

There is no difficulty in, and, I think, there is good warrant for affirming, in opposition to Whitehead and Hartshorne, that all unit realities, whether ultimate or more complex, have an integrity of their own, with distinctive privacies, but that only the complex are able to be conscious and therefore to feel, that they alone can persist unchanged for indefinite periods, and that they are affected not only by cosmic conditions but by any living beings within whose confines they happen to be. I know that these claims are ignored by Whitehead and expressly rejected by Hartshorne, but it is hard to find good reasons for their decision to go so counter to their own desires to do justice to what is known about men and nature. Perhaps there would be less reluctance to acknowledge the irreducible reality of men and other complex unitary beings, each persistent, active, with its own characteristic privacy, were it more clearly seen that the rejection of traditional atomism does not leave one with just irreducible momentary units which, despite all lack of evidence, are to be taken as centers of feeling. There seems no reason to deny that those units exist through indivisible stretches of time, privately undergone. Nor need one hold that those stretches all have the same length. Different ultimate units, like complex beings, have no antecedently prescribed common span. Some may outlast others.

We are now, I think, in a position to take account of occurrences which so far have been deemed unacceptable to Whitehead, Hartshorne, and other process thinkers, though I think their acknowledgment makes the view more viable, comprehensive, and accurate. One must find a place for complex unit-beings, or be left with the unsolvable problem of knowing why ultimate units are bunched and separated differently in different places and at different times. Peirce thought that the fact could be explained by referring to the workings of a cosmic chance. The supposition is gratuitous. Units are bunched and separated because they are confined within and partly controlled by unitary, more complex living beings which subject their contained organs, cells, and eventually the smallest units in these to new conditions, adventures, and controls. When and where complex beings act, there the parts of them are to be found, kept together, redirected, brought into relationship with others in ways that no common cosmic conditions or self-creativity by distinct beings could explain.

Living beings are *natural individuals,* encompassing a multiplicity of other beings for which they inevitably provide careers, opportunities, locations, and neighbors they otherwise would not have. Unlike *natural wholes,* such as stones and streams, whose careers are a function of the parts within them or are due to the actions of those who use them, natural individuals act as units, limiting and affecting what they contain, and limited and affected by these in turn. The *natural world* encompasses all natural wholes and individuals and therefore, all ultimate units so far as they are joined with some and separated from all the others in ways not cosmically determined. Because a cosmology which is restricted to the study of the interplay of ultimate units and final conditions has no place for natural wholes or natural individuals, it cannot account for all the ways in which the parts of those wholes and individuals, and eventually the ultimate units within those wholes or individuals, are interrelated. Instead, it must content itself with taking the ultimate units where it finds them, bunched and separated in ways it cannot explain.

Natural wholes and individuals are not isolated. The individuals, particularly, have their environments, their fellows, and their enemies. They exist together as members of groups. Each interplays with others and with the very conditions with which the others interplay. *Nature* is the locus of the natural wholes and individuals in their severalty and as together. Because the individuals in nature act in ways they would not, were they entirely cut off from one another, or were they just indifferent to one another's presence, the ultimate units in them are bunched and separated in additional ways.

Societies, like the natural individuals they contain, specialize the conditions which directly interplay with ultimate cosmic units. But like wholes, societies lack privacies and are unable to act. Natural individuals, though, not only can confine and affect what they encompass; they are able to initiate acts resulting in still other changes. Were one to deal with ultimate units cosmically, but as subject to the conditioning of just one final reality (let us say, with Hartshorne, a God), one would have to add that the final reality is specialized in the form of the unitary natures of living beings. Those beings are· able to modify the effects directly produced by the interplay of the God and the ultimate units.

Natural wholes and individuals, the natural world which embraces them, and the nature where the individuals are grouped, all make a difference to the functioning and interrelationships of the ultimate units contained within the individuals and what these use. The conditions and the units together constitute the cosmos.

An adequate account of what occurs requires one to supplement a cosmology of atoms and final conditions with an account of complex beings. The acceptance of that addition would enable a process philosophy to soften its now hardened opposition to what it calls a "substantialist" view. That would still not be enough. To do justice to the facts, it is necessary to go further.

Men are individuals severally and together in nature. They also contribute to distinctively human enterprises, helping constitute cultures and civilizations. In these, the activities and relations that men have to one another, and the activities and interrelationships of the ultimate units that they contain, diverge from those they exhibit in the cosmos, as well as from those they exhibit in nature. Men create works of art. They participate in sports. They speak, inquire, work, forge symbols, vitalize traditions, make and manipulate diagrams, pray, and involve themselves in such diverse disciplines as science, politics, history, and philosophy. In these and other ways they produce *domains*. In these they interrelate created objects, while bounding them off from all else. The material used to produce the objects—paintings, games, discourse, legislation, sacral objects, mathematics, theories, constructions, and the like—is subject to distinctive conditions operating in those domains. This is enough to make a difference to what the objects in those domains encompass. The parts of a dancer's body and therefore the ultimate units which are within the boundaries of her body are joined and separated by that body. They are also brought into new relations to one another and to what is in the bodies of others. Her dancing makes a difference beyond that which is produced by her as a natural individual.

The study of domains is both vast and neglected. Universal, final conditions operate in each, but only through the help of creative men. These join conditions to natural objects and thereby produce new entities. To neglect domains and their contents is to overlook what makes a difference to the functioning and relationship of what is encompassed by natural wholes and individuals, the natural world, and nature. The danger is not avoided by those who attend only to ultimate units and the final powers with which they interplay.

A *civilization* is a set of domains, each bounded off from the rest. There, the values and concerns of men are transformed and preserved. At different times, different domains are to the fore, with the others recessive. At different times, consequently, ultimate units and thus what is cosmically knowable, are subjected to still further conditioning, not explicable by attending only to what is pertinent to the ultimate units indifferently, or even to them as affected by natural individuals, the natural world where these are together, or the nature in which they exist both by themselves and together.

The cosmos is the locus of ultimate units in direct interplay with what is final. Within the limits of that cosmos there are more complex realities specializing those conditions and thereby making the ultimate units within them be affected in additional ways. Once it is recognized that the complex realities impose intensified, limited versions of final conditions on their parts, and eventually on a limited number of ultimate units, one is no longer tempted to speak only of cosmic powers, cosmic conditions, and ultimate units, but will also acknowledge both nature and man, and the differences they make to what they encompass. Their acknowledgment does not require a change in a cosmological account focused on ultimate units and final realities. It adds to this, explaining what otherwise would be inexplicable. In addition, it takes notice of realities that can be encountered. But this requires one to resist the reductive tendencies of almost every cosmology, even one, like Whitehead's and Hartshorne's, where the ultimate units are supposed to be living and self-creative. Real natural objects and men obviously cannot be in a cosmos which has a place only for atoms interplaying with final, empowered conditions. But the objects and men are surely real.

The cosmos contains conditions and ultimate units interplaying with these. It also contains specializations of those conditions as well as a limited number of units with which the specializations interplay. But natural objects and men, and what these produce, are not in the cosmos so far as they have or can make use of private, creative powers. Not to accommodate them in this guise is not to accommodate what is part of them in their full concreteness. The accommodation, however, will require one to supplement a cosmological account with a metaphysics. Nothing less than the two together will do justice to the presence and action of what the universe contains. A cosmology of interplaying ultimate units and empowered final conditions necessarily presupposes a metaphysical account of the reality of the units and the conditions, as able to act in these ways.

In order to provide a single, integrated, self-critical, controlled philosophy, able to be shared in by others, it is necessary to abandon Whitehead's project of providing a likely story. Instead one must proceed step by step, first analyzing what is empirically known into its irreducible factors, then passing intensively toward them as able to affect one another, and finally showing how they in fact interplay. If one proceeds cautiously, defending every move, one will replace a view which seems as arbitrary as it is odd, more an exhibition of Whitehead's genius and ingenuity than an account of what is, by one which rests on evidence, and will clarify what now is obscure.

The view at which we have now arrived is not far from one I have developed in other places. But until now I did not see how well some of it, while it diverges and goes beyond, still allows for an appreciation of some of the main cosmological claims which Hartshorne has urged over the length of his distinguished career. The fact makes me confident that what I have maintained is not altogether in error. I hope the indications here given of the way Whitehead's and Hartshorne's views are to be altered, and how they could be extended and filled out—while maintaining their characteristic thrust and flavor—will be accepted by Hartshorne as a tribute to the strength and promise of what he has already so splendidly achieved. I think his account still has grave, perhaps insuperable, difficulties with motion, perception, obligation, responsibility, action, human interchange, contemporaneity, God, and community. But I do hope that the present discussion will allow one to see that the scrawny and rather skeletal creature, unable to move, or to last for more than an atomic moment, which Whitehead brought to light fifty years ago, and whose lineaments have been somewhat altered and whose virtues have been extolled so insistently and sometimes stridently by Hartshorne over the years, has now been given some necessary transplants, been filled out a little, been given the capacity to endure, and has finally been turned into a creature that can grow. Perhaps in the form I have given it, it is even ready to be roasted.

Response by Charles Hartshorne

Paul Weiss, to my delight, has written what I take to be one of his most brilliant essays. I also find that he has given what for me is the best brief defense in all his writing of his own system. He claims, with some plausibility, that he takes various religious views into account better than my

Protestant view, as he regards it, can do. He can also, with some plausibility, claim that he does more justice to ordinary good sense, by recognizing persons and animals as natural individuals, as well as natural wholes.

We should remember, I think, that Weiss and I, unlike any third person, had, before or early in our teaching careers, the experience simultaneously of working with the writings of Peirce as a whole and of trying to digest the flood of new ideas that Whitehead was pouring out in the late nineteen-twenties and early thirties. Moreover, if I am at all right, metaphysics in this century has to take seriously what Peirce, Bergson, Whitehead, and a few other leading process philosophers have in common in their rejection of a number of traditional Western beliefs. Hence to defend a metaphysics today one must relate it to the challenge of the process view. This Weiss does in the essay before us better than he has hitherto. It is a generous essay, and intellectual penetration requires thinking with the minds of others as well as with one's own; it requires intellectual sympathy, and from this to generosity is not an unlimited distance.

There is some overstatement in Weiss's formulation of the issues between us, but it stops short of the degree of caricature in which philosophers sometimes indulge. I suppose we nearly all grant ourselves this indulgence sometimes, but I regard the extent to which we do so as one negative measure of our intellectual objectivity.

Concerning the religious aspect, numerous enthusiasts for my neoclassical theology in recent decades have been Catholics, and I hold a Catholic honorary degree. I have written evaluations of two Islamic thinkers, one medieval and one recent, and in neither case does my Protestantism have much to do with my valuations, which in the second case are largely positive. As for Judaism, I wrote an essay for a symposium which failed to find a publisher but in which I made it clear that in some ways I am closer to Judaism than to much historical Christianity. I believe that we shall never overcome anti-Semitism until we are able to admit that on some issues Jews have been more nearly right than Christians throughout the centuries. I was interested to learn that one of my most influential former students, Schubert M. Ogden, is the only writer who has formulated a theory of Christian incarnation that, in a scholarly study of incarnation doctrines, escaped censure on the ground of anti-Judaism. There is a branch of Hinduism, with some millions of followers in Bengal, two of whose monks have found my views congenial, as I do theirs.

That Buddhism presents a difficult problem for me I grant. But it may mean something that Suzuki, who ought to have known, said that he was not sure Buddhism was nontheistic. In any case I have definite reasons for holding that the Buddhist Nirvana has no unambiguous meaning on a nontheistic basis. The Buddhist poses a problem of the transitoriness of all things and values, but never quite tells us how nevertheless an infinitely precious something called Nirvana can abide. Whiteheadian objective immortality in God can tell us.

How best to conceive natural individuals is one of the subtlest of meta-physical issues. For *many* purposes what Weiss means by this concept is what Whitehead (and here my view is exactly his) means by "societies," especially those with personal order (meaning the temporal order a,b,c, . . .), or by societies in which there is a dominant society with personal order. A human person, mind and body, is indeed an extremely "complex" individual. But its conscious reality in a sufficiently short period of time—in the human case a smallish fraction of a second—is for me or Whitehead a single actual entity, an ultimate unit, in Weiss's language. Of course its body, some actualities of which it most directly prehends, is a nonpersonally ordered society, dominated by a personal one.

My reality now, in the present actual entity, is a complex act of pre-hending predecessors in such a way as to influence successors. And I-now more or less intend such influence. Slightly indirectly I-now act on my extra-bodily environment, more directly on my inner bodily environment. And of course I-now am influenced, slightly indirectly, by you as at a little earlier.

Is I-now abstract? Certainly not. What is abstract is what I-now and I-a-year-ago, still more what I-now and I-as-an-infant, even what I-now and I-as-a-four-week-old-fetus, or a mere fertilized egg, all have in common. Surely that is somewhat abstract, for it is what is left when everything my develop-ment has added to the egg or fetus is abstracted from. Is the whole society up to now abstract? Of course not. Its constituents are concrete actualities. For my human prehensions, they are abstract, but that is because my prehensions are not divine. For God, my career up to now is one of the most concrete, though plural, realities there now are.

There are only three basic options about genetic identity, identity through change. There is the strict-identity view of Leibniz, which holds that in me at birth, or before that, my manner of finally dying was included, along with my entire earthly career. This is the paradox that change is neither gain nor loss but simply a series of states all mutually implying one another and all timelessly included in my individual essence. This view, as Bergson says in another context, spatializes time. The opposite extreme is the Hume-Russell view of entire nonidentity. Each successive state is externally related both to its predecessors and its successors. This is again a symmetrical view. The third option is the asymmetrical one: states include and are constituted by predecessors but not by successors. This is the view of *partial* identity. It is genuine, but not complete, identity. My very past is there in me now. But my present was not in that past.

There seems to be no fourth equally clear possibility. There are only various nuances in the third or asymmetrical view concerning just how impor-tant or adequate the one-way inclusion of, or dependence upon, the past may be. It is plain that Weiss rejects the two symmetrical extremes, since he holds that the future is open and that absolute determinism and predestinationism are false, but does not go to the opposite or Humean extreme of a mere plu-ralism of states. Weiss's and my views are two ways of trying to state the asymmetrical view of partial identity. It may be that no way of stating it has all the advantages and none of the disadvantages of the others. If there were such a possibility, philosophical disagreements would be less intractable than history seems to show that they are.

I prefer the language of actual entities, taken as ultimate, to the language of Western substantialism or individualism, for several reasons. It is more analytic, and yet it is reasonably compatible with ordinary language, because the context of use ordinarily tends to imply the qualifications which the theory of actual entities makes to genetic identities, so that for most purposes it is not necessary to be so analytic. In physics and metaphysics, however, including metaphysical aspects of theology, I hold that it *is* necessary.

There are two ways of avoiding contradiction in analyzing change. In one, the nonidentity of the subjects—say I-now—is determined by the times; in the other it is the predicates that include the temporal designations, say well-at-time-t and not-well-at-t'. But to me it seems clear that it is the business of predicates to be strongly time-independent while logical subjects are strongly time-dependent. There are, on almost any theory, many new persons every moment, but "well" and "not well" have had an abstract identity of meaning for many centuries and many people.

Weiss argues that the admission of substances explains the order in individual careers which otherwise may be hard or impossible to explain. I do not see the force of this reasoning. It is only knowledge of the orderliness of careers that leads us to speak of a career as that of a substance. The substantiality and the orderliness is the same thing expressed in two ways. Moreover, we still need to explain order between, as well as within, substances. With the Buddhists of two millennia I deny that the causal order and the substantial order must have two simply different principles of explanation. With Whitehead I hold that prehension (including divine prehensions of all actualities and every creature's prehension of divine actuality) is the only positive explanation of order among events. Weiss has little chance to talk me out of that conviction. I consider it one of the greatest intellectual discoveries ever made. Alas, philosophers cannot agree. I do agree with Weiss that we must, to carry out the idea, specialize, as he puts it, our idea of deity to account for the order of our cosmic epoch. I consider natural laws as divine decisions influencing creaturely actualities through their prehensions of deity.

Part of the explanation of order is in terms of creaturely intentions mutually to order themselves and their neighbors, including their inner bodily neighbors. Divine ordering leaves details only approximately or statistically specified. Each of us now is an orderer in our corner of existence. But the laws of nature go deeper than any nondivine decisions.

Weiss's splitting up of finalities into deity and four others reminds me of Santayana's doctrine that medieval theology put into its idea of God several ultimate aspects of reality that need to be distinguished—thus truth, spirit, matter or power, and essence. I hold that it is more intelligible to put these things back together as the medievals had them, except that I would, in partial agreement with Santayana, say that the ultimate potentiality, or "matter," is, as David of Dinant is reported to have said, also divine. The aspects of deity, as such, or in its essential or eternal nature, form the whole of the strictly ultimate, necessary, or eternal. The essence of worldliness, or of the non-divine as such, is simply whatever nondivine realities God is *essentially* aware of. God-with-creatures, some creatures or other, is no more than God; for God simply alone, the supreme Creator with no creatures, is an absurdity.

What divine creativity and nondivine creativity have in common, that is, creativity as such, is not something simply outside or additional to God, whose creative action makes divine use of all creaturely action. God is thus the uniquely inclusive reality, not as all determining, for possession is prehensive, that is, partly passive and receptive. In Heidegger's phrase, it "lets things be." To fully know all is to possess all. What God necessarily and eternally possesses is whatever it is that is eternal or strictly necessary. And only divine possession is unqualifiedly adequate, or the definitive measure of the possessed. To know God fully is to know all there is. But only God knows God fully.

The "still center" between contrasting finalities, to which Weiss takes some oriental philosophies or religions to be especially sensitive, I should say was close to, but less illuminating than, the abstraction Whitehead calls creativity, of which divine creating is one aspect and nondivine creating the other. It is not more real than this duality, for its abstractness (or perhaps I should say ambiguity, or simply vagueness) does not measure reality. But allowing the idea to be so vague or noncommittal that the duality in question is not apparent may have its rewards. All perils and troublesome problems disappear. As the Vedic hymn puts it, where there is no other, no multiplicity, what is there to fear? I agree also with the Vedantists that creativity is not a merely objective thing, but is somehow the ultimate form of subjectivity. But ultimate here merely means common to all forms of reality. If it is taken to mean the supremely good or worshipful form, then the contrast with lesser and nonworshipful forms is essential, and many branches of Hinduism have acknowledged this. The principle of contrast is a criterion of metaphysical reasoning. What is true of simply everything is nothing very valuable all by itself.

I agree with Weiss that we must put the human being in the center of things in the methodological sense that our human self-knowledge is the necessary basis for giving meaning to our universal categories. We ourselves are, for ourselves, *the* samples of reality, more adequately, variously, and distinctly known than any other samples. This doctrine is found in Whitehead, Heidegger, Peirce, Bergson, Leibniz, and many others. Generalization has to be by analogy from human experiences. But that is why we cannot set up a sheer dualism of experience and nonexperience, mind and matter, sentient and insentient. Weiss seems to hold that, though all actuality has privacy, not all has feeling, memory, valuation, the psychical in its broadest sense. What privacy totally vacuous of psychical predicates may be, I, like Leibniz, Peirce, Bergson, and many others, seem unable to understand.

The biggest difference between us, perhaps, is in method, in what we take as good evidence in philosophy, in our criteria for, or means of achieving, clarity, also in how we seek to learn from the history of philosophy, and in our views of the role of formal logic in metaphysics.

As example of all this, take the ontological argument. I have not used this argument as *the* way, or even as, by itself, a very good way, to justify belief in God. I have used it primarily to *disprove* certain assumptions about the nature of existential questions. I hold that Anselm discovered certain limits of empiricism. Observational facts cannot, as such, verify or falsify theism. It is a misunderstanding to suppose that we can conceive possible experiences that would contradict theism.

Weiss says that an idea cannot establish existence. If by idea he means a verbal definition or formula, I agree. But if by idea he means a formula *whose coherent significance is known,* then either it is the idea of a contingent existent, and then of course the idea does not guarantee existence, or it is the idea of a kind of thing that becomes contradictory or incoherent when taken as nonexistent, and then the only logically permissible conclusion is that it exists without possible alternative. In the case of theism, coherent conceivability is the same as existence. Aristotle said it: "With eternal things, to be and to be possible are the same." I am an Anselmian insofar as I am an Aristotelian or Peircean in theory of modality. My use of logical formalism in the ontological argument was to make clear the distinction between two assumptions of Anselm that depend on ideas, or meaning-postulates, other than logical constants and rules. I could then argue that one of these assumptions was valid if Aristotle, and many others besides Anselm, were right on the point mentioned above. I could give reasons for agreeing with them in this, and finally could draw the conclusion that the real weakness of Anselm's position was that he not only gives no cogent reason for his other premise (that his definition of deity makes coherent sense) but that his argument itself can, as Findlay pointed out, be used to show the lack of coherence in the definition.

Very reasonably Weiss asks if the ontological argument does not apply to other ultimate abstractions besides deity? I have discussed this at length and have argued that it applies to all concepts on the same level of abstraction as deity. Hence it applies to the idea of nondivine reality as well as to divine reality, for the negation does not increase the concreteness, or introduce contingency. Hence though any particular world is contingent, world-as-such, some world or other, cannot be an empty, uninstantiated idea. However, world-as-such is not in the primary sense individual, but a necessarily nonempty class of individuals. Deity I interpret in the classical manner as not a class of individuals. Divine states I hold are indeed a necessarily nonempty class, but they are actual or possible states of one individual being, which I, but not Whitehead, interpret as a society—a difficult point I admit. Deity is necessarily concretized somehow, but no multiplicity of divine individuals results. Nondivine reality is also necessarily concretized, but in a multiplicity of individuals or societies. Moreover, I interpret the contingency of divine states and of nondivine individuals by the same ultimate principle, which is the Leibnizian one of incompossibility—applied, however, to God as Leibniz did not apply it. All concrete actuality is contingent; for it involves mutual incompatibility between positive alternatives, for example, green here-now or red here-now. God can have the one, or the other, in divinely prehended content, but not both.

In philosophy it is scarcely possible to overestimate the importance of ambiguity or the extent to which philosophical differences are verbal. Of course there are "natural individuals," unitary beings other than Whiteheadian actual entities. But how strict is the "unity" in question? If there is no qualification, then we are, in a crucial point, back with Leibniz. If there is qualification, just what is it? Today or yesterday I am *largely* the identical being, whose "*identifying* characteristic" (note the first word in this Whiteheadian formula) includes a certain birth eighty-four years ago, a certain body, not that of Paul Weiss or any person other than Charles Hartshorne), and above all a huge mass of largely unconscious but selectively accessible memories not those of any other person. We are not speaking of mere qualitative sameness of the person through change, but of numerical identity in *much* of the content prehended through memory and perception. Weiss is rightly thinking of the huge gap between Humean pluralism and what he sees as genetic identity; but he is thinking too little, I suggest, of the huge gap between his view and the Leibnizian one whose distinctive trait is its absolutization of genetic identity. He is subtly caricaturing the Whiteheadian-Hartshornean view of the individual, which, like his own, is intermediary between sheer oneness and sheer plurality in successive states of an individual.

The issue of individual identity arose in Buddhism, though differently than in European religions. The Hinayana was a radically pluralistic view of successive states of an individual; the Mahayana was also pluralistic in accepting the numerical multiplicity of states as more ultimate than personal identity, but with the understanding that there is a mysterious identity of *all actualities whatsoever,* transcending the difference between persons altogether. Leibniz thought the Mahayana view was comparable to his doctrine of monads (by divine selection) mirroring one another, although logically they "have no windows" or are wholly independent. *No* Buddhist had such a view. An individualistic pluralism, such as Europe has tended to have since Aristotle, the Buddhists deliberately avoided, except that the Hinayana in practice to some extent perhaps implied it by seeking salvation for self, with less stress on the Bodhisattva ideal of postponing complete Nirvana for self until all have attained it.

In Weiss's series of contrasts between Whitehead's and my idea of God, except for the first two phrases ("exists moment after moment, and . . . is a kind of society"), I would qualify every one of the contrasts, whether from my point of view or Whitehead's. I do not simply deny eternal objects but limit them to categorial and mathematical abstractions, holding with Peirce, for example, that particular color qualities are emergents. I find a distinction in Whitehead's theism as well as mine between "an abstract and an accidental dimension"; for me "the world," our world, is one among the many God prehends or will prehend, unless by "world" is meant the mere idea of the nondivine as such. I hold that God as consequent or concrete is indeed a "primordial creature" of primary creativity in whatever (somewhat ambiguous) sense Whitehead admits this creativity. Again I find in Whitehead the clear affirmation that God suffers with and loves the creatures, and (in aesthetic richness of content) is forever increasing, and in that sense getting better. I agree with Weiss that Whitehead and I do not regard "angry" as equally applicable to God as "loving." This may be partly temperamental. Human "righteous anger" has always been for me a dubious quality. I may have failed to think this question through. It certainly seems that if God can approve, God can disapprove, evaluate negatively. But if (human) love is blind, human hatred and anger are more so.

I am still farther from Weiss than Whitehead is in that I make God *the* finality, not one among others. Nature is what God knows as the present cosmic epoch in the creation of nondivine reality. The idea of deity as self-created goes back thousands of years in the Old World and many centuries in the New. What Whitehead adds is that nothing is merely self-created or merely created by others but always both. This, too, has been implicit in some older views.

I agree that only the complex individuals (i.e., societies) are able to be conscious, but I note the ambiguity of "and therefore to feel." Whatever is conscious feels, but "whatever feels is conscious" is valid only if the term "conscious" is used in the most general possible, and doubtfully useful, sense. An infant feels, but does it think to itself that it feels? Consciousness, as Whitehead and I use the term, is a special high-level case of sentience, not the universal case. That human beings are either conscious or (to their later memory at least) without feeling is because that is the human way (after infancy at least) of being sentient. It need not hold for all lower creatures.

I am especially pleased by Weiss's noting that my philosophical theology is not the whole of my attempted contribution. In two of my books, one the earliest and the other almost the latest, there is no explicit mention of that or any other theology.

Another agreement I have with Weiss is that the Einsteinian or Whiteheadian conceptions of contemporaneity are not the whole story. But introducing a finality called Substance or Existence or Unity seems scarcely more than a verbal solution. I do agree that contemporary individuals interact, but I analyze this into a complex of one-way actions of each individual's momentary states upon later states of the other. It is supposed to follow from quantum physics (Bell's theorem) that not all influences are limited by the speed of light. The account of time in physics is an extremely difficult, controversial, technical subject. I am appalled by the difficulties.

What Weiss means by "privacy" as not necessarily psychical is perhaps to be related to Dewey's contention that, although qualities as well as relations are everywhere, feeling or sensing need not be everywhere. Yet definite qualities are knowable only by sensing or feeling them. Shapes, say right-angled triangles, can be known by conceptual means, but mere concepts, apart from quite particular sensations or feelings, will not give us "blue." And I take experiences of pain or physical pleasure to exhibit in paradigm cases what Whitehead means by "feeling *of* feeling," which for Whitehead is what direct experience or prehension of concrete actualities universally is. My first book was in support of this idea. Weiss has suggested that this is my best book. It is certainly as original as any.

Well did Descartes say that in talking about pain we are discussing we know not what—unless, I add, human pain is a human feeling *of* the feelings of subhuman bodily constituents—a view that in Descartes's time no one held. Descartes at least saw the problem. Pain is psychical but it is also physical, direct awareness of a bodily process. So is physical pleasure, a fact of which philosophers generally seem even less aware than they are of the similar status of pain. It is false that pain or pleasure tell us only of our own mental states. They tell us directly of bodily states. Doctors know this with respect to pain. Referred pain is no counterinstance. The bodily injury is always there, its spatial localization is a partly learned and fallible process involving more than one sense organ.

I close as I began by noting the high quality of this essay by Weiss. It does credit to both of us. I am deeply grateful.

Manley Thompson

7

Hartshorne and Peirce
Individuals and Continuity

Peirce scholars are indebted to Charles Hartshorne not only for his work in coediting with Paul Weiss the first six volumes of the *Collected Papers of Charles Sanders Peirce*,[1] but also for three stimulating papers on Peirce's theory of categories.[2] In the second of these papers (1964) Professor Hartshorne argues that ''Peirce's greatest single mistake . . . was his 'Synechism', which consisted in trying to make continuity the key principle to every relationship, both of actuality and possibility'' (MR, 467). This same theme is argued again in the most recent paper (1980). I want to explore briefly Peirce's use of continuity in his account of individual existence and then to review this account in the light of Professor Hartshorne's criticisms.

I

''Our initial hypothesis,'' Hartshorne declares, ''should be that actuality is discrete, but with our minds open among the unlimited conceptual, but mutually incompatible possibilities for discontinuity,''; Peirce, on the contrary, ''wanted actuality . . . to be continuous'' (M, 286). Yet as Hartshorne, of course, realized, Peirce clearly wanted it both ways. Actuality is in a sense discrete and in a sense continuous. As Pierce developed his position, actuality or existence is the mode of being of individuals as opposed to reality, which is the mode of being of universals. According to his preferred definition, ''an individual is something which reacts'' (3.613).[3] Actuality (existence, secondness) consists in reactions, and reactions as instantaneous must be discrete. After giving his preferred definition of an individual, Peirce remarks that it is no objection to the definition that it makes an individual unintelligible, for an individual is unintelligible in the sense proclaimed by the definition. As he declares about this time (1902-3), in another context, ''An

130

existing thing [an individual] is simply a blind reacting thing to which not merely all generality, but even all representation is utterly foreign'' (5.107).

The unintelligibility of individuals as discrete existences is emphasized again and again in Peirce's later writings, and he was well aware that with this position he was left with the problem of explaining how we can ever talk about individuals—how we can ever represent them. We experience them through sensations of brute reaction, and these sensations are not re-presentable. I am groping my way about in the dark. My outstretched hand meets a solid object that resists further forward movement of my arm. The resistance that I feel—the sensation of reaction—is something absolutely discrete and individual. When I put my withdrawn arm forward a second time, I may say I feel it again, but the ''it'' in this case refers to the object I take to be causing the resistance and not to the sensation of reaction I felt a moment before. In judging that I feel the object again, I assume that the object, unlike my initial sensation of reaction, continued to exist during the interval between my first and second sensations. I say that I had different sensations of the same individual object. I have thus said something about an individual and not merely experienced it through sensations of reaction, but I have done so only by invoking continuity as well as discreteness. I represent the individual as having continued existence through time while my sensations of reacting with it remain instantaneous and discrete. My representation is cognitive, intelligible, judgmental. It may be false. The object I felt the second time may not be the object I felt the first time, no matter how short the interval between my two sensations. But my sensations are noncognitive, unintelligible, nonjudgmental. They are neither true nor false; they simply are. An individual taken simply as that which reacts is simply that which is experienced in a sensation of reaction. As such it is unintelligible, unrepresentable.

Peirce seems to have had considerations like the above in mind when, after defining an individual as something which reacts, he went on to proclaim that ''everything whose identity consists in a continuity of reactions will be a single logical individual'' (3.613). If the identity of an individual consists in its reactions, it retains its identity—remains one and the same individual— only to the extent that it continually reacts. My judgment that I felt the same individual twice can be true only if the individual retains its identity during the interval that separates my two sensations. But I can represent it as thus retaining its identity only by thinking of it as continuing to react during the interval, even though it is not reacting with me. For my judgment implies that if I had put my arm forward at any point during the interval I would have reacted with the object at that point. The object was then reacting with something (with the air or other objects in its surroundings) and it would still have been reacting with me if I had been in an appropriate position. If I think of the object as having ceased to react during the interval, I think of it as having ceased to exist, and I must then judge that my second sensation is of a different object.

Murray Murphey finds Peirce's declaration that individual identity consists in a continuity of reactions to be inconsistent with "either the definition of reaction or of continuity—there cannot be a continuum of instantaneous events."[4] Peirce, of course, entertained different definitions of continuity, and his views on the subject changed. When he gave his definition of individual identity, the view of continuity he had in mind would seem to be the "common sense" one he came to through a modification of Kant's definition "that a continuum is that of which every part has itself parts of the same kind" (6.168). While this definition, Peirce adds, "seems to be correct . . . it must not be confounded (as Kant himself confounded it) with infinite divisibility." For it "implies that a line, for example, contains no points until the continuity is broken by marking the points." It thus "seems necessary to say that a continuum, where it *is* continuous and unbroken, contains no definite parts; that its parts are created in the act of defining them and the precise definition of them breaks the continuity." Peirce ends the paragraph by remarking that this "common sense idea of continuity" is not that found in "the calculus and theory of functions," according to which continuity "is only a collection of independent points."[5]

Whatever Peirce meant by declaring individual identity to consist in a continuity of reactions, he did not mean that it consists in a collection of independent reactions. The point is not that each reaction consists of shorter reactions, or that between any two reactions there is always a shorter. Infinite divisibility in this context can never yield more than a collection of independent reactions. The point is rather that indicated by a remark he makes to underscore his contrast between the common-sense idea of continuity and that found in the calculus and theory of functions. "Breaking grains of sand more and more will only make the sand more broken. It will not weld the grains into unbroken continuity" (6.168). Peirce wants a notion of individual identity according to which reactions are welded into unbroken continuity.

The inconsistencies Murphey finds in Peirce's attempt to define individual identity are unavoidable if one begins with the assumption that the identity of an individual consists in a collection of independent reactions. The infinite divisibility of every item in the collection will not weld the items into an unbroken continuity that constitutes the identity of an individual. Peirce, as I read him, never made this assumption. The assumption he made instead is that the existence of an individual, but not its individual identity, consists simply in reaction, opposition, pure secondness. "[T]he mode of being of the individual thing is existence; and existence lies in opposition merely" (1.458). An individual in its mode of being is thus unintelligible; it is experienced, bumped up against, reacted with, but never cognized as an identical object. Cognition always involves thirdness, the mode of being of a universal or general idea. While "a reaction may be experienced . . . it cannot be conceived in its character of a reaction; for that element evaporates from every general idea" (3.613). Yet this is not to say that we have no concept of individual existence, that we cannot conceive of it in general. "Existence, though brought about by dyadism, or opposition, as its proper determination, yet, when brought about, lies *abstractly and in itself considered,* within itself'' (1.461, Peirce's emphasis). We thus come to the concept of ''numerical identity, which is a dyadic relation of a subject to itself of which nothing but an existent individual is capable.'' This identity, unlike that ''of a quality with itself'' is not ''empty verbiage'' but ''a positive fact.'' Red is always red and never anything else, but an individual that is now red may change its color. Yet, no matter how much its qualities change, an individual does not lose its numerical, its individual, identity. ''Throughout all vicissitudes its oppositions to other things remain intact, although they may be accidentally modified; and therein is manifest the positive character of identity.''[6]

The subtle point Peirce seems to be urging here is the difference between experiencing individuality (existence, actuality) and conceptualizing that experience. As experienced, individuality is simply a sensation of brute reaction, and as such it is unintelligible. As conceptualized it is simply that which reacts, an individual, and as such it is intelligible as that which remains numerically one and the same throughout its reactions. This is not to say, however, that since an individual retains its identity whatever its reactions may be, its identity is intelligible without reference to its reactions. Existence consists in reaction, and an individual maintains its identity only as long as it exists. But since it always exists through a time and reactions are instantaneous, its identity is not that of a single reaction. But then how is a collection of reactions welded into a single individual?

For Peirce, this is like asking how a collection of points is welded into a single line. The question is put the wrong way round. One begins with the notion of a line and asks how it consists in a collection of points. The answer then is that the identity of a line consists in an unbroken continuity of points, but that none of its properties is determined until certain of its points are actually fixed, e.g., by specifying numbers or laying down certain conditions for a geometrical construction. There is no question about how the points once they are fixed are welded into a line. One begins with the concept of line identity and fixes points in order to determine properties of a particular line. When two points are fixed, the identity of the line connecting them consists in an unbroken continuity of intervening points. As such, the points on the line are already welded into a line and actually fixing any of them simply breaks the continuity. It is senseless to ask how these fixed points are welded into a line, for there is no question of constructing the line out of fixed points but only of fixing points on the line. It is of course impossible actually to fix them all, even with the completion of an infinite enumeration, since their multitude is nondenumerable. The properties of a line are determined only by fixing points. But its identity as a line does not consist in a continuity of fixed points; it consists in the unbroken continuity of all the points on the line.

In this geometrical illustration, a point by itself apart from the concept of a line is unintelligible. It is the geometrical analogue of a reaction. Just as one has first the concept of line identity and then fixes points in order to determine properties of a particular line, one has first the concept of individual identity and then experiences a reaction that determines properties of a particular individual. When my outstretched hand meets a solid object as I grope my way about in the dark, the reaction fixes a "point" in my spatial environment. I already have the concept of individual identity. The reaction I experience is individual and discrete; as such it is unintelligible. But through the concept of individual identity, I conceptualize the experience as an encounter with an individual existent.

It is not necessary for this conceptualization that I experience more than a single reaction and then judge that I encountered the same object twice. The conceptualization is not simply an objectification of the sensation of reaction, merely the conceiving of this sensation as a single instantaneous object. The sensation itself is not the object with which I react, but something in me and not something outside of my consciousness that opposes me. To take the conceptualization in question here as simply the objectification of the sensation would be to conflate what Peirce called "the feeling-element of sense" with "the compulsion, the insistency, that characterizes experience" (6.340). With conceptualization merely of the feeling-element, I could say only that I felt hardness or solidity. I could not say that I felt a hard or solid individual object. In conceptualizing the object I cannot take its individual identity to consist in its hardness, solidity, or any other quality. The qualities of an indvidual, "however permanent [and peculiar] they may be, neither help nor hinder its individual existence . . . they are but *accidents;* that is to say, they are not involved in the mode of being of the thing; for the mode of being of the individual thing is existence; and existence lies in opposition merely" (1.458).

To conceptualize the object merely as that which stands in opposition to me—to my sensation—I must conceive of it as opposed to sensation in a respect that is both basic to sensation and yet has nothing to do with sensory qualities. The only thing basic to sensation apart from its feeling-element is the respect in which it involves a sense of reaction, and in this respect "it does not involve the sense of time (i.e. not of a continuum)" (8.41). It is sensed as discrete and instantaneous. The respect in which I conceive of an individual object as distinct from my reaction with it is then that I conceive of the former but not the latter as retaining an identity through time. When I judge on the basis of a single reaction that there is an object there in the dark I have bumped against, I must apply the concept of individual identity as consisting in a continuity of reactions. I cannot conceive of the identity of the object as consisting in the single reaction I experienced, for a single reaction as such is unintelligible. Individual existence is intelligible, as opposed to being merely experiencable, only as something that persists through time. And this persistence is intelligible only as a continuity of reactions; a collection of discrete reactions can never be welded into an individual identity.

Actuality or existence is thus discrete in the sense that "the compulsion, the insistency, that characterizes experience" is discrete, but it is continuous in the sense that an individual existent retains its identity through time. It seems to me that Peirce's use of continuity in his account of individual existence as I have sketched it is open to some but not to all of the criticisms Hartshorne has urged against it. I turn now to these criticisms.

II

Hartshorne objects (1) that although Peirce "had an ontology of relations in the idea of relative actualities, he lacked any definite terms or subjects for the relations. There seems to be a succession of experiences, but (if the succession is a continuum) there are no single experiences" (M, 286); (2) that Peirce "fell into a subtle but complete mistake" when he held that since "continuity leaves open possibilities which discontinuity excludes . . . the burden of proof is upon discontinuity" (MR, 467–68); (3) that "he could not, in the continuum of becoming which he posited, give meaning to the idea of a definite single event" (M, 287).

(1) The first objection, I think, is the one against which Peirce has the clearest defense. The succession of experiences is discrete as a succession of sensations of reactions, and there are single experiences in this sense. But as single the experiences are unintelligible. Intelligibility is obtained through the concept of individual identity as consisting in a continuity of reactions. With this concept Peirce could account for definite singular terms in general, though he could not with his "pragmaticistic"[7] theory of meaning distinguish one such term from another as he could distinguish one general term from another. "[I]t must be admitted," he wrote, "that pragmaticism fails to furnish any translation or meaning of a proper name, or other designation of an individual object" (5.429). Yet this failure does not prevent the pragmaticist from granting "that a proper name . . . has a certain denotative function peculiar to that name and its equivalents" and "that every assertion contains such a denotative or pointing-out function." While this function "in its peculiar individuality" must be excluded from "the rational purport of the assertion . . . *the like* of it, being common to all assertions, and so, being general and not individual, may enter into the pragmatistic purport." The generality intended here is supplied by Peirce's concept of individual identity. His next sentence is: "Whatever exists, *ex-sists*, that is, really acts upon other existents, so obtains a self-identity, and is definitely individual."

The denotative function of a proper name that enters into the pragmaticistic purport (the intelligibility) of every assertion is the function performed in quantificational logic by individual variables. When a variable is replaced by a proper name or other designation of an individual, no new element of intelligibility is added. The function performed by individual variables in general is then performed by one symbol in particular. It is the function of singling out a subject of which a certain general term or predicate is true. The function is the same whether the subject is any, at least some one or other, or only a single individual. What is singled out is intelligible not as an individual in its individuality (what Peirce sometimes called a "hecceity")[8] but only as that which continually reacts through a period of time and thereby remains one and the same.

With this denotative function common to all assertions Peirce has a way of accounting for definite terms or subjects for relations. Complications arise when an individual is considered to be spatial as well as temporal. But these complications relate to Hartshorne's third objection, and I will postpone consideration of them here.

(2) Peirce's defense against the second objection, that he fell into a subtle but complete mistake when he thought the burden of proof was with discontinuity, lies in his use of Kant's distinction between what is constitutive and what is merely regulative of experience. In the passage Hartshorne cites, Peirce is concerned with proclamations of discontinuity as assumptions that "block the road of inquiry" (1.170). His examples are the questions of how one mind can act on another and how one particle of matter can act on another at a distance from it. He objects to what he calls the "nominalistic" assumption that, because there is ultimate discontinuity between one mind and another, and between one particle and another, these questions are absolutely unanswerable. He acknowledges that, with the state of physics at the time of his writing (c. 1897), we can only say "that we know that one thing does act on another but that how it takes place we cannot very well tell." But this uncertainty in no way licenses the assumption that, since we have not succeeded in telling exactly how they act on each other at a distance, particles of matter must be ultimately discontinuous. Such an assumption blocks the road of inquiry, whereas the assumption that all particles of matter may be continuous leaves the road open to the possibility of eventually explaining action at a distance, starting with the hypothesis "that one portion of matter acts upon another because it is in a measure in the same place."

Peirce remarks in the next paragraph: "The principle of continuity is the idea of fallibilism objectified. For fallibilism is the doctrine that our knowledge is never absolute but always swims, as it were, in a continuum of uncertainty and of indeterminacy. Now the doctrine of continuity is that *all things* so swim in continua" (1.171, Peirce's emphasis).

From these remarks, it would seem that fallibilism is the regulative principle that no hypothesis should be regarded as absolutely determinate and certain, while the doctrine of continuity, or "synechism," as Peirce usually called it, is the corresponding constitutive principle that the things constituting reality are never absolutely determinate and discrete. But this view conflicts with a later statement (1902): "Synechism is not an ultimate and absolute metaphysical doctrine; it is a regulative principle of logic, prescribing what sort of hypothesis is fit to be entertained and examined" (6.173). I do not think the conflict here is serious. The word 'fallibilism' occurs in the *Collected Papers* as the expression of a doctrine only in 1.171 and in another fragment (1.8–14) of the same date (c. 1897), and I have never seen the word used in this way in writings not included in the *Collected Papers*. Even in 1.170 Peirce advocated the assumption of continuity in things (minds and particles of matter) because it avoided blocking the road of inquiry. He did not also claim that it was metaphysically true. So even here the assumption is, in the Kantian sense,[9] regulative of inquiry rather than constitutive of experience. Constitutively, experience is discrete; it is constituted by sensations of brute reaction. But as such it is unintelligible. Intelligibility arises only when reactions are followed by judgments concerning what is experienced, and judgments as regulated by the principle of continuity are always fallible. The judgment that one particle of matter is spatially separated from another may be true in a sense but false when taken as implying an absolute separation in reality.

Although Peirce's use of the regulative/constitutive distinction may provide a reason for his belief that the burden of proof is with discontinuity, I think there is more than a use of this distinction underlying Hartshorne's charge that with the belief Peirce fell into a subtle but complete mistake. The further issue, however, seems to me best approached in the light of Hartshorne's third objection.

(3) In discussing the first objection, I remarked that complications arise with Peirce's account of definite terms or subjects for relations when an individual is considered to be spatial as well as temporal. After declaring that "everything whose identity consists in a continuity of reactions will be a single logical individual," Peirce explained: "Thus any portion of space, so far as it can be regarded as reacting, is for logic a single individual; its spatial extension is no objection" (3.613). But how is a portion of space to be determined, and how are we to decide when it can be regarded as reacting? A few sentences later Peirce remarks that "space is nothing but the intuitional presentation of the conditions of reaction, or of some of them." This remark suggests a Kantian position according to which space is the form of outer sense. Whatever is outer, external to my consciousness, and therefore capable of reacting against me, is spatial. As long as my outstretched hand continues to encounter resistance as I move it about spatially, I determine a portion of space I regard as reacting and judge to be a single individual.

Peirce never accepted just this Kantian position, but he remained close to it. While he rejected the view that space and time are forms of intuition, he retained the Kantian notion of outer and inner sense corresponding, respectively, to space and time (cf. 8.41, 8.330). He thus was prevented by his philosophical position from conceiving of space-time as a four-dimensional continuum. Peircean individuals, like Newtonian and Kantian particles, are located in space *and* time, not in space-time. I see no defense for Peirce against Hartshorne's third objection, that he could not give meaning to the idea of a definite single event. For the idea Hartshorne intends here, I think, is that of an event in space-time, and Peirce could give no meaning to this idea because in his philosophy he lacked any notion of space-time. I suggest that it is to the reason for this lack rather than, as Hartshorne avers, to an "uncritical love for continuity" (M, 286), that we should look when we want to account for Peirce's failure to develop the idea of a definite single event. I will return to this point shortly.

III

I remarked that I think there is more than a use of the regulative/constitutive distinction underlying the objection that Peirce places the burden of proof on discontinuity. The further issue is the basically epistemological and Kantian orientation of Peirce's philosophy, early and late. Like Kant in his critical period, Peirce's initial philosophical stance is that of a knower with human cognitive faculties for processing given input into cognitions of reality. Reality is then what is represented in the final output of the unlimited community of such knowers. But then how is the reality of the original unprocessed input to be explained? If this input has no contact with reality, if it is not in itself real, how can any processing of such input, even when indefinitely prolonged, result in a representation of reality?

These questions present no special difficulty if one's philosophical stance is external to the human knowers one is considering as subjects; if, in other words, one speaks of knowers only in the third person. Original input is then simply the stimulation of a subject's sensory receptors; there is no question of its reality because it is in direct causal contact with reality. Nor need there be a question of how the subject is conscious of the stimulations, since with a third-person perspective one may remain a radical behaviorist and agree with Quine: "What to count as observation now can be settled in terms of the stimulation of sensory receptors, let consciousness fall where it may."[10] But the question of consciousness can of course not be dismissed when the philosophical stance is that of oneself as a human knower; and if cognitive consciousness is always the result of processing an input, as it appears to be with Kant's doctrine of synthesis, consciousness of the input cannot be a cognition of reality. Any such cognition from this first-person perspective will be output. As Barry Stroud has put it recently, "In my own case I have nothing but 'output' to work with."[11]

In his early papers on cognitive faculties, Peirce held that every cognition was determined by a previous cognition. There was thus only output. He argued that the assumption of an absolutely first cognition (one not determined by previous cognitions) is no more required to account for the fact of cognition than the assumption of an absolutely first distance to be traversed is required to account for the fact that Achilles overtakes the tortoise (cf. 5.263). The argument leaves untouched the question of how a cognition is ever in contact with reality and not just with previous cognitions. With regard to this argument alone, it might seem plausible to think of Peirce as misled by an uncritical love for continuity. He seems to have seen only the logical problem of accounting for the completion in a finite time of a process for which it is impossible to specify an absolutely first beginning. He missed entirely the epistemological problem of explaining how cognition is initially in contact with reality. But if it was from an uncritical love of continuity that he missed the problem, it was also from a love of what he regarded, by the time had come to see the problem, as a confusion of infinite divisibility with true continuity.[12]

In Peirce's later philosophy, cognition is initially in contact with reality via a perceptual judgment, which is "the cognitive product of a reaction" (5.156). As we have already noted, reaction in its mode of being as an existent is unintelligible. What is intelligible is not its existence but its individual identity as consisting in a continuity of reactions. Yet the continuity here is not the infinite divisibility of discrete items in a collection but the unbroken continuity that welds the items into the identity of an individual. Continuity in this sense is regulative of experience which, constitutively, is discrete, being nothing but sensations of reactions. Input as input is simply the brute reaction of experience; its contact with reality is immediate, for existence simply consists in reaction. But any judgment as to individual identity is output and is regulated by its principle of continuity.

With a basically metaphysical stance, on the contrary, what is viewed constitutively is not experiential contact with reality but reality itself. Reality is then constitutively continuous as possibility or potentiality, but in actuality it is discrete. To place the burden of proof on the assumption that there is ever discontinuity is then tantamount to skepticism as to whether there is any ultimate actuality—whether there is a real external world as opposed to the infinite possibilities realizable in thought. This attitude toward discontinuity inevitably appears as skepticism when one begins with a metaphysical stance that takes a real world of existing actualities as given. The reverse is the case, however, with Peirce's epistemological stance. Nothing existential is given but sensations of reaction that give rise to cognition of reality. With this cognition, reactions are welded into a continuity of reactions constituting an individual identity, and an individual is cognized as instantiating a real universal or law. The reality of a law does not consist in a collection of independent individuals any more than a line consists in a collection of independent points. A real law, like a line, is an unbroken continuum.[13] Ultimate discontinuity, with this epistemological stance, is ultimate inexplicability, brute facts unrelated by laws. Any hypothesis of ultimate discontinuity blocks the road of inquiry and appears as dogmatic skepticism—a proclamation of absolutely unknowable reality. Hypotheses of this sort are excluded from inquiry regulated by synechism.

It is not enough with Peirce's epistemology to say merely that "an individual is something which reacts." The essential point epistemologically is "that it might react, or have reacted, against my will" (3.613; cf. 8.41). It is only as it reacts against my will (e.g., my will to move straight ahead in the dark) that I receive input from which I construct cognitions that for me determine reality. As reacting against my will, an individual must exist external to me, and I must therefore conceive of it as located outside my consciousness. This location cannot be temporal, for its reaction against my will and the sensation I internally experience occur at the same time. As external to me, it must have spatial location; it must be "a portion of space" that "can be regarded as reacting." When I conceive of its individual identity as consisting in a continuity of reactions, I am conceiving of a portion of space continually reacting.[14]

If I were to say instead "a portion of space-time," I would have no way to draw the epistemological distinction between internal and external that is central to the Kantian orientation of Peirce's philosophy. If I were to conceive of both myself and the object as world-lines in space-time that intersect on the occasions when the object reacts against me, I would view myself as an object in the world of existents and there would be nothing external to me in the epistemological sense of an external world. I would have no reason to conceive of the object as having an identity consisting in the continuity of the reactions of a portion of space while I conceived of my own identity quite differently.[15] I would have the idea of a definite single event as an event in space-time, and I could conceive of both my own identity and that of the object as consisting in a collection of events. Though discrete, the events would not be independent but internally related, for unlike Peircean reactions and mathematical points they would not be in themselves unintelligible. Such events through their internal relations are "welded into an individual identity," to borrow Peirce's language. There is no need to conceive of the identity as consisting in an unbroken continuity—as something whose mode of being is distinct from the mode of being of the events. The fact that Peirce conceived of individual identity in this way is not, I would urge, simply the result of an uncritical love for continuity. It is rather the result of a basically Kantian orientation that permeated his philosophy and rendered the notion of space-time foreign to his thought.

I want to close with some brief comments in which I expand a bit on what I mean by a Kantian orientation and its philosophical consequences.

IV

I do not intend by my remarks about space-time to imply that, if Peirce had known relativity physics, he would have given up his notion of individual identity as consisting in a continuity of reactions and accepted the idea of a definite single event as intelligible by itself. I do not know whether he would have done this or not, since I believe that with his pragmatism he might have accommodated relativity physics without altering his epistemology, though I cannot go into the question here.[16] What seems to me clear is that the philosophical issues underlying Hartshorne's criticisms of Peirce cannot be settled by theories of physics or the mathematics of continuity. I will try to give some indication of what I mean, starting with a few remarks by Whitehead.

In the Preface to *Process and Reality* Whitehead declared that "in the main the philosophy of organism is a recurrence to pre-Kantian modes of thought."[17] Later in the work he explained: "The philosophy of organism is the inversion of Kant's philosophy. The *Critique of Pure Reason* describes the process by which subjective data pass into the appearance of an objective world. . . . For Kant, the world emerges from the subject; for the philosophy of organism, the subject emerges from the world."[18] With Peirce's pragmatic definition of reality, the world emerges from the inquiry of the unlimited community. But such inquiry presupposes individual inquirers who process given input into cognitive output that to some extent represents a determination of reality. The concept of individual identity as consisting in a continuity of reactions functions as a regulative principle for the process that renders the output (ultimately the world) intelligible. In the pre-Kantian philosophy of Plato and Aristotle, individual substances have specific identity by participating in or being essentially constituted by intelligible form, and rational subjects emerge (are actualized) in the apprehension of such form. The apprehension constitutes the actualization of the subjects but not of the world.

There are, to be sure, aspects of Peirce's philosophy that appear to represent a return to pre-Kantian modes of thought, notably his "scholastic realism." But his is a unique sort of scholastic realism; its orientation is epistemological rather than metaphysical. Real universals are defined with reference to the output of scientific inquiry rather than to the input that makes such inquiry possible. *Pace* Whitehead, Peirce has real universals emerging from inquiry rather than inquiry emerging from real universals. His "scholastic realism," despite appearances to the contrary, hardly represents a return to pre-Kantian modes of thought. I think a similar remark holds for his cosmic evolution, his logic of events, his objective idealism, and other parts of his metaphysics, although I admit that the point needs to be argued.

The notion of space-time is not difficult to fit into pre-Kantian modes of thought. In a recent elementary text on relativity physics, the author begins with space-time as "the collection of all possible events" and proceeds to develop the notion first in terms of what he calls "Aristotelianized space-time."[19] I have difficulty conceiving of Kantianized space-time, and I suspect Peirce would have too. But I do not think the philosophical issues concerning the epistemological role Kant assigned to space and time as forms, respectively, of outer and inner sense, are simply resolved by introducing the notion of space-time in physics. Whether in philosophy one should conceive of actuality as comprising individuals that maintain their identity in portions of space continually reacting through time, or as comprising events in space-time, is not a question of physics or of mathematics. Hartshorne's criticisms of Peirce seem to me to assume that the second alternative is the philosophically sound one.

Notes

1. Charles Hartshorne and Paul Weiss, eds., *The Collected Papers of Charles Sanders Peirce* (Cambridge, Mass.: Harvard University Press, 1931–58). Volumes 7 and 8 were edited by Arthur W. Burks.

2. "The Relativity of Nonrelativity: Some Reflections on Firstness," *Studies in the Philosophy of Charles Sanders Peirce,* ed. Philip P. Wiener and Frederic H. Young (Cambridge; Mass.: Harvard University Press, 1952), pp. 215–24. "Charles Peirce's 'One Contribution to Philosophy' and His Most Serious Mistake," in *Studies in the Philosophy of Charles Sanders Peirce, second series,* ed. Edward C. Moore and Richard S. Robin (Amherst, Mass.: University of Massachusetts Press, 1964), pp. 455–74. References to this paper are given in the text as MR followed by page number. "A Revision of Peirce's Categories," *Monist* 63, no. 3 (1980):277–89. References to this paper are given in the text as M followed by page number.

3. This reference is to volume 3, paragraph 613 of the *Collected Papers of Charles Sanders Peirce.* All references in the text to this work are given in this fashion. In contrast to his preferred definition, Peirce gave a "more formal" one: "an individual is an object (or term) not only actually determinate in respect to having or wanting each general character and not both having and wanting any, but is necessitated by its mode of being to be so determinate" (3.611). I have discussed these two definitions in "Peirce's Conception of an Individual," in *Pragmatism and Purpose: Essays Presented to Thomas A. Goudge* (Toronto: University of Toronto Press, 1981), pp. 133–48.

4. Murray G. Murphey, *The Development of Peirce's Philosophy* (Cambridge, Mass.: Harvard University Press, 1961), p. 398.

5. Peirce elsewhere referred to this mathematical idea of continuity as yielding a "pseudo-continuum." Cf. 6.176.

6. In his logical algebra and logical graphs, Peirce regarded identity as a second intentional relation (cf. 2.315, 2.548, 3.398, 3.490, 4.80ff.). But he never confused this logical notion of identity ("things are identical" when "every predicate is true of both or false of both" [3.398]) with the notion of individual identity through time, which is at issue here.

7. In his later writings (1905 and afterwards) Peirce sometimes referred to his own position as "pragmaticism" to distinguish it from what James and others were calling "pragmatism." Cf. 5.414.

8. Hecceities are "determinations not of a generalizable nature" (3.612).

9. That Peirce had Kant in mind when he spoke of a regulative principle is indicated by his reference to Kant in 3.612.

10. W. V. Quine, *Ontological Relativity* (New York: Columbia University Press, 1969), p. 84.

11. Barry Stroud, "The Significance of Naturalized Epistemology," *Midwest Studies in Philosophy, VI,* ed. Peter A. French, Theodore E. Uehling, Jr., Howard K. Wettstein (Minneapolis: University of Minnesota Press, 1981), p. 464.

12. Cf. 6.168, where Peirce says he himself initially fell into Kant's confusion of continuity with infinite divisibility.

13. I have discussed this point in "Peirce's Verificationist Realism," *Review of Metaphysics* 32, no. 1 (1978):74–98.

14. I ignore here the question of motion, which requires identifying portions of space in a way that allows for change of relative position. Such identification must be given by scientific laws. I consider this question in my "Peirce's Verificationist Realism."

15. Cf., e.g., the remarks on the nature of a person in 5.421 and the remarks in 6.338 beginning: "All thought is dialogic in form."

16. I have in mind passages like 5.496, in which the relations between metaphysics and epistemology are reassessed in the light of pragmatism.

17. A. N. Whitehead, *Process and Reality* (New York: Macmillan, 1929), p. vi.

18. Ibid., pp. 135–36.

19. Robert Geroch, *General Relativity from A to B* (Chicago: University of Chicago Press, 1978), p. 11.

Response by Charles Hartshorne

Manley Thompson has chosen to deal with an extremely subtle aspect of Peirce's philosophy. So far as I can judge, his account of Peirce's view is essentially faithful to the evidence in Peirce's writings. Peirce did make use of a rather unusual notion of individual identity as analogous to a continuous "line," a continuity, of reactions. Continuity here means, as Thompson says, "containing no definite parts," such as points. Now this is why I have trouble finding in Peirce's doctrine definite terms for definite spatial or temporal relations. If individual X reacts now to a remembered past experience (as in what Peirce calls immediate memory), it is the individual *now* that reacts to the individual *then*. But with continuous change what is the now? A point-instant? Thompson's discussion seems to limit "reaction" to transactions with simultaneous or contemporary entities; but Peirce as I read him allows memory (as in surprise) to instantiate secondness or reaction.

The lack of definite parts is the reason for Peirce's denial that we ever, in a single definite experience, intuit or know a single other definite experience. Hence his rejection of the claim to immediate intuition. Always we are remembering an infinite series of remembering of remembering of . . . whatever we want to intuit, no matter how close to the present it is. And always, if we first intuit red and then yellow, we have, in any finite time, however short, gone through a continuum of intermediate hues. It is such contentions that seem to me to indicate an overattachment to continuity. Thompson may be right, and I believe he is, that Peirce had other reasons or inclinations (including an influence of Kant) supporting his conclusion; but it is demonstrable from his own language in praise of the wonders of continuity that he did have *this* reason. So did his father, as the latter's philosophical writings show.

It is hardly mere coincidence that Peirce not only had no encounter with quantum theory, with its emphasis on discontinuity, but that he did not want physics to develop any such theory. He tried to derive indications from his philosophy concerning suitable further developments in physics. This was to be one of the tests of the philosophy. Yet he never dreamed of anything like quantum physics. This is all the more remarkable in that it was the introduction of quanta which first caused physicists generally to take seriously the idea, so courageously defended by Peirce, of a tychistic or random aspect of the physical world. As Thompson says, Peirce had an argument favoring his synechism: since all things swim in continua, measurement is inevitably inexact, more or less indefinite or approximate, so that absolute determinism could never be observationally confirmed. I see a subtle error here. True, where continuity is in question, exact measurement is out of the question, whereas quanta can in theory be counted. However, the combination of quanta and continuity is, if possible, even more obviously recalcitrant to exact observation than either is alone. And the point is that laws, to be useful, must deal with possibilities as well as actualities, and the ultimate possibilities are, as Peirce rightly says, continuous. The wave functions of quantum theory illustrate this.

Consider light reflection. The amount of light going through a glass depends on the angle of incidence. The angle can presumably vary continuously. Alter the angle slightly, and more or fewer photons will be reflected in a given time; alter it *sufficiently* slightly, and it may not be enough to cause a single added or subtracted photon. What it will do is alter the probability of such an addition or subtraction. Consider the all-or-none law in neurology. Alteration in the forces at a synapse means either no change, or a fixed finite amount of change, beyond the synapse. Again, the law must be a probability law as to the number of discharges, each of fixed amount. Still again, an atom of uranium decays into an atom of lead—when? No law prescribes the time for a single atom. But half of a large collection of such atoms will decay in a time fixed by the law. Probabilistic causality fits the case, not classical causality. Did Peirce realize this consequence of quanta? It favors his tychism at least as well as his synechistic view does.

Thompson mentions another argument that I consider fallacious—that continuity allows for all possibilities, whereas discontinuity excludes some possibilities, so that we should initially approach reality with the completely open idea of continuity. But sheer continuity excludes an infinite variety of possible discontinuities and is thus the most exclusive view of all, *unless* discontinuity is simply impossible, inconceivable. Peirce himself in "The Logic of Continuity" seems to argue that it is primordial possibility that is continuous and that actualization consists in introducing some kind of discreteness, as when we draw a chalk line on a continuous blackboard.

I am puzzled by Thompson's suggestion that Peirce can talk about definite experiences as sensations of reaction, whereas the continuity is in the reactions, not the sensations. Would Peirce's argument against definite intuitions then not hold?

Thompson is right of course that synechism was put forth by Peirce as regulative, not constitutive. The arguments given were indeed for it as regulative, yet even as such the arguments seem misleading. The very idea of atomism, so immensefully fruitful in the history of science, was always a kind of departure from synechism, so far as I can see. I suspect the better regulative principle is to seek the right combination of continuous possibilities and discrete actualities. The wave-particle complementarity seems to indicate what this amounts to. "Wavicle" is perhaps a good term for the idea.

The important argument for synechism—that merely discrete entities cannot intelligibly influence each other—is not necessarily unambiguous in excluding all discreteness. We have here the question of internal relations. It is of first importance not to forget that Peirce is definitely and unambiguously committed both to external and to internal relations. His definition of firstness is one of the most precise definitions in the literature of the idea of external or nonconstitutive relation, and the definition of secondness is equally precise as definitive of internal or constitutive relations, except for the arbitrary limitation to dependence upon just *one* other entity. In my revision of the categories I remove this limitation. Events, as I construe Peirce (also Whitehead), depend on their predecessors; *perhaps* they depend also on their contemporaries (Peirce is less clear as to that), but not on their successors. Relations to the future are not to particular later events but to more or less general aspects of the future as expressed by probabilistic laws, laws tolerant of a tychistic aspect. Peirce suggests that things are where they act, but it does not follow that things act, or are, everywhere throughout space and time. We cannot act on our remote ancestors, and are not in their world at all, though they are in ours, which is why we can talk about them as they could not about us.

Peirce was an immense genius, but he was a physicist perched in a world with a physics about to change to the foundations. Thompson wrote in his book on Peirce that Peirce's idea of existence calls for clarification in the direction of an Aristotelian or similar conception of individual substances. I agree that clarification is needed, but perhaps it should be in a less traditional direction, or, taking the Orient into account, in a more Buddhistic direction, into a clear doctrine of change as succession of acts of becoming, not instantaneous but unitary.

Peirce's phrase "the logic of events" points forward to contemporary physics and Whitehead, as much as, if not more than, back to Aristotle or other pre-quantum thinkers. Note, too, that Peirce greatly admired Buddhism and made declarations that in some ways are the most nearly Buddhistic to be found in American philosophy before Whitehead. Here the influence of synechism was relatively helpful. We are, as Saint Paul had it, "members one of another."

A strong argument against unqualified synechism is given by Von Wright. Peirce himself somewhere says that an individual is determinate, conforming to the law of excluded middle as to predicates; but he also says, and by his tychism must say, that according to this definition there are no individuals, strictly speaking. Now Von Wright argues that continuous change makes it impossible to have any wholly definite actuality. In any time, however short, a subject will be first P and then not-P, with respect to some predicate or other. With continuous change, only in an instant could this contradiction or violation of excluded middle be avoided, but then in an instant nothing can happen. Time does not consist of instants. Would Peirce have accepted this? Whitehead had a somewhat different form of Zeno argument.

Peirce admired Aristotle as cordially as anyone ever has, calling him "by far the greatest intellect" in human history. I incline to call Peirce the greatest modern Aristotelian. But he wanted to go beyond Aristotle. In his theory of time as "objective modality," in some aspects of his theories of firstness, secondness, and thirdness and of his synechism, I think he did so. But perhaps one has to go further still away from Aristotle. Once when I was standing beside Bochensky and he heard me remark to a third person, "Reality consists of events," Bochensky said, "*Aristotle* says that. He didn't dot all the i's or cross all the t's. . . ." I often think about this remark of Bochensky's. Peirce dotted some of the i's and crossed some of the t's. But are there not more to be dotted or crossed?

Peirce's idea of a continuum of reactions as defining individuality in a seemingly strict sense is troublesomely abstract, oversimplified. A human person seems to be only intermittently conscious, What is reacting when the person is in dreamless sleep? The body? But that is billions of cellular individuals, and far from an identical collection of them from moment to moment. Peirce was not unaware of the complexities of human personality. Consciousness, he wrote, is a sort of public spirit in the brain cells. The process theory of sequential societies of actualities, each of which is created and then persists thereafter as an objectified datum of prehension in later actualities, seems calculated to take the complexities into account more definitely and naturally than any talk about a rigorous continuity of action defining a single, identical, yet changing individual.

Peirce himself says that a person is an idea. I recall Whitehead independently saying to Raphael Demos, "There's the Demos idea" and going on to explain how this was the "identifying characteristic" which made the society called Demos the same from moment to moment. There are indications that Peirce was to some extent, in Matthew Arnold's words, "between two worlds, one dead and the other powerless to be born." So were countless other people at the time. Only in some ways, as in his logic, his tychism and probabilism, was Peirce well into the new world.

I agree with Thompson that Peirce is not a systematic writer. He has materials for a system, clues to one, but it never quite crystallizes. He even had a theory to justify this. He forces one to make one's own system. In some ways I find Peirce more helpful than Whitehead, for instance, in the Peircean theory about the primordial continuum of possible qualities out of which anything so definite as blue (or a certain quality of emotion) is an emergent, not an eternal object.

One of the subtleties of the question of continuity is that, even if one accepts the theory of discrete actualities, the limitations of our powers of introspection (which is really, as Ryle says and Whitehead implies, a form of memory) prevent us from clearly identifying definite intuitions of or by single experiences. Rather the discreteness is blurred for our awareness, as Whitehead admits. There is reason to think we come close to single experiences in noting the number of successive musical notes we can be aware of in a second. So, although for practical purposes our lack of intuitive certainties is much as Peirce says, theoretically we can say what we mean by definite relations and definite terms, and this seems an advantage.

Permit me to summarize my view about Peirce on continuity and individuality. When Peirce discusses individuals, he is writing about what for me are sequential societies of actualities, not single actualities. About these societies I, with Whitehead and the Buddhists, would accept much of what Peirce says about individuals. Their relations to our knowledge and to each other are very much as Peirce says. The disagreement concerns rather their relations to their own momentary states, also the details of the mind-body distinctions involved.

Individuals or societies are not wholly definite; their identifying traits are partly conventional or arbitrary (When did I first become myself? When will I cease to be myself?). Societies are not "simply located" in space but are partly internal to one another. Also the distinction between a person's experiences and the person's bodily states is extremely complex and subtle. The body is a vast society of societies; the mind or psyche is a single, personally ordered society whose primary immediate data are indistinctly intuited momentary actualities forming the bodily societies.

My criticism of Peirce's synechism concerns primarily his assertion that *actual* becoming is continuous and that, in a finite time, we have an infinity of experiences, each infinitesimally short, temporally.

My accusation that Peirce made a definite mistake in arguing that the initial assumption of inquiry must be that actuality is continuous, since otherwise one would be ruling out possibilities, may be put as follows. A continuum is indeed an infinity of possibilities, but none of these possibilities is realizable except in an actualized discontinuity. An actualized continuity is an impossibility, and this impossibility is all that the assumption of discreteness rules out. It does so on the ground that, just as continuity is the order among possibilities, so discontinuity is the order among actualities. Any particular discontinuity rules out all the other possible ones in a given case. Hence no particular discontinuity should be assumed a priori. That there must in every actual case be *some* discontinuity or other, rules out no particular discontinuity, and hence no possibility. Peirce's argument is invalid.

That individuals are not wholly external to one another (not simply located in space) is acceptable, but only in terms of a real discontinuity of momentary actualities. Only past actualities are internal to a present actuality. However, an actuality in my personal series may be internal to a later actuality in yours, and vice versa. In this way we are internal to each other, react to each other. Peirce has not reached the final level of analysis. Nor had Kant reached it.

Do I not react continuously? If "I" refers to me as conscious individual, then in dreamless sleep what is my reaction? I see none. Commonsense individuals are not ultimate terms of analysis. The Buddhists saw that so well.

Peirce's own doctrine that dichotomies are crude tools of analysis may be cited here. Besides universals and changing individuals there are actual entities which are created but do not change. Also a human person or metazoan animal is not merely a single individual but many individuals on various levels.

I do not recall "instantaneous reactions" as Peirce's doctrine. For me an actual entity reacts or has secondness to its predecessors in a finite portion of time, and this action is a creation, not a change. The finiteness is not an internal trait of the entity but measures it in relation to other actual entities and their time of becoming. In the fraction of a second it takes a single actual entity on the human level to become, a multiplicity of briefer entities can become on subhuman levels. But in this we are deep in difficult problems of physics and biophysics, also in the problem of relating quantum theory and relativity theory, a problem about which no one seems completely happy.

I congratulate those who arranged these meetings upon their including a real expert on the philosopher whose writings were one of the big things in my life. I have never regretted time spent reading Peirce. It was a huge piece of luck to be given as a task an occupation which was an education and a delight throughout. That it was so much a delight as it was, especially in the latter part of the job, was partly because of a second piece of luck, Paul Weiss's turning up to help with a substantial part of what, as a one-man job, would have been excessively difficult and have taken up too large a portion of the career of one as eager to do his own writing as I (or as Weiss) was.

My cordial thanks to Manley Thompson.

John B. Cobb, Jr.

8

Overcoming Reductionism

Process philosophy has undertaken to overcome the reductionism of the New-tonian world view within a naturalistic context and guided by the actual course of scientific thought. The greatest single contribution to this work has been by Alfred North Whitehead. Yet there are limitations to his achievement as well. In *The Nature of Physical Existence*[1] Ivor Leclerc has both acknowl-edged Whitehead's crucial contribution to the philosophy of nature and crit-icized him for continuing reductionistic tendencies. The purpose of this paper is to set Charles Hartshorne's contribution to the overcoming of reductionism against the background of Whitehead's work.

Section I briefly clarifies what is meant by reductionism and its status in the current discussion. Section II presents Whitehead's systematic refutation of reductionism. Section III describes and evaluates Leclerc's critique of Whitehead. Section IV reviews Whitehead's position in the light of Leclerc's critique. Section V describes Hartshorne's distinctive contribution.

I

The problem of reduction is often discussed today in terms of levels and their relations. Different sciences treat the world at different levels ranging, for example, from the level of subatomic particles, through molecules and cells, to the level of human behavior. These sciences have demonstrated that much can be learned about each level without referring to other levels. Hence a considerable degree of autonomy is possible for theory at each level without referring to other levels.

On the other hand, the study of one level is sometimes able to illumine what is taking place at a higher level. Chemistry clarifies biological phe-nomena, for example, and physics throws light on chemistry. A great deal of scientific advance has taken place by interpreting phenomena at one level in terms of events at a lower level.

Indeed, many scientists have believed that the complete explanation toward which science moves is necessarily reductive in this sense. If biological phenomena are fully understood, this will be through biochemical explanation. If all physical events could ever by fully explained, this would be in terms of the behavior of quanta. This is the view of thoroughgoing reductionism.

Historically, reductionism has been associated with materialism and determinism. The units of which the world is made up were thought to be material particles which remained unchanged in themselves as they moved about in space and formed the diverse configurations which made up the physical objects in our world. Some thinkers still picture the world in this way. They interpret the principle of indeterminism as indicating limits on the possibility of human knowledge of this world but not as indicating that the cosmology is incorrect. Even if the shift from deterministic to statistical laws with respect to these physical existents is accepted as reflecting an actual indeterminacy in their behavior, the reductionism is not greatly affected. The ideal remains that events at other levels are to be explained in terms of these statistical laws governing events at this basic level.

By no means all scientists today accept this ideal of reductionism. Many are impressed by the degree of autonomy characterizing phenomena at other levels. They do not deny that some levels have been reduced to others and that further reductions are possible, but they see that success in reduction has often been exaggerated. Rather than assume that reduction must ultimately be possible throughout science, they take it as an open question whether particular physical existents at higher levels are reducible to physical existents at lower levels.[2]

For the philosopher of nature this raises an interesting question. Since complex physical existents can be broken down into component physical existents, how can they have properties that the components lack? The tendency is to answer this question in terms of structure or architecture or system. When smaller existents are organized in a certain pattern, the properties of the patterned system will be different from the properties of the elements that constitute it.

There can hardly be any doubt that this is true, in some sense. Even a pile of rocks will have properties that none of the rocks individually possess— instability for example—but this is hardly a significant challenge to the reductionist goal. The properties of the pile, while not characterizing the individual rocks, can be derived from what is known of rocks and their behavior in external relation to other rocks. From the time of Democritus, reductionists have never questioned the importance of spatial arrangements.

The kind of structure which is now emphasized is quite different from this. It makes possible complex interactions among the structured elements so that the whole structure operates in relation to other structures in ways quite unlike the operations of the components apart from that structure. It is highly improbable that laws describing the behavior of the particles within this structure and information about spatial relations could ever explain the behavior of the structure as a whole.

This is remarkably like the old organismic view which held, rightly, that the whole is more than the sum of its parts. But like the earlier view it is weak in explanatory power. It is now evident that the properties of the whole are not found in the parts except as they are organized into that whole, and that for this reason the reductionistic program is not successful. The question remains, Why? Is there, as vitalists supposed, in addition to the mechanism some other principle at work? If so, What? If not, how does the arrangement of the parts produce properties which are not ultimately functions of the parts together with their spatial relations?

II

Much of Whitehead's cosmology is a response to questions of this sort. This response is rich and complex. There are three major ways in which his philosophy opposes reductionism.

1. The most fundamental basis for rejecting reductionism as adequate to explain the physical world is his doctrine of prehensions or internal relations.[3] According to this doctrine the relations of one entity to others are constitutive of the entity in question. It is for this reason that the properties of a system cannot be derived from the properties of its constitutive parts, that is, from the properties possessed by these entities when outside the system. It is well known, for example, that a virus outside a cell lacks important properties it exhibits when in the cell. But in less dramatic ways this is true of atoms and molecules. Molecules exhibit properties that cannot be derived from the properties of the atoms constituting them when these atoms exist outside the molecular structure. If the properties of the molecule are derivative from those of the atoms, this can only be from the properties which the atoms have in this molecular structure.

The doctrine of internal relations has important implications for the scientific enterprise. That enterprise has been for the most part committed to analysis. The doctrine of internal relations explains why analysis is of limited, although real, value. Alongside the autonomous study of phenomena at each level and the reductive study of phenomena at one level in terms of those at a lower level, we need a study of phenomena at each level as they are shaped by phenomena at a higher or more inclusive level.[4]

The effect of the doctrine of internal relations on the understanding of the nature of the physical existent is radical. It destroys the notion of material substance and substitutes that of an event in which "the many become one, and are increased by one."[5] Since both relativity and quantum theory up until now have been couched in terms of substance, the theoretical effects of a shift to event thinking would be vast. These effects might provide the basis for the still needed synthesis of relativity and quantum theories. But that is not the project of this paper.

2. At least in the instance of the living cell, Whitehead believed that the constitutive entities are not all physical in the usual sense. There are entities or events also in the empty space. It is these events, and not the molecular structure of the cell, that account for the life of the cell. The molecules provide the necessary stability, but only the occurrences or "occasions" in empty space are capable of the novelty and spontaneity that are the distinguishing mark of life. Thus Whitehead posits a type of entity wholly neglected in ordinary reductionistic accounts.

3. The doctrine of internal relations and the assertion of occasions in the empty space of living cells still do not do justice to the reasons that complex entities cannot be explained in terms of the simpler ones of which they are composed. Whitehead saw that in the human instance we have immediate understanding of ourselves as unified experiences that cannot be identified with the experiences of the physical units making up our bodies. These human experiences are the dominant, presiding, or final percipient occasions which constitute us as "living persons." Similar occasions are to be found among other high-grade animals. Hence the full analysis of these animals requires not only the recognition that all the entities that make up their bodies are internally related to other such entities but also that there is present another set of entities of a much higher grade of experience which constitute the psyche, soul, or mind of the animal. These psychic experiences are internally related to the bodily ones, and the bodily ones are internally related to them.

III

In his renewal of emphasis upon the philosophy of nature, Ivor Leclerc has recognized the importance of the contribution of Whitehead. Indeed, much of Leclerc's writing has been an explanation and defense of Whitehead's project. However, Leclerc is an original thinker in his own right, and in *The Nature of Physical Existence* he criticizes Whitehead in important ways, especially for what he sees as a remaining tendency to reductionism. It will be useful to examine his criticisms, and to reexamine Whitehead in their light before presenting Hartshorne's contribution to these central issues.

Leclerc recognizes that Whitehead tries to deal with the properties of larger and more complex entities in his doctrine of societies. But Leclerc believes there are limitations in Whitehead's solution of this problem. He insists that such compounds of lower-level entities as atoms, molecules, and cells must be recognized as having individual existence in their own right, whereas he finds Whitehead attributing to them only social unity. Leclerc develops his own position through a double criticism of Whitehead.

Leclerc's first criticism centers on the doctrine of causality. In Leclerc's interpretation of Whitehead, activity or agency is located entirely in the perceiver. What is perceived functions as a passive datum for the new event or occasion. Leclerc interprets Whitehead's position to be like that of Leibniz in presenting the cause-effect relation as one of perception. This implies that no force is exercised by the datum perceived. The agency is entirely in the perceiver.

Leclerc juxtaposes to this the proposal that acting be "conceived as an 'acting on' and thus as a 'relating'."[6] He believes that among the entities composing a compound "this reciprocal acting constitutes a tie or bond between them, this bond being the relation—which exists only in the acting, and not as some *tertium quid*. The word 'relation'—in this respect like the word 'perception'—connotes both the act, the rela*ting,* and *what* the act achieves."[7]

Up to this point, I believe, Leclerc's differences are not with Whitehead's philosophy as developed in *Process and Reality* and *Adventures of Ideas*. They are with earlier writings in which the doctrine of causal efficacy was not developed. They are also with Whitehead as interpreted in some secondary writings, including Leclerc's own otherwise valuable commentary in *Whitehead's Metaphysics: An Introductory Exposition.* In that book he repeatedly cautions the reader not to take Whitehead's language at face value, since Leclerc is sure that Whitehead could not mean what the language says. For example, whereas Whitehead consistently speaks of past occasions as actual, Leclerc says that Whitehead could not mean this. In Leclerc's interpretation, "only concrescing, i.e., 'acting' entities are *actual* in the full, proper sense. The acting of antecedent actualities is completed; as such they are, in the strict sense, no longer 'actual'."[8] Whereas Whitehead speaks of past occasions as "functioning" in the self-creation of new occasions, Leclerc tells us that in Whitehead's systematic position this "functioning" cannot imply agency.[9] He adds: "This should be stressed because the contrary supposition might arise from Whitehead's statement . . . that upon objectification an actual entity 'acquires causation whereby it is a ground of obligation characterizing creativity'."[10]

My point is that, at the time Leclerc wrote his interpretation of Whitehead, he understood Whitehead's systematic position to be that past actual entities function in the present concrescence only as passive perceived data, not as truly causally efficacious. His interpretation of Whitehead did not change as he came later to recognize that this is not an adequate doctrine of cause. The results are odd. Whereas Whitehead repeatedly stressed that it is the distinctive task of his philosophy to show how one actual entity is constitutively present in other actual entities, Leclerc criticizes Whitehead for picturing past entities as remaining passive data for perception. Whereas Whitehead understands an actual entity to be constituted by the creativity which he defines as the many becoming one and being increased by one, Leclerc criticizes him for thinking that the many merely characterize a creativity which then leaves them behind as it constitutes a new entity.

Although it is unfortunate that Leclerc has in this way introduced confusion into the discussion,[11] it is fortunate that we have his strong and independent corroboration of the importance of a doctrine of real causal relationality bonding the entities of the world together. Whitehead would certainly agree with Leclerc that actual entities exercise true agency on other actual entities, and that this "acting constitutes a tie or bond between them, this bond being the relation—which exists only in the acting and not as some *tertium quid.*"[12]

Although Leclerc's criticism of Whitehead's doctrine of causality is based on misinterpretation of the texts, Leclerc goes on to draw antireductionistic conclusions beyond those of Whitehead summarized in the preceding section. The passage just cited continues as follows: "This means that by virtue of the mutual activity of relating, there exists a form or character common to the entities acting. This form or character is not one inhering in each entity separately and individually—in which case the character would be a mere class name—but is a character of a relation."[13]

These sentences are not entirely clear. They could be interpreted as saying nothing different from what Whitehead asserts, namely, that in the case of a society the form or character common to the entities is derived by all subsequent ones in their prehension of earlier ones. But Leclerc elsewhere makes clear that he means more than this. "Specifically the question here is: which are to be identified as 'acting' entities in the primary sense—as opposed to being only derivatively acting, that is, by virtue of the acting of the constituents of the entity in question? For example, are we to conceive chemical atoms as active in the primary sense while molecules are active only derivatively? But atoms, in current theory, are themselves composites; does this then imply that they too are derivatively active, it being their constituents, electrons, protons, etc., which are primarily active? But some at least of these constituents, e.g., protons, would themselves seem to be composite, so that by the logic of this argument the truly active entities must be identified with the ultimate constituents, those which are not themselves composite."[14]

Leclerc finds that the evidence of modern science counts against such a reduction. "The action of one compound 'atom' on another is not, by the scientific evidence, an aggregate action of the electrons and protons individually on each other."[15] Molecules and cells also function as units of action, hence as real individual physical existents or substances.

Leclerc believes that when the subordinate entities in a compound act upon one another in a fully reciprocal way, so that they share in one another's constitution, the whole attains a unity that is not attributable to its parts. This whole he calls the dominant monad. "There is a most important difference between the dominant monad and the other constituents of the 'corporeal substance'. The dominant monad will not be simply one monad among others, differing from them only in having a greater internal complexity—having consciousness, for example; the dominant monad will in a certain sense be inclusive. . . . What has emerged in this new position is the conception of a monad or substance which is not a constituent of a compound but itself a compound."[15]

This does not mean for Leclerc that the constituent parts lose their identity in the compounds. "The actual unity of necessity transcends the constituents individually, and since it is the *unity* which is actual, *in relation to it* the constituents must necessarily be potential; this is necessarily entailed in the relationship. In themselves, however (that is, not in reference to the actual unity) they are actual substances, and must be in themselves actual in order to be able to be constituents. Furthermore, they must be in themselves actual in order to be able to act; the actualized unity is not due solely to the acting of the dominant or unifying monad, for the latter acting to be an 'acting on' requires a responsive acting in the others."[17]

IV

Leclerc pictures the world as composed of a hierarchy of individuals each of which is compounded of smaller individuals until the ultimate stratum is reached. A similar vision can be found in Whitehead, especially in *Science and the Modern World*. For example, after asking whether a molecule in a human body is affected by the decisions of the dominant human occasion, he says that it would be more consonant with his philosophy to say that the direct effects would be negligible, but that the indirect effects would be important. "We should expect transmission. In this way the modification of total pattern would transmit itself by means of a series of modifications of a descending series of parts, so that finally the modification of the cell changes its aspect in the molecule—or in some subtler entity."[18]

This passage clearly suggests that the bodily organs prehend the dominant occasion, the cells prehend the organs, and molecules prehend the cells. From the point of view established in *Process and Reality*, if prehensions are attributed to organs and cells and molecules, then there are actual occasions at these successive levels. Furthermore, in *Process and Reality*, there are several passages that imply that there are molecular prehensions[19] and others that indicate that there can be occasions at successive levels, for example, electronic occasions and still more ultimate ones.[20] Hence it is misleading for Leclerc to contrast his view so sharply with Whitehead's on this topic. Something like Leclerc's doctrine can be derived from Whitehead's. Also, Leclerc's critique ignores other features of Whitehead's way of overcoming reductionism which were discussed in Section II.

Nevertheless, there are differences between Leclerc's position and the one that is most fully articulated in *Process and Reality*. As Whitehead developed his doctrine in that book, he seems to have conceived all actual occasions as minuscule in size. This is true not only of physical ones but also of those in the empty spaces of the cells and those constituting the animal psyche. Despite the indications, just noted, that there are occasions at various levels, such as subelectronic, electronic, and molecular, his most detailed analysis indicates that the larger units are societies of mutually external smaller entities and do not have the unity of actual occasions. The animal does have a series of unifying, dominant occasions which jointly constitute the psyche, but even these can exist only in the interstitial spaces in the brain.

The most interesting case, and the one to which Whitehead gave most attention, is the living cell. For Leclerc the cell is a dominant monad which is a compound of all its subordinate elements. Whitehead's analysis was discussed in Section II where the important concept of occasions in empty space was discussed. The question now, however, is that of the unity of the cell. Does the cell have the unity of an occasion so that the cell as cell prehends and acts? Or are all the prehensions and actions of the cells the prehensions and actions of its constituent parts, either those constituting the molecules or the occasions in empty space?

In the analysis of the cell Whitehead introduced the distinction between the nonsocial nexus of living occasions in the empty space of the cell and societies of occasions (e.g., molecules) constituting its physical components. In this connection he considered the possibility that the living occasions in the cell might constitute a single personally ordered society rather than a nonsocial nexus.[21] That would mean that at any moment there would be a single living cellular occasion internally related to the world rather than a great multiplicity of minuscule occasions to which severally the internal relations of the cell must be attributed.

His reason for rejecting this theory is interesting. He had in view at that point in his writing two types of occasions: those socially organized and those not organized into societies. Social order was constituted for him by deriving a common character from antecedent events. In short, social order involved repetition of form. In a nonsocial nexus, on the other hand, the unit events could be spontaneous. They need not derive their character from antecedent events. Given these choices, social order explains the mechanical character of relationships. To explain life one must turn to occasions in nonsocial nexus. Hence to see the cell as governed by a single personally ordered society would deny the life and spontaneity which was the reason for turning to the occasions in the empty spaces.

There are obvious problems with this position. Whitehead at that point was forced to explain the order in the cell in terms of its molecular structure, to which spontaneity was denied, and to explain the life of the cell in terms of the events in its empty space, which he depicted as radically unordered. It is hard to think that this combination can account for the type of order and the type of spontaneity actually exemplified in a cell.

Whitehead recognized this problem, and even while writing *Process and Reality* he advanced beyond this point. He developed an understanding of another type of entity which combines order and life.[22] He did so because he recognized that there is something like social order in the human soul and that this is combined with life and freedom. If successive human experiences constituted simply a nonsocial nexus, they would lack significant connection through time. But for them to constitute a society, as Whitehead had conceived of societies up to that time, each would have to repeat identical characteristics derived from antecedent members. Experience would have to be either chaotic or endlessly repetitive. In fact it is neither.

Whitehead saw that the problem had arisen because he had described societies in terms of the derivation of a common character from antecedent members. That meant that the more social an occasion is, the more it is conformal to its past. But another pattern is possible. The main requirement for social order is derivation of its characteristics from some aspects of the past members of the society. This derivation can be from their originative elements rather than from those that they have derived from *their* antecedents. In Whitehead's terms, an occasion may prehend the conceptual feelings of antecedent occasion, not only the physical feelings of those occasions. In this way spontaneity in one moment can be transmitted to the next as the base from which its own spontaneity arises. Whitehead called this quite different ordering of occasions a "living person."

In *Process and Reality* Whitehead did not employ this new concept in conceptualizing the cell. Indeed, he explicitly rejected such application.[23] But in *Adventures of Ideas* his comments on life suggest that he may have changed his mind. There he stressed that it is the coordination of spontaneities that constitutes life.[24] His discussion is more reminiscent of what he said in *Process and Reality* about a living person than of what he said about a nonsocial nexus.

Even if Whitehead had clearly affirmed the presence of a cellular "living person" and also of molecular and atomic ones, there would remain a difference with Leclerc. The locus of the cellular living person would not have been the cell as a whole but the empty space within the cell. Even in the case of the human living person the locus is not the brain as a whole. Instead, Whitehead posits that the "route of presiding occasions probably wanders from part to part of the brain."[25] Whitehead seems to have thought that all occasions, including dominant or presiding ones, must occupy spatio-temporal regions external to the regions of all other occasions. In this sense, even dominant occasions do not include other occasions in the spatial sense but lie alongside of them.

In summary, although Whitehead developed categories for understanding the unity of a society as more than the commonality of its tiniest parts, he applied these categories explicitly only to the higher animals. Even here his account indicates that he thought of the dominant monads as spatially minuscule in extension rather than as spatially inclusive of the occasions at lower levels. Hence, despite Whitehead's extremely important contributions to overcoming reductionism, Leclerc is not wrong in detecting a continuing tendency to a particular type of reductionism. He affirms complex societies, and

societies of societies, in some of which there are dominant occasions or monads. But the dominant monads are pictured as members of the societies rather
than as compound individuals.

V

Leclerc published his theory in 1972. He seems to have been oblivious to the
fact that Charles Hartshorne had published an almost identical theory in 1936,
even using much of the same terminology, in "The Compound Individual."
The chief difference is that, whereas Leclerc developed his views through
criticism of Whitehead, Hartshorne thought of himself as interpreting and
developing ideas partly derived from Whitehead.

Hartshorne focuses on atoms and cells as clear instances of individuals.[26] He notes that "all individuals apparent to the senses are compounded of numerous much smaller individuals."[27] Such compounds are
distinguished from composites in the same way Leclerc distinguishes compounds from aggregates. The constituents of the aggregates lack the degree of
mutual immanence characteristic of those in compounds. Like Leclerc,
Hartshorne, in this essay, uses "substance" as the equivalent of individual.

Hartshorne, like Leclerc, holds that where there is a true compound
individual there is a "dominating unit."[28] For him, as for Leclerc, this includes the constituent entities without reducing their own substantial identity.

To point out the unrecognized similarity of Leclerc's "new" proposals
of 1972 and the position espoused by Hartshorne at least since 1936 is, on the
one hand, to claim originality for Hartshorne and, on the other, to indicate
that the independent and thorough work of Leclerc adds to the credibility of
Hartshorne's speculations. It might also suggest that future work should build
on Leclerc's more recent and better-documented formulations. The remainder
of this essay argues that this would be a mistake—that Hartshorne's formulations have more far-reaching applicability and greater power of illumination.

Leclerc develops his theory in direct consideration of the objects of
scientific inquiry. Like Whitehead prior to *Science and the Modern World*, he
brackets out the human knower from the world he studies. Hence his formulations are adapted to a world of objects and their relations. He does not exclude
certain kinds of subjectivity from this world, indeed he insists on activity in a
sense that goes beyond observed phenomena. But he does not wrestle with the
question of where an instance of such activity can be humanly observed. His
work is, as he states, exclusively in the field of the philosophy of nature.

Whitehead had recognized that our one direct access to a unitary entity
is in our own immediate experience. Much of his analysis of the dynamic
structure of every unitary entity is based on phenomenological analysis of his
own experience. He speculated that to be an actual entity at all was to have a
dynamic structure analogous to that of human experience. Yet much of his
thinking about the natural world was done before he made this move.

For Hartshorne this approach was eminently congenial. In his case it did not have to achieve reconciliation with another, more objective, study of nature that had occupied him for many years. On the contrary, its application in cosmology as in metaphysics was direct and unproblematic. Accordingly, Hartshorne's whole cosmology reflects the model of human experience more directly than does Whitehead's.

From the point of view of cosmology this difference is not entirely in Hartshorne's favor. Cosmology has never been Hartshorne's chief interest, and difficult questions may be too easily answered when one is not immersed, as Whitehead was, in the relevant science and mathematics. Nevertheless, some modifications of Whitehead by Hartshorne, even in the area of cosmology, lead to differences of doctrine which seem to be marked advances.

Since Hartshorne begins with human experience, the first cosmological question that arises for him does not have to do with atoms and molecules but with the relation of human experience to the body, especially to the central nervous system and the brain. Approached in this way the most natural answer is that human experience is the unified subjective concomitant of the complex pattern of physical events that constitute the body or some portion thereof. At different times Hartshorne has written of this as the body as a whole, the central nervous system, and the brain. It is my own judgment that the evidence favors the view that human experience occurs in a more or less extended portion of the brain rather than in the brain as a whole.[29] But discussion of these important topics belongs to another paper. Here the brain will be taken as the physical correlate of human experience, and the flow of human experience will be termed the psyche. The traditional mind-body problem will be discussed as the psyche-brain problem. In these terms, then, for Hartshorne the psyche is located where the brain is located, not in some tiny point within it. The numerous, more limited, brain events occur in portions of the same region in which the unified human experience is taking place.

Hartshorne and Whitehead both assume that evolutionary evidence implies full continuity between human beings and other animals. Hence, where similar physiological structures and behavior occur, both posit that there are unified animal experiences analogous to unified human ones. Neither attempts to identify the exact point at which such experiences emerged in evolution. Both suppose that they are lacking in plants. That means that the internal relations of the plant to its environment are to be found in the parts of the plant as these are discovered in analysis. Both also suppose that the smallest units of reality have a character which resembles human experience at least in that it involves internal relations. But beyond this they diverge.

Whitehead's account showed why complex organisms cannot be reductively explained by the activities of their component parts when these are studied apart from the structures of the organism. It gave additional reasons why the cell cannot be reduced to its molecular components. But when dominant occasions in animals and the occasions in empty space in cells are included in the animal and cellular societies, then the activities of the societies can be explained by the activities of the components when they are components of those societies. In societies other than animals and cells these component parts are finally only the subatomic entities.

Hartshorne proposes that wherever the evidence counts against reduction, we posit that the entities in question are real individual agents, internally related to the environment. The case of the living cell may be taken up again. If the activity of the cell suggests that it is taking account of its environment as a cell, then we should attribute internal relations and unified activity to the cell as a cell. That means that we should view the cell by analogy with our own experience and see the relation of the cell to its constitutive parts on the analogy of the relation of our own experience to our brains. There is no need to locate the cellular experience at some point within the cell, associating it exclusively either with the molecules or with the empty space. The cellular experience is the subjective unification of the whole complex of events. That means also that the cell as cell interacts with other cells in the larger organism.

The structure of the human brain gives rise to unified subjective experience. It does not appear that anything analogous occurs by virtue of the structure of a rock or even of a tree. The question as to whether the structure of a cell is more like that of a brain or of a tree is a factual one. If, as seems to be the case, unicellular organisms are responsive to their environment in their unity, then the evidence supports the attribution to them of internal relations to that environment. In this case the cell constitutes an important level not reducible to lower ones for the same reason that animal life constitutes a level not reducible to physiology.

If this is so, then the internal relations of the tree to its environment can be located in its cells. Does that mean that the level of the tree can be reduced to the level of the cell? No. What happens in the growth and death of the tree can, indeed, be best studied at the cellular level, but the cells in the tree behave as they do because of the structure of the tree. One cannot explain the tree by a study of the cells apart from the tree.

The question of which levels have the radical autonomy introduced by their own internal relations and which are irreducible only by virtue of the internal relations and actions characterizing their parts is always a factual one. Hartshorne attributes internal relations and action to many levels of organization—for example, to atoms and molecules. Clearly these are for him factual questions to be settled by such evidence as we can acquire. It is this freedom from prejudice against the attribution of internal relations and action at whatever level the evidence suggests them that is most promising for guiding further investigation. It is the use of the psyche-brain analogy that provides a clarity to Hartshorne's treatment lacking in Leclerc's and shows that the paradigm that solves an important problem in philosophy of nature also solves a crucial problem in philosophical anthropology.

In employing a single paradigm to solve a variety of problems Hartshorne follows Whitehead's direction. Whitehead taught that all reality should be understood through a common categoreal scheme. Hartshorne's doctrine of compound individuals goes beyond Whitehead but conforms to his spirit and program. It has also helped Hartshorne to formulate a doctrine of God and the world that goes beyond Whitehead's at a point at which Whitehead's doctrine strains his categoreal scheme to the limit.

That God is different from everything else is to be expected. If God were not profoundly different, God would not be God. On this point there is no disagreement between Whitehead and Hartshorne. But both are also convinced that to view God as an exception not only to the general character of creaturely beings but to metaphysical principles as well is to render talk of God finally nonsensical. They declare that God is not an exception to the categories but instead their chief exemplification.

Hartshorne takes an additional step. He has already used the psyche-brain analogy to understand the world of physical existents. He proposes that we use it also with respect to God.

Such a move was not available to Whitehead. For him the soul at any moment is located at some one point in the brain. To think of God as similarly located at one point in the cosmos would be absurd. It would not help to think of God as flitting around in the interstices. Accordingly Whitehead opted for thinking of God as unlike everything else in that God is nonextended spatially.

When Whitehead declared God to be without spatial extension, he had the primordial nature chiefly in view. The primordial nature is God's mentality, and in Whitehead's scheme mentality is not, of its own nature, spatio-temporal in character. Hence no problem arose. But Whitehead went on to affirm that God has a physical pole as well which feels all the feelings of the world. This seems to introduce something like spatial extensiveness into God. In the world it is physical relations that are in their very nature extensive. Whitehead does not explain how the physical feeling of the world in God leaves God free from the extensiveness of that which God feels. It is also not clear how God has this immediate feeling of all feelings without being spatially proximate to the feelings felt.

Answers to these questions are possible within Whitehead's framework, and speculations about God are notoriously difficult. But where a simpler and more satisfying answer is available, obscurity and complexity appear unnecessary. Hartshorne offers the simpler and more satisfying answer.

Hartshorne conjectures that God is related to the universe as we are related to our brains. We are not our brains, but what happens in our brains is immediately related to our experience. We are spatially immediately present to every event in our brains. We are coextensive with the sum of these events. But we are numerically different from the sum of these events, and our experience is not exhausted by them. For example, we enjoy consciousness, whereas probably none of the brain events are thus favored. Further, our decisions affect the events in the brain just as these events affect us.

This doctrine does not differ greatly from Whitehead's. It may even be that he in fact adopted something very like it, for in *Modes of Thought* he identified God with the whole in a way that is highly congenial to this doctrine. In traditional terms this is the doctrine that God is everywhere instead of the doctrine that God is nowhere. Both conceptually and religiously it seems superior.

All analogies have limits. The limits of this one appear quickly. We have no conscious awareness of the events in our brains, even though they largely determine the content of our consciousness. Our consciousness is directed to the external world. God has no external environment. God's consciousness is of those events that, for God, are analogous to the brain events for us. That would indeed be a very different mode of consciousness! But this model does not pose the radical puzzle of nonextensive experience of extensiveness.

Conclusion

Hartshorne has understood himself more as a metaphysician than as a cosmologist. His concern is more with the question of what anything must be to be at all than with determining which entities in the universe have which characteristics. On the whole he has accepted and adopted Whitehead's cosmology. Nevertheless, much in his thought is distinctively his own, and this is true of some of his cosmological ideas. In this paper I have argued that his wide extension of a paradigm derived from reflection about the relation of the psyche to the brain has proved fruitful in carrying forward a basically Whiteheadian way of overcoming reductionism.

Notes

1. Ivor Leclerc, *The Nature of Physical Existence* (London: George Allen and Unwin, 1972).

2. For a recent mainstream discussion of levels and the possibility of reduction, see John Cowperthwaite Graves, *The Conceptual Foundations of Contemporary Relativity Theory* (Cambridge, Mass.: MIT Press, 1971). Graves writes on page 20: "I will assume, along with Carnap, Nagel, and most other philosophers of science, that a theoretical reduction of one level *A* to another level *B* requires the following two things: (1) Each term that appears in *A* should be definable in terms of the language of *B*. At best such definitions should be explicit, but if this fails one can use something like a system of 'reduction sentences.' Putting the same point in more ontological terms, each entity in *A* should be fully characterized in terms of the properties and relations of the entities in *B*. This would constitute a reduction of the material aspects of *A* into the language of *B*. (2) Once this translation has been

carried out, we can express the laws of *A* in terms of the language of *B*. But at this stage these *A*-laws will appear only as unjustified assertions within *B*. To complete the reduction, we must also show that the *A*-laws as expressed in the language of *B*, can indeed be derived from the basic laws of *B* by some deductive procedure. Success here would constitute a reduction of the formal aspects of *A* to those of *B*." While not denying that in specific cases this reduction can be carried out, Graves sees no evidence of its universal success.

3. Alfred North Whitehead, *Science and the Modern World* (New York: Macmillan, 1925), p. 152.

4. In *Science and the Modern World,* pp. 115–16, Whitehead wrote: "The concrete enduring entities are organisms, so that the plan of the *whole* influences the very characters of the various subordinate organisms which enter into it. In the case of an animal, the mental states enter into the plan of the total organism and thus modify the plans of the successive subordinate organisms until the ultimate smallest organisms, such as electrons, are reached. Thus an electron within a living body is different from an electron outside it, by reason of the plan of the body. The electron blindly runs either within or without the body; but it runs within the body in accordance with its character within the body; that is to say, in accordance with the general plan of the body, and this plan includes the mental state. But the principle of modification is perfectly general throughout nature, and represents no property peculiar to living bodies."

In *Process and Reality,* corrected edition, ed. David Ray Griffin and Donald W. Sherburne (New York: The Free Press, 1978), p. 100, Whitehead wrote: "The first stage of systematic investigation must always be identification of analogies between occasions within the society and occasions without it. The second stage is constituted by the more subtle procedure of noting the differences between behaviour within and without the society, differences of behaviour exhibited by occasions which also have close analogies to each other. The history of science is marked by the vehement, dogmatic denial of such differences, until they are found out."

5. *Process and Reality,* p. 21.

6. *The Nature of Physical Existence,* p. 309.

7. Ibid., pp. 309–10.

8. Ivor Leclerc, *Whitehead's Metaphysics: An Introductory Exposition* (London: George Allen and Unwin, 1958), p. 101.

9. Ibid., p. 110.

10. Ibid.

11. In his presentation at the First International Whitehead Symposium at Bonn, August 25–28, 1981, Leclerc repudiated his earlier interpretation and criticism of Whitehead on this point, recognizing that Whitehead seriously intended to affirm the causal efficacy of past occasions.

12. *The Nature of Physical Existence,* p. 309.

13. Ibid., p. 310.

14. Ivor Leclerc, "Some Main Philosophical Issues Involved in Contemporary Scientific Thought," in *Mind in Nature,* ed. John B. Cobb, Jr., and David Ray Griffin (Washington: University Press of America, 1977), pp. 103–4.

15. *The Nature of Physical Existence,* p. 311.

16. Ibid., p. 303.

17. Ibid., p. 305.

18. *Science and the Modern World,* p. 215.

19. *Process and Reality,* p. 323.

20. Ibid., p. 91.

21. Ibid., p. 104.

22. Ibid., pp. 106–7.

23. Ibid., p. 107.

24. A. N. Whitehead, *Adventures of Ideas* (New York: Macmillan, 1932), p. 262.

25. *Process and Reality,* p. 109.

26. Charles Hartshorne, "The Compound Individual," in *Philosophical Essays for Alfred North Whitehead,* ed. F. S. C. Northrop (New York: Russell and Russell, 1936), p. 193.

27. Ibid., p. 194.

28. Ibid., p. 215.

29. Hartshorne's formulations are sometimes quite similar to this, e.g., "a man's consciousness is everywhere in some limited area in his nervous system, rather than localized in a point." Charles Hartshorne, *A Natural Theology for Our Time* (LaSalle, Ill.: Open Court, 1967), p. 95.

Response by Charles Hartshorne

Cobb's account of Whitehead and Leclerc I find highly illuminating. His account of me is entirely acceptable. The issues between Leclerc and Whitehead have always seemed to me rather difficult to grasp. So far as I understand them, they are as Cobb says.

It is true that I am more a metaphysician than a cosmologist (student of the special structures of this cosmic epoch). I know the history of philosophy far better than I do current science, except some small parts of the latter having to do with sensation and animal behavior. I do know with some intimacy what it is to be an empirical scientist, but only as dealing with some very special ranges of phenomena.

Cobb does not mention the fact that my application of the mind-body analogy to the idea of God is Platonic. I refer to the idea of the World Soul in the *Timaeus*. As a Harvard student of philosophy I chose Plato and Spinoza as my special topics in the history of philosophy; and I have always been something of a Platonist; though never much of a Spinozist. I have been strongly influenced by the challenge Spinoza issues to us all to take seriously the question of the modal structure of reality. We should learn from him to choose among: complete necessitarianism or denial of any contingency at all; a wholesale contingency of the system of nondivine things, between the parts of which there is no further contingency; piecemeal contingency among the parts of the system as well as of the system as a whole. Spinoza took the first of these options. But his reasons are unconvincing, once one sees that his definition of God as absolutely infinite substance is either meaningless or contradictory, since there are incompossible yet positive possibilities. As Whitehead saw, and so many have not seen, "all actuality is finite," only possibilities can be absolutely infinite. Definiteness is "the soul of actuality," and definiteness means this but not that, or that but not this, where this and that are alike possible, genuinely conceivable. One cannot prove anything by assuming the logical coherence of the classical idea of an *ens realissimum* or unsurpassable actuality, for this coherence is in no way known or knowable. In addition the sheer denial of contingency violates the principle of contrast. "Everything is necessary" deprives 'necessity' of any distinctive meaning.

Granting contingency, which alternative is more reasonable: within the world there is no contingency, all is tightly interlocked, there are no open possibilities for choice or decision; or there are such inner-worldly open possibilities? That there is this world, not some other, is without ultimate necessity, and so it exists by free choice or mere chance, yet within the world there is no chance or free choice at all—is this a reasonable view? Theistically it amounts to giving God and God alone effective freedom to decide; for the rest there is just the content of the divine decision. In that case how could we, who have no libertarian freedom, conceive the freedom we attribute to God? Linguistically (linguistic analysts please note) this is an incoherent position. If our apparent freedom to select among truly open possibilities is not genuine, neither can we know what such freedom would be in God.

If all is to be conceived by analogy with our human nature, then *either* Spinoza is right and the eternal, immutable essence of the cosmic soul necessitates everything in the cosmic body, and there is no chance, randomness, or genuinely open alternatives either within the world or as between this and other possible worlds; *or* there is freedom both in our decisions and in God's. Either only the real is possible, or, in both the human and the cosmic mind-body relation, there is contingency. Contingency is not an irrational idea; deductive reason is subsidiary to the ultimate rationality, which, as Whitehead says, is the wise, free creation of novel orders. Causal explanation is misunderstood if taken as the effort to show necessities. Rather it is the effort to show possibilities and impossibilities, so that we avoid wasting our energies attempting the latter and make reasonable choices among the former.

Spinoza does give one a sense of the unity of the world and of the world with God, even though he exaggerated this unity, or conceived it too simply. But his predecessors mostly underestimated the unity in both respects. Above all they attempted to combine belief in divine knowledge devoid of inner contingency or change with the assertion, rejected by Aristotle for clear and logically cogent reasons, that the world known by this knowledge is contingent. Aristotle avoided the contradiction by denying divine knowledge of the contingent aspects of the world, Spinoza, by denying all contingency. There remains the admission of contingency both in the world and in God as knowing that world. Socinus took this remaining option and Spinoza noted the fact. Too bad that so few others did note it. They might have learned something. For, unlike Spinoza, they were unwilling to deny all contingency.

I do not comment in detail on Cobb's paper. He is as clear as I can be about the things he discusses. It is gratifying to be so well understood as I feel I have been by the four former students participating in this volume, the other three being Peters, Alston, and Ogden.

George Wolf

9

The Place of the Brain in an Ocean of Feelings

Some months ago, in the midst of working on this paper, I happened to run across Charles Hartshorne at a symposium. I asked him what had led him to write the *Philosophy and Psychology of Sensation* (PPS), his first book and the impetus for this paper. He answered by telling me a little story about how one day, as a young man, he stood on a cliff on the coast of France and beheld a scene of great natural beauty. Suddenly he saw "into the life of things" and at that moment gained a sense of all of nature being alive and expressing feelings. Hartshorne spent the next two decades trying to make sense of what he saw that day.

The book appeared in 1934. It presents a theory of experience—the "doctrine of affective continuity"—which tries to unite philosophic ideas and scientific knowledge about sensation. The theory proposes that each sensory quality, such as yellowness, or the taste of an apple, or the buzz of a bee, is composed of a particular combination of basic dimensions of feeling—for example, intensity, pleasantness, proximity to self, and activity-passivity. Therefore, according to this theory, sensations differ in degree and not in kind. Hartshorne suggests that the theory is relevant to science in three ways. First, it accounts for the diverse qualities of experience in terms of a single idea—all qualities are forms of feeling. Second, it is supported by experimental data in sensory psychology. Third, it has empirical implications that suggest new lines of experimentation.

The theory of affective continuity never received much attention from the scientific community. It was too phenomenological, speculative, and general to arouse scientific interest in an era dominated by behaviorism and positivism. But there are recent indications that the *Zeitgeist* may be changing, especially in the neural and behavioral sciences. Researchers like John Eccles and Roger Sperry are addressing the philosophical problems of mind and brain, and there is an increasing interest in theories of mental functions. This seems like a good time to revive Hartshorne's pioneering endeavor to unite process cosmology and scientific research and see if we can advance it in the light of modern neurobehavioral research. I will try to begin this here.

I also have had experiences like Hartshorne's that set me to wondering how we perceive the world and led me to both process thought and science. But whereas Hartshorne approached the problems of spanning these two modes of thought from a background in philosophy, I come to them from a background in science. I am interested in the consequences of adopting a framework of process cosmology for research in the neural and behavioral sciences. In this paper I will try to show that the world view of process cosmology is reasonable from the standpoint of ordinary mechanistic, reductionistic science. I will also discuss how process cosmology can enhance science by suggesting new interpretations of facts and raising new questions for research. In the first part of the paper I will evaluate the reasonableness of two central concepts of process cosmology—concrescence and self-creation. In the second part I will discuss the usefulness of a process framework for scientific explanation and inquiry.[1]

Reasonableness

Of Concrescence

I stand on a high knoll in an apple orchard and look at a panoramic landscape that connects the bright red-and-green apple trees close by with vague, gray mountains in the distance. I'm struck by the incredible variety of forms and colors that I take in with a single glance. I find myself wondering, "How does all this fit inside my head?" It must be represented in my brain, bit for bit. And yet it's not in my brain; it's out there, big and bright. I can walk out there and touch each thing I see—it would take days to get to those mountains.[2]

Process cosmology tries to make sense of this experience by means of the notion of concrescence. It asserts that my experience of the countryside is really out there where it seems to be. I am continuous with the countryside— it is *in* my experience. According to the notion of concrescence, objective facts and subjective experiences are not really separate things but are mere abstractions. What is concretely real is the process by which diverse facts are united in an occasion of experience. Finally, concrescence includes not only the facts that I consciously perceive but all the facts that constitute the whole antecedent universe.[3]

Consider now the compatibility of concrescence with scientific facts and principles. First of all, how can we reconcile the idea that the countryside is contained in my experience with the scientific fact that there are photons and nerve impulses that intervene between the countryside and my experience of it? In fact this is not hard to do. To say that the countryside is contained in the experience does not mean that there is nothing between the two, it means that the countryside is contained within each of the intervening entities in much the same way that it is contained in my experience. Is this, in turn, compatible with scientific notions of causality?

A familiar model of a causal sequence which is often associated with science pictures each event as a link in a chain—a separate thing distinctly located in space. In contrast, the notion of concrescence pictures each (elementary) event as a cone that opens endlessly into the past to include the whole antecedent universe within it. So a causal sequence is like a stack of time-cones. (To be more accurate, I should say that each cone is stacked on a bundle of innumerable cones because each actual occasion that it prehends is itself a cone.)

The chain model and the time-cone model of a causal sequence appear to be incongruous. But, it turns out that the chain model is, in fact, a less accurate representation of the scientific notion of causality than the time-cone model is. This is because there is a sense in which any particular event is dependent on every event in its causal past. For example, consider a particular event—say lighting a match. This particular flame involves particular molecules of oxygen. If each of the molecules had not been just where it was, this flame would not have been just the flame it was. Now, if my understanding of statistical mechanics is correct, the chances are infinitesimally small that a given configuration of air molecules in the atmosphere would be just what it was if *any* configuration in its causal past had been even slightly different. If we interpret this implication of statistical mechanics to mean that every past event is involved in each present event, then we are coming close to the meaning of concrescence.[4]

There is another way that concrescence might seem to be incongruent with science but, in fact, is not. If the whole world is involved in every concrescence, then what is the function of the sensory systems? In other words, why did special sense organs evolve if every organism can feel everything in the world anyway? No notion can be considered credible if it is out of line with the "golden thread of biology"—the theory of natural selection.

We generally assume that primitive organisms are not sensitive to as many different kinds of stimuli as higher organisms are and that the sensory systems evolve to give organisms access to more and more types of stimuli. In the framework of process cosmology this can be interpreted differently. All organisms are sensitive to all possible stimuli right from the start (because all the data of the actual world are involved in every concrescence). But for primitive organisms the sensitivity is not differentiated and for higher organisms it is. The reason why the sensory systems evolve is to enhance the differentiation between stimuli that are relevant for life and those that are not. Each sensory system is like a special channel for a particular type of stimulus. Since there is an upper limit to how many data a finite organism can handle, opening a channel for one stimulus type automatically results in a filtering out or dampening of other types. In this interpretation the notion of concrescence is entirely in accordance with the evolution of the sensory systems.[5]

Now I want to turn to the meaningfulness of concrescence. Does it make sense? What does it mean to say that the universe is unified in each concrescence? The objective meaning seems fairly clear. Each event is the outcome of its entire causal past, and this can be understood in terms of statistical mechanics. But the subjective meaning is cloudy. I understand to some degree how the perceptible features of the world are unified in my experience. But how is the world beyond this countryside *in* my experience (not just the world behind the mountains but the imperceptible things between the mountains and me)? Perhaps I experience it unconsciously. But I'm not sure exactly what this means, and I have no good idea of the sense in which the unconscious experience is unified with what I experience consciously. Furthermore my experience of the countryside is supposed to be conveyed through the experiences of the intervening photons and neurons. Now, am I to believe that these entities experience the red apple that I see before me in the same way that I do? If not, then what is the relation between the redness I see and the object that I am looking at? I don't know of any good answers to these questions. Still, the notion of concrescence does not strike me as so unreasonable when I consider the alternatives. For instance, if photons and neural impulses are really no more than what the textbooks say they are, then I have to believe that this bright, beautiful, panoramic experience miraculously arises out of insentient chemical reactions inside my brain. I wouldn't accept this alternative for a minute.

Of Self-Creation

As I look over this countryside, I feel that I have some control over what I perceive and what I do with myself. I can look at the apple trees, or I can listen for the sound of bees, or I can sniff the scents of autumn in the breeze. I deliberate about whether to go back before it gets late or stay to watch the sunset. I can decide to be practical and go, or I can yield to my inclinations and carry on a while.

Traditional notions of causality only allow for two ways of accounting for my decisions—either they are caused or they are uncaused. Insofar as they are caused, they are the inevitable outcomes of antecedent events. Insofar as they are uncaused, they are haphazard. Neither of these alternatives captures what I feel at this moment or accounts for the free agency that my everyday concerns presuppose.

Process cosmology has a different notion of causality—the notion of self-creation. According to this notion, my impressions and presuppositions about my decisions pretty much reflect what is really going on. Self-creation incorporates both order and freedom in a single process. Also, self-creation is completely general; it is not limited to human decisions but is the basic process of all causality from subatomic events to social interactions. This sounds wonderful, but what is this notion exactly? Does it make sense in itself, and is it compatible with scientific thought?

Since it would take too much space to describe all that is involved in the notion of self-creation, I will focus only on the features that I find most problematic. It will be convenient to begin by considering whether the notion makes sense and then to consider its compatibility with science.

I will consider two problems concerning the sense of the notion. The first has to do with mind-body interaction and the second with temporal sequence. Self-creation is a subjective process that stands between every objective cause and objective effect. Objective causes constitute the data which are brought together by the self-creative act to form a new objective datum (the effect). This general idea is clear enough, but I do not have a clear idea of just how these transformations take place. Exactly how does a physical fact enter experience, and exactly how does experience become a physical fact? To answer this by saying that a physical fact is *prehended* into experience or that experience becomes a physical fact through *concresence* does not quite satisfy me. I do not mean to say that these technical terms have no explanatory value; they convey images that make a certain amount of sense to me. But they don't get to the crux of what I want to know here—I am still in the dark. Of course, I don't really expect an entirely satisfactory answer to this question, because I agree with process cosmology that, after all, subject and object are merely abstractions from the concrete unity of the world process. This means that on the one hand no analysis of subject or object alone can be complete, and on the other hand the togetherness of the two in their full concreteness cannot be fully comprehended.

The second conceptual problem involves temporal sequence. In order for a decision to be free of the past but still be based on reasons rather than being merely haphazard, not all of the reasons for the decision can precede the decision in time. According to the notion of self-creation, the final reason for the decision is created by the decision itself. This is the essence of self-creation. But how can a cause follow its effect? The theory of epochal time was formulated to avoid this logical inconsistency. In this theory the act of self-creation takes place within an epoch of time which contains no temporal sequence. Now, it is not at all clear to me how one can conceive of a process of self-creation in which one thing "follows" another unless one thinks of it as a temporal sequence. It seems that the theory of epochal time involves a trade-off of logical inconsistency for incomprehensibility. One might conclude that the temporal epoch is merely a kind of neat little black box for tucking away the ultimate paradoxes of freedom and causality. On the other hand, one might conclude that it is a better way of framing the problems of freedom and causality because the problems it solves are more significant than the ones it creates.

Let us go on to the question of whether the notion of self-creation conflicts with any scientific principles. It is obvious that self-creation is not compatible with strictly deterministic concepts of natural law. However, it is compatible with predictability of any degree short of perfection in any physical system from atom to man. Therefore it is entirely in accordance with probablistic concepts of natural law, and these are acceptable to many, if not most, scientists today.

On the other hand, self-creation seems to be discordant with the first law of thermodynamics. This is most apparent in the case of human behavior. Insofar as a decision is free, it must be independent of the ongoing flows of physical energy in the brain. But if the decision is not part of the flow, how does it affect that flow to produce a bodily action? Where does the energy come from? I discuss this problem and its theoretical and experimental implications in more detail elsewhere.[6] All that needs to be added here is that, although this is a most serious problem, it is not necessarily incurable; after all, the laws of thermodynamics are open to reinterpretation.

Before drawing any conclusions from these analyses, I want to discuss briefly the validity of my criteria and norms of reasonableness. The criteria were (a) clarity, consistency, and completeness of meaning and (b) compatibility with scientific facts and principles. While these are presumably relevant criteria, I am not sure that adequately objective measures of them are possible. Certainly, they were applied rather informally in this study. Norms are also a problem. It is obvious that my norms for reasonableness here have been low compared to norms of ordinary scientific discourse. However, this seems appropriate if one accepts Whitehead's distinction between speculative and scientific reasoning.[7] The concreteness and generality of speculative notions such as self-creation and concrescence preclude the precision of meaning that is possible for abstract scientific notions such as homeostasis or momentum. Nevertheless, one might still judge the present norms as too low for any reasonable domain of discourse.

In view of these considerations, I will speak only for myself. The notions of self-creation and concrescence seem reasonable enough to me. Insofar as these notions embody the basic categories of process cosmology, the system as a whole should pass my test of reasonableness along with the notions. At the same time the problems inherent in these notions are bewildering. However, I believe that metaphysical presuppositions are inevitable in any form of inquiry, so we are stuck with notions like these whether we consider them reasonable or not. The question is whether the present notions are less reasonable than the conventional alternatives. My analysis thus far has convinced me that they are at least par for the course. For example, when I scrutinize, in the same way that I scrutinized the notion of self-creation, modern physical notions of what goes on when one billiard ball strikes another, and when I try to understand my sense of agency in terms of an admixture of physical causes and random happenings, I find myself just as bewildered—and a little more forlorn.

Usefulness

For Explanation

I'm having a hard time getting myself to leave this lovely place. I muse over what this implies about my sense of agency. Suddenly, a bee interrupts my reveries. As it hovers before my eyes, insisting on itself, I find myself confronted by more limits upon my freedom. My eyes react like an electronic camera. As they focus on the bee, the apple trees I was just looking at dissolve into a blur.

Ordinary science can give a good account of involuntary reactions, such as focusing reflexes. Starting with the entry of the stimulus through the lens of the eye and progressing to the neural reflex mechanisms in the roof of the midbrain, it gives a step-by-step account of how a small moving object in the field of vision can cause a shift in the focus of attention. The account involves simple physical and logical principles such as those governing the focusing of a camera and the operation of a servomechanism in a computer.

For all practical purposes this kind of account is useful, informative, interesting, and complete. Additional information about my feelings and intentions is not relevant here. I am not asking questions about agency because I was not functioning as an agent; my attention seemed to shift itself, and my eyes focused reflexively. Therefore, my curiosity is pretty well satisfied by a purely mechanistic answer to my question.

Is there anything that process cosmology can add to this kind of explanation? It seems to me that as long as we are looking for practical knowledge about how aggregates work, and our criteria of understanding are based on prediction and control, we do not gain much from process thought. The language of science is tailor-made for talking about what aggregates do and how they do it.[8] In contrast, the language of process cosmology does not seem very useful for talking about aggregates. The basic concepts of process cosmology are about individuals, and all explanations are in terms of prehensions of individuals. In a sense, process concepts should still be applicable to aggregates because aggregates are supposed to be composed of individuals at some level or another, and mechanistic functions are due to the coordinated acts of these individuals. But how could such an account be of any value to ordinary science?

I do not know how to investigate the prehensions of the constituent individuals involved in mechanical functions. All I can do is infer what the prehensions are from my scientific studies of the mechanistic functions. But then the process account seems superfluous. For instance, once I have determined the physical and chemical mechanisms of muscle contraction, an additional account in terms of subjective aims and physical prehensions that are manifested in the contractions of muscle cells does not add anything of practical value to my understanding. In fact, this additional account seems incongruous with scientific method, for we are introducing unnecessary entities into our explanation and thus violating the principle of parsimony.

Still, I don't see any reason to close the doors to further inquiry into the possible benefits of process concepts for scientific explanations. Maybe we will discover radically different ways to envision aggregate functions, ways that involve thinking in terms of populations of individuals acting in concert. I am not suggesting a return to primitive animistic notions but an advance to new forms of animistic explanation through process thought. For instance, Hartshorne has described the functions of aggregates of cells in terms of "waves of mob feeling." I think it is important to let ideas like this stimulate one's imagination and to try to apply them to a variety of phenomena. Although it does not make much sense now, it is not inconceivable that we might find ways of understanding the operations of ordinary machines like, say, a diesel engine in terms of feelings of pressure, friction, fatigue, and so on in the constituent occasions. It might turn out that animistic interpretations informed by process thought will give us a richer understanding of how both organic and inorganic mechanisms work and lead to unique predictions and new methods of control.

Another door might be opened by the discovery of phenomena that do not fit neatly into the ordinary scientific scheme and can more easily be understood in terms of process concepts. We may be close to this in some areas of brain research. One of the most interesting phenomena that is currently being studied is the emergence of two separate individuals when the connections between the cerebral hemispheres are severed. The concepts of the theory of societies seem to apply particularly well to this phenomenon, and they may provide a better explanation of it than to ordinary scientific concepts. But all this is just conjecture, and the immediate fact is that there is no obvious way of enhancing scientific explanations with process concepts. In the meantime, I think it will be more fruitful to look elsewhere for the immediate value of process cosmology for neurobehavioral research.

For Inquiry

It's beginning to be dawn on the knoll. I can make out the shapes of leaves and apples against the eastern sky. How do I know what these thing are? How do I prehend the shapes of aggregates? The data of prehensions are the objective features of individuals and nothing else. The shape of a leaf as a whole can't very well be a feature of the individuals that make up the leaf. It must be that the leaf is part of an overarching individual so that the shape of the leaf is an objective feature of the overarching individual that I prehend. Maybe we are inside a cell. How can we find out?

Process cosmology raises new questions, and I believe that this is where its immediate value for scientific research lies—it expands the range of inquiry. In the remainder of this paper I want to show how process concepts can give rise to new hypotheses, new areas of experimentation, and new methodologies. To illustrate the scope of the research implications, I will describe several different hypotheses and experiments that range from the ordinary to the extraordinary. Also, I will cover three diverse fields of research in the neural and behavioral sciences, namely, neuroanatomy, psychophysics, and comparative psychology. (See reference in note 6 for additional experiments in neurophysiology.)

I would like to begin by returning to the wealth of ideas for research that are suggested by Hartshorne's speculations in PPS. For instance, the notion of affective continuity among the senses has implications for neuroanatomical research. Recall that Hartshorne proposes that all sensory qualities are composed of some combination of basic dimensions of feeling. This suggests several hypotheses that can be tested by routine neuroanatomical procedures involving methods of histochemistry and electrophysiology. For instance, according to the theory, particular sensory qualities are innately related to particular emotional qualities, e.g., yellowness is related to gaiety. We know that certain groups of neurons respond to yellow stimuli and certain other groups mediate positive affects. We might expect to find histological or physiological evidence of special connections between these groups of neurons.

There are also implications for comparative neuroanatomical studies. We might look for evidence that the sensory and the emotional-motivational systems of the brain evolved from a common pool of primitive neurons. There is already evidence that discrete sensory pathways have gradually replaced a relatively undifferentiated network of neurons (the reticular system), which initially mediated all sensory input. The primitive neurons of this network, which still function in our brains, typically do not discriminate distinctly among the different sensory modalities. But they seem to be sensitive to common dimensions of feeling, such as intensity and hedonic tone. As one might expect, the emotional-motivational system is still closely connected to these primitive neurons.[9]

Process concepts also suggest more creative possibilities for neuroanatomical research. For instance, according to the theory of societies, we can envision the structures which we find in the brain as being products of social interactions among individuals. Understood in this way, these structures can serve as clues to the nature of the social organizations and of the individuals that make up the brain. One might look for aesthetic or symbolic forms that are found in human societies or even for familiar artifacts of everyday life. It is not clear where this line of research might take us, and this is part of the adventure here. Let me give an idea of what one might find.

With the aid of modern techniques of microscopy and a little imagination, one can find plenty of evidence of hierarchies of individuals and complex social interactions among and within brain cells. For instance, motion pictures of living brain cells taken through a microscope reveal tiny microglial cells that look like spiders and climb the trunks and branches of neurons cleaning up debris and performing who knows what other functions. At a higher level of magnification you can see inside the neurons where little corpuscles stream down the long axons like traffic down a highway. You can see collisions and traffic jams. At yet higher magnification, a slice through a neuron viewed in an electron microscope looks like a landscape seen from an airplane—one anatomist calls it the "cytoscape." At the highest magnifications we begin to see things that look like spiral galaxies.

Turning now to the field of psychophysics, let us consider some of the implications of the notion of concrescence here.[10] This notion raised a question about the evolution of the sense organs. The answer I proposed suggests that we should be able to receive some kinds of information from our environment in the absence of normal sensory functions. Let me make this more explicit. Recall the idea that each sense organ is like a selective channel for a particular type of data. The data coming through each channel can be thought of as forming a peak of distinctness in our experience. The "landscape" of our experience generally has several peaks, one for each sensory modality. But, according to the notion of concrescence, no data are completely excluded from experience, and so, between the peaks of ordinary sensory input should be troughs of vague feeling that seep in diffusely through other routes. These are the primitive modes of knowing the world that are largely walled out in evolution as the selective sensory windows evolve. Let us refer to these modes that fill the gaps between the senses as "intersensory prehensions" and see how one might find evidence for them.

First of all, the kind of information conveyed through intersensory prehensions might well involve ordinary physical energies such as electromagnetic waves. Second, there is little reason to expect intersensory prehensions to be particularly distinct or complex, not necessarily anything like some of the remarkable phenomena studied by ESP researchers. What I would look for first, to test the hypothesis of intersensory prehension, is straightforward, reliable evidence of a vague awareness of presences (a feeling of feelings in the environment) in the absence of normal sensory input. For instance, there have been studies of the ability of blindfolded people to estimate locations of large objects such as a wall nearby. It was found that people were able to use such cues as heat radiation to make estimates. Another phenomenon that is well established is the ability of some people to identify colors by touch. This also seems to be a function of sensing different frequencies of radiation. In gifted people this phenomenon is robust and highly repeatable. The influence of ambient electromagnetic fields on experimental animals is currently being studied by neuroscientists, and it seems that certain frequencies and intensities can affect brain function and behavior.

These lines of research have not been of major interest in sensory psychology, and possibly one reason is that they have not had interesting theoretical implications. However, in the framework of process cosmology these lines of research become much more interesting. One might want to explore the range of intersensory prehensions by determining the types of environmental stimuli that people can detect, the degrees of accuracy that are possible, and the conditions that enhance or impede detection. Furthermore, one can think of specific hypotheses that can easily be tested. For example, hybrid physical prehensions should be intersensory insofar as they involve something other than ordinary sensory stimuli. Therefore, one might predict that people deprived of ordinary sensory input will detect the presence of other people in a room more reliably than they detect the presence of aggregates such as a piece of furniture.

The evolutionary considerations also suggest other hypotheses that are easy to test. For example, if intersensory prehensions are primitive modes of feeling that are suppressed during the course of evolution, then one might predict that lower animals will perform better in detection tasks when deprived of sensory input than will people. Also, insofar as ontogeny recapitulates phylogeny, children should perform better than adults.

Finally, let us look at the empirical implications of process cosmology for research in the field of comparative psychology. Hartshorne's concept of social feeling is especially relevant here because it is a version of prehension that emphasizes the empathic nature of human experience and the commonality of feelings among all species of individuals. This concept led to Hartshorne's ethological research on bird song. In *Born to Sing* he presents a novel interpretation of bird song that is based on his empathic impressions of the feelings that birds have when they sing.

There are especially difficult experimental problems involved in testing hypotheses about the experiences of other individuals. I think it is possible to get relevant empirical evidence, but we will probably have to be satisfied with less conclusive results than we get in other fields of research. One reason for doing research in this field is to find out just how much we can learn here. Consider the possibilities for the following method of inquiry.

According to the concept of social feelings, under appropriate conditions people should generally agree in their empathic impressions of a given individual's feelings, be it a human, a bird, or an atom. If this is true, then we should be able to get reliable indices of the feelings of an individual by using a "behavioral assay" method for feelings. What this would involve is using people's empathic reactions to an individual as an index of that individual's feelings. This procedure is analogous to the bioassay method commonly used in biology. Here the presence of substances whose chemical structures are unknown is inferred on the basis of the reactions of living tissues to the substances.[11]

I have done a little work on developing model behavioral assay procedures for studying the experiences of laboratory rats. Such procedures might be helpful in identifying subtle effects of nutritional, social, or other environmental variables upon an animal's emotional life. We must first find out what happens when people are asked to respond empathically to individual rats and determine optimal conditions for empathic studies.

In contrast to the common stereotype, rats that are raised as pets are gentle and friendly creatures that enjoy interacting with people. They can conveniently be housed on a card table that contains a shelter, playthings, and food—sort of a "rat plateau." In one preliminary study students were assigned a small family of tame rats to take home for observation and interaction. In this study the student is not a detached observer, but he or she enters into the life of the subjects. The student is instructed to interact with the rats as though they were little people and to anthropomorphize freely in describing their behavior.

I have been more interested in the empathic responses of the students than in the behavior of the rats in these studies. One rather consistent finding is that before long the students begin to feel affection for the rats. At first one rat seems like another, but after interacting with them for a while, the students usually find themselves responding differently to different individuals. Some students believe that they can recognize distinctive personalities in the individual rats, and that they can tell what a rat's experiences are like in much the same way that they can tell what another person's experiences are like.

What should be done next is to determine the reliability and the validity of the empathic impressions. Will different persons give the same descriptions of individual rats? Can a person identify individual rats on the basis of anthropomorphic descriptions of their personalities? Will empirical implications of empathic impressions consistently be verified by objective behavioral and physiological tests? Even if it turns out that there are no useful applications of behavioral assay methods with rats, these studies should be interesting in themselves because they may tell us something about our ability to determine what it is like to be another organism.[12]

There are also possibilities here for entering more novel areas of inquiry. For instance, astronomers have been searching the macrocosmos for signals that might indicate the presence of intelligence. Process cosmology suggests that we look into the microcosmos as well and that we use our empathic powers to find signs of sentience, as well as use our usual analytic methods to find signs of intelligence. To illustrate the range of possibilities for this line of research, I will describe a *gedanken* experiment in which a behavioral assay of feelings is employed to test the hypothesis that atoms are sentient individuals.

First of all, we will have to monitor spontaneous, complex events in individual atoms and transduce these events into a form that can readily be perceived. Suppose, for example, we could record the pattern of emission of nuclear particles from a radioactive atom. The pattern can be presented to people for behavioral assay in various ways—it can be stretched out or compressed in time; it can be presented in a sequence of auditory, visual, or tactual stimuli; or it can be transformed to a spatial pattern. For comparison similar patterns can be generated by random procedures or by mechanical means. Now we want to find out if people react differently to the atomic and the control patterns. Suppose it turned out that people regularly sense something aesthetically or emotionally familiar in the atomic patterns but not in the control patterns? This would not by itself be convincing evidence that there is sentience present. But it would raise interesting questions for further inquiry.[13]

Now, that was just a *gedanken* experiment, one not really feasible with current technology. But if we move up the hierarchy of individuals to the level of cells, then many experiments like this become technically feasible. I would like to offer an empathic interpretation of a cellular event that is easy to monitor, and let the reader think of experiments to test it.

I recently visited a laboratory in which the activities of individual neurons were being monitored by transducing the neural impulses to pulses of sound. In the midst of the "popping" sounds of the neural impulses I heard a soft moan. The researcher told me it was the sound of a dying cell—a high-frequency discharge as the cell's life ebbed away. Here is my empathic interpretation of this event which you may treat as an empirical hypothesis. I believe that the moan was an expression of a feeling that all sentient creatures share—it was a feeling of perishing.

How do I know this?

> I have a mind myself and recognize
> Mind when I meet with it in any guise.[14]

Notes

This work was supported by Grant GM 30777 from NIH. I thank Robin Frost, Nora Peck, and Lisa Wolf for editing this paper.

1. I limit this discussion to what I shall refer to as "ordinary science"—traditional mechanistic, reductionistic approaches to research. Other approaches, such as general systems theory, have somewhat different relations to process cosmology, which I do not consider in this paper. Also, the process cosmology I speak of is that of Hartshorne and Whitehead only.

Also, some comments on my biases and some qualifications are appropriate here. My scientific thinking has been most influenced by the liberal behaviorism of Neal Miller and the psychobiology of Curt Richter—rough-hewn, pragmatic, common-sense approaches. At the same time, my perception of nature is more akin to that of Anglo-American Romanticism. Thus I feel most closely connected to the strand of thought in American philosophy that runs from Pierce to Hartshorne and intertwines empirical and romantic approaches to nature.

In view of this rather anomalous combination I want to qualify the claim that my judgments represent contemporary thought in the neural and behavioral sciences. I do believe that my analyses reflect sound scientific thinking. But there are many intangible factors that result in divergences in final judgments between me and my colleagues. We may agree that a notion is reasonable in terms of its compatibility with scientific facts and its clarity, consistency, and completeness of meaning, but at the same time differ in our judgment of its plausibility. In my experience many scientists find the notions of process cosmology hard to believe (and also hard to understand). For instance, after I had presented a long and careful account of the notion that the basic actualities that make up the world are sentient creatures, a very intelligent and scholarly neuroscientist said to me, "I still can't imagine what it would be like for an atom to have feelings, and I still can't see any good reason to believe this in the first place." This notion about basic actualities and reasons for belief in them arise from a different way of seeing the world in the first place. Certainly process cosmology has a more immediate appeal to a person who sees experience at the heart of nature than to one who perceives the world as an insentient mechanism.

2. I'd like to quote a poem by Emily Dickinson which expresses what I am trying to say here in a most remarkable way.

> The Brain—is wider than the Sky—
> For—put them side by side—
> The one the other will contain
> With ease—and you beside—
>
> The Brain is deeper than the sea—
> For—hold them—Blue to Blue—
> The one the other will absorb—
> As Sponges—Buckets—do—
>
> The Brain is just the weight of God—
> For—Heft them—Pound for Pound—
> And they will differ—if they do—
> As Syllable from Sound—

3. Concrescence is a complex notion, and this account describes only one aspect of it which is particularly relevant to science. However, I want to mention briefly the essential role of feeling in concrescence because the ability of process cosmology to explain the kinds of experiences that I am con-

cerned with in this paper depends on it. Also the notion of feeling will come up again in later sections of the paper, and so I want to state my understanding of it explicitly.

The time-cone of concrescence is nothing but a creative synthesis of feelings. Hartshorne states the thesis plainly—"all experience is feeling of feeling." What this means is that the actual world that enters into a concrescence is ultimately made up of sentient individuals, and the facts of the world are the objective manifestations of their feelings. Likewise, everything in subjective experience is a form of feeling—the colors and palpable textures, the thoughts and intentions as well as the emotional tones are all articulations of feelings derived from the world. I will have to bypass the many interesting implications and problems of this "social theory of feeling" because they are too complex to deal with adequately in the space available here.

4. There is a more general issue that arises from this analysis of concrescence. I have shown that the objective meaning of concrescence is compatible with the scientific notion of causality. But concrescence also has a subjective meaning; it states that every elementary event involves an experience. Is this compatible with scientific method, which eschews subjective language and adheres strictly to the law of parsimony? I think it is. To show how, I would like to rephrase the question as follows. Should the ontology of the cosmological framework of science be as limited as the ontology of science itself? It seems that many scientists would like the two domains to be congruent. The apparent advantage of this is that science then ranges over all of reality; it can potentially explain everything that exists. But this is accomplished by a contraction of the domain of existence; it is too easy. Insofar as speculative cosmology aims for more generality and concreteness than science does, it needs a richer ontology. In fact, at the final metaphysical level, one should want the richest ontology possible, because each thing that is omitted from the ontology is a thing whose possible mode of existence is no longer subject to inquiry. Finally, there is no reason to think that a rich ontology in the framework will intrude into the limited domain of science within the framework. Scientific method automatically insures against that. Abstraction is the natural mode of scientific thought. It isolates relevant variables and disregards the rest. So, while it may be true that science functions best in a "desert landscape," it is also true that there is plenty of room for such a landscape in the endless domain of speculative cosmology (a sort of "garden of delights").

5. This brief account omits many details and problems. This is not the place for a technical discussion of concrescence and evolution, but I would like to clear up one bit of confusion that the account might have generated. In what sense can one say that there is a limit to how many data an organism can handle if all the data of the actual world are involved in the concrescence? The limit is manifested in the number of data that can be harmonized in the satisfaction. This is finite. The remaining data which are discordant are also in-

volved in the satisfaction but do not contribute to the intensity of the experience. What the sensory systems do is begin the process of sorting out relevant and irrelevant data on the way to the final percipient occasion.

6. See my paper "Psychological Physiology from the Standpoint of a Physiological Psychologist," *Process Studies* 11 (1981): 274–91.

7. Whitehead discusses this in *The Function of Reason* and in the first chapter of *Process and Reality*.

8. I use Hartshorne's terminology of "individuals" and "aggregates" according to the following understanding of these terms. Individuals correspond roughly to Whitehead's personally ordered societies. When time is reduced to a limit, "individual" becomes roughly synonymous with "actual occasion." Hartshorne gives as examples of individuals: animals, cells, and atoms. It is important to keep in mind that to call a thing an individual does not imply that the thing is an individual all the time. For instance, a cell might have only brief moments of unified experience—in the case of a neuron this might occur only at the moment when the membrane potential reaches the threshold for triggering an all-or-none impulse. At other times the cell would be just an aggregate. The term "aggregate" includes anything that is not an individual (more precisely, that does not attain moments of individuality). Examples of presumed aggregates are a leaf, a machine, any assortment of things. The distinctions between different types of aggregates are not relevant to the present discussion. But it is worth mentioning that there are important problems here and that approaches such as general systems theory attempt to work out taxonomies of aggregates and to identify characteristics of aggregate hierarchies that are necessary and sufficient for emergence of various forms of holistic functioning, including individuality. It is also worth noting here that the theory of societies envisions everyday physical things (individuals or aggregates) as made up of hierarchies of individuals and aggregates. For example, an animal (individual) is made up of organs (aggregates), which are made up of tissues (aggregates), which are made up of cells (individuals), and so on down to basic actualities which have to be individuals (assuming that there *are* basic actualities).

9. Recently, a study was published that addressed the problem of reconciling the neuroanatomical structure of the sensory projection areas with their functions. The study involved commentaries by thirty-six neuroscientists and philosophers. The problem was how to resolve the merely *quantitative* neuroanatomical differences among the various cortical projection areas with the *qualitative* differences among the sensory experiences mediated by these areas. Although this problem is more philosophical than experimental, I mention it here because of the striking relevance of the theory of affective continuity to it. (See R. Puccetti and R. W. Dykes, "Sensory Cortex and the Mind-Brain Problem," *The Behavioral and Brain Sciences* 1 [1978]: 337–76.)

10. Psychophysics is a field of research which measures the relations between changes in the physical properties of stimuli and changes in the

evoked sensory experience. Strictly speaking, the research I describe here asks some questions which extend beyond the ordinary boundaries of this field. But I think it is appropriate to put this work under the heading of psychophysics because they both arise from the same tradition of thought. Psychophysics was founded by Gustav Fechner, unquestionably a predecessor in the field of modern process cosmology, and the long history of this field is evidence of the value of this kind of thought for research in the behavioral sciences.

11. One might ask whether this analogy is misleading. The inference from the bioassay can potentially be confirmed by chemical tests, but how can we confirm the inference from a behavioral assay? Although there is obviously a sense in which we can not get at subjective features in the same way that we can get at objective features, this does not preclude the efficacy of converging operations for confirming hypotheses about subjective features. For example, if the individual whose feelings are being inferred is a person, or even a higher animal, we can potentially confirm empathic judgments by looking at neurophysiological data. Suppose, for instance, that we have an empathically derived hypothesis that a bird is experiencing pleasure when it sings. Suppose we had identified a particular brain chemical that is released from binding sites whenever animals are placed in conditions that are usually associated with pleasant feelings. Suppose further that we confirmed this with tests on our own brain when we were having pleasant feelings. Clearly if we found that this chemical were released whenever the bird began to sing, this would be a strong bit of evidence in favor of our hypothesis. There are other ways to get converging evidence on empathic hypotheses that can also strongly affect our confidence. For instance, if we judge that an individual is having a pleasant experience, we would expect him to favor conditions that produce this experience. Here we could use behavioral preference tests to get empirical evidence. Still, when it comes to making judgments about another individual's subjectivity, we can always be fooled in the end—it could be an insentient computer, after all. But in the meantime we can increase our confidence in our empathic hypotheses without limit so long as successive converging operations confirm our expectations. I do not ask more from ordinary science than this. And finally, returning to our bioassay and chemical tests, we can always be fooled in the end here too—it could be gremlins, after all.

12. I think it is important to be especially concerned about the welfare of the animals in this kind of study. Unlike research aimed at important practical goals such as medical treatment, this highly speculative research does not justify causing the animals any undue discomfort. Besides, it would be entirely contrary to the spirit of this kind of inquiry.

13. One factor that I overlook in this design is the contiguity of the feeler and the feeling felt. It seems to me that something important might be lost by recording the objective display of the feeling and interjecting it between the feeling and the feeler. But I cannot imagine how this could be done otherwise in this case.

Finally, if it turns out that it is indeed possible to transform the behavior of imperceptible individuals into a form which can be appreciated empathically by people, then we could conceivably use behavioral assay procedures to look for macrocosmic as well as microcosmic individuals. Giving imagination free play for a moment, one can conceive of behavioral assay studies of immense, slowly changing entities. For instance, what might we see if we looked at a time-lapse telescopic motion picture of some large segment of the universe taken over a period of millions of years and played back within the period of an hour? Perhaps we might see some familiar-looking actions—perhaps something resembling organismic, purposive behavior.

    14. And then Robert Frost adds,

> No one can know how glad I am to find
> On any sheet the least display of mind.

Response by Charles Hartshorne

The researches (for several years intensively pursued) which were part of my preparations for the book on sensation to which Wolf reacts so generously and imaginatively were made about a half century ago. (The book is still in print.) The basic theory of sensation the book presents came to me sixty years ago and is the subject of one chapter of my doctoral dissertation, written in 1923. The experience in France referred to by Wolf was in 1917 or 1918. I then knew almost nothing of the many evidences in the history of philosophy and psychology that various philosophers and psychologists have had somewhat similar intimations that reality *as immediately given* is indeed an "ocean of feelings." I refer to some of these writers in the book mentioned. They all show a phenomenological thread in the history of speculative idealism, a thread less manifest in Husserl's writings than in those of Heidegger, and, before him, in writings of Berkeley, Goethe, Rickert, Croce, and many others. One of the ways in which philosophers differ in personality, and, in part, a cause of their theoretical differences, is in their sensitivity, or lack of it, to certain aspects of experience.

The sensation book pleased a few psychologists, e.g., Carroll Pratt, author of an excellent book on the psychology of music, who some years ago told me he thought my book was in some respects well ahead of those by the general run of psychologists. One prominent psychologist, misled by a misprint (one of only two in the book) which happened to come early (p. 27) and seemed to imply that I did not know the difference between millimeter and millimicron, saw little merit in the book. In fact it was not I that put "millimeter'' in the manuscript but an editor at the press who made no other serious mistake. What I had put was an abbreviation, two Greek letters—$\mu\mu$—for millimicrons. I corrected in the galleys the erroneous spelling of the abbreviated word but by a moment of carelessness missed its persistence in the page proofs—the worst proofreading error of my career. No student of Leonard Troland (parts of whose great psychophysiology I almost memorized) could fail to recall his frequent use of ''millimicron,'' and I knew that millimeter is a very different magnitude. Another psychologist who praised the book became an administrator and was not prominent as a researcher thereafter. Some philosophers did think highly of the work, including, oddly, a self-styled materialist. Wolf's explanation of why the book did not exert much influence is to the point. An additional reason, though, is that the work has some flaws of presentation which, again unluckily, but also partly arising from inexperience (it was my first book), occur quite early and so might easily lead some to stop reading further. The flaws included an indulgence in some arguments so vague that now I wonder if they are anything but special pleading. I had enough more definite arguments to make my case, which was only weakened by attempting the doubtful ones. Another mistake was to show more scorn than was tactful or altogether seemly in an outsider, a nonprofessional in psychology, for some standard psychological notions.

I still think, however, that in some ways psychology has tended to miss the biological-emotional function of sensation, which is far deeper than mere ''associations'' and individual learning. Natural sweet-tasting substances are nourishing, and the taste encourages us to eat them; natural sour, bitter, or salty-tasting substances tend to be unnourishing or even poisonous, especially in substantial quantities, and the tastes discourage us from eating or drinking such things, e.g., sea water. The evolutionary explanation is obvious and has nothing to do with personal learning. My thesis is that something less obvious, but in basic principle similar in biological-evolutionary meaning, is true of *all* sensations. And I am sure that the psychology of music or painting will never go very deep until it is realized that underneath the role of personal learning is an innate basis in the sense organs themselves, or the sensory areas of the brain, which gives sounds and colors their emotional character. This is part of the explanation of the fact that bird song is intelligible as music to mammals such as ourselves, crossing a deep gulf between classes of animals. It is why no one has to *learn* what a growl, by which a newborn infant would be frightened, means. It means danger, and does this for inherited evolutionary reasons, not reasons of individual experience.

My work on bird song was my other attempt to be an empirical scientist, somewhat more successful than the other in getting the attention of experts. In 1973 I knew better how to relate to professionals than I did in 1934. And I did far more direct observing and simple experimenting, such as replaying songs, sometimes at slower speeds. Also I got help from those who knew how to use computers.

Although I was trying to get at birds' feelings, in the process I discovered objective, quantitative facts not hitherto observed, facts for which my "aesthetic hypothesis" is an intelligible explanation. No alternative explanation for them has been found. The standard account of why song evolved in certain animals is not such an explanation; for my theory is a special form of that standard account, and only what is special about it explains the objective behavioral and environmental facts in question.

Evolution explains the adaptiveness of certain behaviors of singing animals, but there are two ways of conceiving adaptive behaviors. One is to take them as merely mechanical, like some contrived feedback arrangement (my father made one for our furnace when I was a child). The other is to suppose that the adaptive behavior is motivated by certain *feelings*, as avoidance of painful burns is motivated by the pain itself, or engaging in sexual reproduction is motivated by the pleasure of the action. Adopting the second view not only fits our natural intuitions of the other animals, especially the higher forms, but fits also the evolutionary scheme according to which our human traits are intensifications and elaborations of traits found in our prehuman ancestors. It also, I argue, explains certain special facts about the distribution of singing skills among species and about *how* birds sing (avoiding monotony, for instance, in a fashion not explicable by mere chance, and adaptive only on the hypothesis that to act in certain useful ways it is necessary to have and satisfy the emotional motivations that favor such acting. Scientists today do not usually deny feelings to other animals, as the Cartesians did, but, as William James shrewdly noted, they often proceed as if for all practical purposes animals were indeed mere insentient machines. Any feelings that might be there are treated like "idle wheels" that do nothing.

Wolf uses the word "dismal" in connection with the view of nature as an assemblage of mere mechanisms. Only extreme materialists fail to feel this dismalness. But there are two ways of trying to escape from it. One is to suppose that, while most of nature is purely mechanical, at some point in the evolutionary ascent there appears a new principle, either life or mind, depending upon where the point is supposed to be. This is the dualistic way. Traditional vitalism was of this kind, in Driesch, for example. Theories of emergent evolution generally took this form. Wolf is an example of a scientist who feels that dualism is an unsatisfactory compromise, with some of the disadvantages of both extremes. The other way of escaping the dismal view, or what Fechner called the "night-view," is to reject mechanism altogether, so far as it is supposed strictly true of even the most "inanimate" parts of the world. A distinguished biologist, the entomologist Wheeler, once remarked that while philosophers and biologists were arguing about mechanism and vitalism the physicists took mechanism and "quietly dumped it into the sea." The first physicist to do this, I like to insist, was not any quantum theorist but the chemist, physicist, astronomer, logician, mathematician, and philosophical idealist Charles Peirce, our American universal theorist, who had no notion of quantum theory. Before Peirce the most definite anticipation was in the system of the Greek materialist Epicurus, for whom even atoms had some freedom.

The details of Wolf's speculations I leave to others. I am not well equipped to make useful comments on them. These are large, difficult issues about which scientists and philosophers may have much to say. In any case I lack the energy at a busy time, and probably should not take the space, to deal with them. But I do wish to say that in all my many contacts with George Wolf for nearly two years now I have found him an admirable example of a scientist who is also by nature a philosopher, or one who wishes to retain the sense of the larger whole while he plies his limited specialty. It has been a privilege indeed to know him.

Some final remarks. Throughout this conference it has been made clear that process philosophy is not a panacea, a magic formula, thanks to which we can soar above our human limitations and all agree upon the perfect truth. Every speaker has felt that there are difficulties still, topics that we scarcely know how to deal with, or upon which we cannot agree. If the search for the truth is better than simply having it (Lessing), we can be content for the search to go on while the species endures—if, in spite of its appalling quarrelsomeness, it can manage to do so.

Long ago I heard a professor in the Harvard Divinity School, the learned George Foot Moore, remark, "It is civilization that destroys nations. What else could destroy them?" We can today see the element of truth in this more easily than the man who said it or his hearers could. Whatever our philosophy, we had better use it to moderate the tendency that is in all of us to look to violence to settle issues between groups in a world whose technology makes violence against groups ever more likely to destroy all who participate in it, or advocate it, along perhaps with nearly everyone else. Neither process philosophers nor any other philosophers have yet shown us the way out of this terrible impasse. We Americans have relied on nuclear weapons to make up for the inferiority of our conventional arms and training. Now that our enemy is similarly equipped to join us in destroying mankind, the whole matter must be reconsidered. Our own invention has been reduced to a ghastly absurdity. This result was predictable enough; but who of us had the courage to face the prospect and draw a rational conclusion?

What is the relation of process philosophy to this grim dilemma? At least this: To do justice to the issue it is necessary to care deeply about goods and ills far transcending one's own personal career. For most of us are old enough to hope that the unthinkable catastrophe will most likely come after our career is finished. Moreover, believing in an "afterlife" has only ambiguous implications for motivating our behavior. If what really matters is achieving, or being granted, heaven, and escaping hell, even nuclear warfare may seem not our major concern. Dying soon or late is after all a very minor matter, compared to life everlasting, either in very happy or more or less unhappy circumstances. The Buddhist-Whiteheadian view of the self implies with radical clarity that the rational aim of the individual must in principle transcend any mere good of that individual, whether between birth and death or everlastingly. We are nothing apart from what our moments of living contribute to future life, and this means to some or all of the following: our own future experiences; future experiences of other human beings, nonhuman animals, or plants; divine experience, this last contribution containing *all* the value whatsoever that our moments can have. This is the meaning of loving God with all our being. We contribute ourselves to enriching the lives of others, all such enrichment being entirely embraced in its objective immortality in the Life of lives. An incinerated earth will certainly enormously curtail our possible direct or indirect contributions.

Whatever our philosophies, and it seems clear that human beings are not about to agree to any one philosophy, we are all mortal, and even the lower animals act as if their aims stretched beyond their own lives to their offspring. And the Marxists, too, are critical of merely self-regarding views of life's meaning. This conference is a remarkable illustration of cooperation on a very high level. Perhaps we can take it as a sign that our species can somehow surmount the worst of its threats for the near future.

To George Wolf, and to all the other contributors, and to the planners of this conference, for the extraordinary pains they have taken for this occasion, thanks are due not only from me but, no doubt, from many others who were present or who may benefit from its results.

Contributors

William P. Alston is professor of philosophy at Syracuse University.

John B. Cobb, Jr., is Ingraham Professor of Theology, School of Theology at Claremont, and Avery Professor of Religion at Claremont Graduate School.

Franklin I. Gamwell is associate professor and dean at the Divinity School of the University of Chicago.

Charles Hartshorne is Ashbel Smith Professor Emeritus of Philosophy, the University of Texas at Austin.

R. M. Martin is recently retired professor of philosophy at Northwestern University and presently research associate at the Boston University Center for the Philosophy and History of Science.

Schubert M. Ogden is University Distinguished Professor of Theology, Southern Methodist University.

Eugene Peters was professor of philosophy at Hiram College, upon his death in 1983.

John E. Smith is Clark Professor of Philosophy, Yale University.

Manley Thompson is professor of philosophy at the University of Chicago.

Paul Weiss is Heffer Professor of Philosophy at the Catholic University of America.

George Wolf was research professor in the Department of Psychology at New York University, New York City, upon his death in 1983.

Index of Persons

Index of Subjects

Absolute, the, Royce's argument for, 103
Absoluteness, as divine attribute, 79, 81–83
Abstract/concrete: as problematic distinction, 48; as logical-type distinction, 23
Acceptance, as pragmatic reaction, 48
Active singularity, criterion of, 29, 160
Actuality: as definite, 165; distinguished from existence, 55, 75; as finite, 165
Actuality, Peirce's account of: as continuous, 135; as both continuous and discrete, 130
Adaptive behavior, as mechanical or as motivated by feelings, 186
Affective continuity, doctrine of, 186; and neuroanatomical research, 175
Aggregate: anything not an individual, 182; a logical type, 23
Analogical terms, in relation to logical types, 24–33
Analogy, Hartshorne's theory of, 21–36
Animals, as compound individuals, 159–60
A priori, as experiential, 48
Arguments: formal, in Hartshorne's concept, 48; as relative to a system, 46, 71
Aspects, logic of, and Fregean Under-relations, 47
Atomism, process version of, 116–18
Atoms, as individuals, 158

Becoming, asymmetry of, 110
"Behavioral assay": and bioassay, 183; as method for comparative psychology, 177–79
Bell's theorem, 129
"Better than," as nearly primitive term, 73. *See also* "Greater than"
Buddhism: doctrine of self, xiv, 127, 188; problems for theism, 122

Causality: models of, 169, 181; reciprocal, 153–154; as self-creation, 170–71; solely in the present, 153
Cells, as compound individuals, 158

Chicago, University of, xvi
Christian theology, as defined by Ogden, 16–17
Civilization, as set of domains (Weiss), 120
Comparative psychology: "behavioral assay" method in, 177–79; and process cosmology, 177–79
Complexity, as divine attribute, 79, 84
Concrescence, 168–70, 180–82; limited by satisfaction, 181–82; and scientific notions of causality, 169; and subject/object distinction, 168; and time-cone model, 169, 181
Concrete/abstract, as problematic distinction, 48
Concreteness, theory of, as including theory of abstractness, 4
Consciousness, as special case of sentience or feeling, 128
Contingency: criteria of, 110–11; defined, 89–90; and temporality and mutability, 88–90, 99–100
Contrast, principle of, as criterion of metaphysical reasoning, 125
Corporeality, as divine attribute, 80, 86–87
Creation (creativity), as ultimate rationality, 165
Creation *ex nihilo,* as divine attribute, 80, 84–86

Determinism, as reductionist, 150
Divine, meaning of, 51
Domains (Weiss), 119
Dual transcendence, doctrine of, 46, 99

Empathic impressions, in comparative psychology, 177–79
Entailment, as semantical notion, 48
Epochal time: as nonsequential, 171; a problematic notion, 171
Eternal objects: Whitehead's doctrine of, 50; qualified, 128
Event, as logical type, 23

193